The Feminist Poetry Movement

The Feminist Poetry Movement

Kim Whitehead

UNIVERSITY PRESS OF MISSISSIPPI
Jackson

Library of Congress Cataloging-in-Publication Data

Whitehead, Kim.
    The feminist poetry movement / Kim Whitehead.
        p.   cm.
    Includes bibliographical references and index.
    ISBN 0-87805-939-3 (cloth : alk. paper).—ISBN 0-87805-940-7
(paper : alk. paper)
        1. American poetry—Women authors—History and criticism.
    2. Feminism and literature—United States—History—20th century.
    3. Women and literature—United States—History—20th century.
    4. American poetry—20th century—History and criticism.   I. Title.
PS310.F45W45   1997
811.009'9287—dc20   96-25920
                                                            CIP

British Library Cataloging-in-Publication data available

for

Audre Lorde

poet

visionary

warrior

Contents

Acknowledgments

First and foremost, for their vision and courage, I am deeply grateful to the poets whose works fill these pages. I am just one of the multitudes of readers for whom their rebellious poetries have been life-altering.

I am indebted to those who listened to my ideas as they took shape, prompted me in fruitful directions, and painstakingly critiqued the manuscript in some or all of its stages. In addition to thoughtful readings, Rebecca Chopp, Robert Detweiler, and Cristine Levenduski consistently offered encouragement and advice. Many, many thanks go to Martha Henn, Kim Loudermilk, Annie Merrill Ingram, and Maria Pramaggiore for their incisive readings and rereadings, and for long hours of companionable exchange; with them I learned the possibility of feminist community. Carole Meyers's readings and support, as well as our discussions about literary history, have proven indispensable. I am grateful to Rosemary Magee for our ongoing conversations about women's writing and to Janet McAdams for her insights into Native American history and literature. Tammy Oberhausen provided invaluable assistance in preparing the final manuscript. Finally, for her patience and her commitment to this project, my enduring thanks goes to Seetha A-Srinivasan.

For their kind assistance, I am thankful to curator R. Russell Maylone and the Special Collections staff who manage the Women's Collection at Northwestern University Library. Most of this manuscript was written while I was at the School of Literature, Communication, and Culture at Georgia Institute of Technology, and I am particularly indebted to my students, who taught me day after day the power of poetry, and all literature, to delight, challenge, and transform.

A host of others have kept me going. Thanks always to Valerie Epifani, whose laugh calls the sun. A lifetime of thanks goes to Susan Peterson, who believes I can do most anything, and Andrew Chancey, who is always there. Among the many women who have provided me both refuge and inspiration, special thanks go to Cynthia Blakely, Suzanne Castro-Miller, Ann Connor, Ann Frellsen, Ellen Garrett, Ami Mattison, Marie Sandusky, Gail Scheu, Melissa Sexton O'Neil, Ruth Sill, and Amy Wright. Any work of mine belongs to them as well.

Finally, I thank my family, and especially my parents Betty Whitehead and Bill Whitehead, whose lessons and love never fail.

Introduction

When Minnie Bruce Pratt accepted the American Academy of Poets' prestigious Lamont Prize for Poetry in May 1989,[1] the poetry "establishment" and the feminist poetry and publishing community convened to honor Pratt's volume of poems *Crime Against Nature* (1990). While numerous feminist writers and editors were on hand to celebrate, the chancellors of the academy (both prominent poets themselves) presided over the event with obvious discomfort. John Hollander and James Merrill fidgeted and passed notes to one another during Pratt's acceptance speech and poetry reading and even interrupted her verbally in the middle of one of her poems to tell her that her time was up. Pratt recalled later that they had not done the same to another honoree (a man) who spoke almost as long earlier in the evening, and that members of the audience were visibly upset by the chancellors' thinly masked hostility. Pratt later asserted that her explicit discussion of her personal experience, both in her speech and in her poetry, was the reason for the chancellors' uneasiness: "It was felt that it was not appropriate for me to be talking about 'that' at the ceremony—although 'that' was the content of the poems I had won the awards for" (Zipter 1990).

This episode illustrates in part the status of the relationship between the feminist poetry movement and the cultural institution(s) of contemporary American poetry a full two decades after significant numbers of women poets first began to address explicitly feminist concerns in their work. At this ceremony, the feminist publishing network presented itself as a strong cultural force peopled by talented writers, committed publishers, and faithful readers. Indeed, Pratt herself exemplifies contemporary feminist poets, who remain steadfastly connected to feminism as a social/political movement, and who continue to search for a unified community ("Woman") as well as to acknowledge and explore the diverse identities and experiences ("women") within that community. At the heart of feminist poetry is still that dictum that drove the early women's movement—"the personal as political"—which means feminist poetics is heavily invested in the details of specific women's lives and simultaneously in resisting the gendered oppression of women as a collective in contemporary America and around the world. Feminist poets still rely on what has developed into a solid feminist readership and professional network of feminist journals and small presses for publication, and their movement now receives measurable respect from other poetry communities.

In contrast, the poetry "establishment,"[2] represented in this episode by Hollander and Merrill, has given, for the most part, only grudging attention to women poets in general and to feminist poets in particular. As Adrienne Rich has noted concerning the Pratt award ceremony, when a poetry is as angry and "undomesticated" as Pratt's, it violates the "ritual space" and "rules of decorum" of the academy (1993, 161). In most ways, these two worlds, the mainstream and the feminist, still do not intersect but remain parallel and contradictory. The case of the Pratt award ceremony clearly illustrates that feminist poets are indeed engaged in an ongoing struggle with the "guardians" of the contemporary American poetry establishment: they are censored or rejected because they self-consciously call on a distinctly feminist poetics, and most especially if they also write explicitly about their personal experiences of not only gender but other differences (in Pratt's case, lesbianism, but also race, ethnicity, and class) that further violate the sameness of white men that has prevailed in the establishment throughout the life of twentieth-century American poetry.

One of the chief ways that feminist poets like Pratt still engage in feminist politics is through their opposition to a dominant poetry culture that does not recognize the primacy of gender and other oppressions. The question of potential points of intersection between these worlds is important, not least for reasons that relate to the health and longevity of the feminist poetry movement itself: among them, that women poets may gain, in increased publicity for their works and the presses that publish them, from the acclaim that poetry prizes and critical appraisal bring; they may benefit from the financial awards often attached to poetry prizes;[3] and this access to the resources of the poetry establishment can advance the goals of feminist poets to achieve a new status for poetry in the lives of American women. However, feminist poets remain concerned with the poetry establishment primarily for the ways they can expose it and/or revolutionize it rather than for the ways they can simply be included in or annexed to it. Therefore, the relationship between feminist poets and the poetry establishment remains primarily oppositional in nature, as feminist poets continue to emphasize the need for a more complete transformation of the American literary tradition in terms of its exclusions of writers based on gender and other identities.

That both sides maintain this opposition remains especially apparent in the fact that feminist poets have largely been ignored by establishment poets and critics who attempt to name and write about what is happening in poetry. (The sole exception to this rule is Adrienne Rich, whose work, like that of Sylvia Plath before her, has been singled out as a/the worthwhile example of feminist consciousness.) But critical inattention is an issue that also highlights contradiction and opposition *within* the women's movement itself, for many self-identified feminist critics wholly ignore the ways that women poets very self-consciously write out of feminist commitment. Therefore, the setting of the Pratt award ceremony only partially conveys the state of the community of feminist poets, feminist publishers and critics, and feminist readers: it accurately reveals the collectivity of these women as they experience in common their opposition to gender oppression, but it masks the gaps in their solidarity, the ways they are different from one another, the ways they explore and express these differences, and the ways they are different from still other feminists who have had the critical say-so to provide discursive labels for what these women are doing literarily and politically. The truth of the matter is that the relationship of poetry to feminism as a social/political movement, and feminist poets' explorations of the relationship of individual women to the category of "Woman," by and large have not been addressed in feminist critical analyses of contemporary poetry. Ironically, as many feminist literary critics have developed readings toward a "women's tradition," they have elided the difference between women poets in general and feminist poets in particular, the latter of whom have developed an identifiable poetry movement out of their concern with women's political struggles and the place of literary expression in women's lives.

An analysis of these poets and their movement first necessitates a model of literary history that does not rely on the idea of a "women's tradition" but on that of a distinct feminist tradition; in order fully to understand the implications of the work of feminist poets, these women can and must be distinguished from American women poets in general and from those other women poets now taking advantage of increased publishing opportunities made available largely as the result of the groundbreaking work feminist poets and publishers did beginning in the early 1970s. Second, this reading requires an understanding of individual voice, collectivity, and difference as aesthetic and political ideas of relationship that function significantly in both the outer-directed cultural critique and the inner-directed self-critique of the women's movement conducted by this distinct group of poets—in the themes and purposes they choose for their poetry, in the ways they view themselves as writing against a larger, hegemonic American literary tradition and culture, and in their explorations of their connections to and conflicts with each other and other women. Finally, this reading must be grounded in a sociologically based understanding of feminist theory and practice that recognizes the diversity of feminists and the existence of feminisms rather than a single feminism based on an essentialist notion of gender or of how gender is expressed textually. In this model, the test for literature is the lives of its multiplicity of writers and readers—their ideological standpoints and political interests—rather than an interpretation of textual value based on a single kind of women's experience (such as white, middle class) or on how "feminine" a text itself is (see Felski 1989).

Using this model of literary history and criticism, I offer this project as a corrective to literary historical and critical models that ignore or downplay the function of feminist thought and the women's movement in contemporary poetry by American women. My central objectives are not only to explore the historical development of the feminist poetry movement but to understand how feminist poets write out of a theorized poetics, how they write both toward "Woman" and out of the difference of "women," and how they do both of the above within the network of feminist dialogue in the ongoing women's movement. The feminist poetry movement was born in the fray of the social/political women's movement in the 1970s and has changed as the movement has; this project focuses on the years 1970–1980 as the formative years for this poetry movement, and the years 1980–1990 as the period of its maturation into an enduring force.

While no final word can be issued on the life of either the women's movement or the feminist poetry movement, as both are still alive and evolving, understanding the ways they were connected during these two decades can form the basis for an important kind of literary study that in turn can affect the direction of these movements themselves. Thus, though historically confined, the critical implications of the project are intended to contribute to the ongoing dialogue about the connections between feminist poetics and political activity.

A Movement of Poets

Feminist poets have enlivened the American poetic tradition by rethinking the function of language and poetry, broadening theme and imagery by grounding them in the experiences of women, and developing a formal reorientation based in a feminist consciousness. As women writing with the interests of other women in mind, these women have developed a poetics grounded in women's individual experiences, geared toward women's liberation from gender oppression, and therefore involving the need for both subjective and collective expression. As a result, they have combined older formal strategies with newer ones. Rooted in the revolutions in American poetry that occurred in the 1960s, and integrating aesthetic elements from diverse cultural backgrounds, feminist poets have produced interesting formal innovations. They have begun to merge the lyric and the narrative to produce a hybrid form; they have used and revised prose poems because of the widespread need to tell individual women's stories and the histories of whole cultural groups of women; and they have used elements of various literary forms from non-Western cultures together with Western ideas about poetry.

The list of poets like Pratt who ascribe to this feminist poetics—and who have produced substantive bodies of work, only to receive nominal critical attention—is long.[4] These poets have been noticed to some small extent by the poetry establishment, have been widely recognized by feminists, both in the publishing community and by readers and reviewers, and have functioned as powerful poetic voices for the continuing women's movement. While they certainly deserve critical attention based on the level of their aesthetic achievement and the ways they have developed a feminist poetics, they also merit it because of what they as a community of poets represent in literary history: they struggle in their poetry to articulate their feminist visions as they have evolved over the last two decades, and they shape their themes, language, and formal strategies in light of these visions. They are very diverse in their experience and training, and certainly in the matters of identity they explore in relation to gender.

These poets do constitute a distinct current in American poetry and among women poets, but it is important to qualify the establishment term "movement" in order to use it in this instance. Delineating feminist poetry as a movement, based on feminist poets' political/literary affiliations, falls within a common form of classification of modern poetry. While contemporary "schools" of poetry are sometimes designated by proximity as well as poetics (the New York poets, the Black Mountain poets), other larger designations are frequently made: the work of the Beat poets, for instance, embodied a distinct set of philosophical and political ideals, and what are now referred to as the antiwar poets of the 1960s were united across form (and across the country) by their political commitment to ending U.S. involvement in Vietnam. Feminist poets certainly resemble the Beat or antiwar poets in this way, for they are self-consciously feminist and consider themselves to be working together toward common poetic and political goals.

This form of classification is also useful because it helps to identify different trends among women poets in general rather than considering them (as many feminist critics do) as a unified group, which is unfruitful in that it relies on the monolithic "Woman" and collapses all distinctions among women. This kind of totalizing move most often marginalizes women of color, lesbians, and others in favor of the "norm," which has been white and middle class. However, it also elides differences among even those women who have received more recognition from the poetry mainstream, and who have employed various and sometimes defeating definitions of "Woman." Louise Bogan, for example, resisted the term "woman writer" altogether because she knew this would mean her virtual exclusion from the poetry establishment. A contemporary example is Diane Wakoski, who even in 1980 resisted the distinction "woman writer" because there had been, to her mind, so few women who had "done things" (1980, 217). Wakoski only transformed her view in the wake of the development of feminist poetry; by the time Florence Howe was preparing a revised and updated version of the anthology *No More Masks* in the early 1990s, Wakoski had come to identify herself as a woman writer quite willingly (Howe 1993, xxvi).

However, the matter of identifying the distinct category of feminist poetry also has the potential merely to repeat the totalizing gesture of applying "Woman" to all women poets; indeed, it is possible to use a totalizing version of "feminist" to unite women who might not even be interested in the designation. Therefore, it is necessary to ground any description of a feminist poetry movement in very specific historical conditions. Perhaps most significantly, these women explicitly refer to themselves as feminist and consistently conceptualize poetry in ways related to their political commitments; that is, they see art and politics as inseparable. A second sign of poets' participation in the feminist poetry movement is the extensive energy they have invested in the on-going national dialogue about feminist issues. In the tradition of poets like Adrienne Rich and Judy Grahn, who were involved in the earliest stages of the contemporary women's movement, these poets have continued to discuss and to act on women's issues, and to compose poetry that directly addresses the feminist concerns prevalent in this conversation and activism. The indications of this interaction abound, but are especially significant in feminist literary publishing. The six poets whose work I will examine in individual chapters provide excellent examples: Judy Grahn cofounded the Women's Press Collective and published her own and other feminist poets' works; Irena Klepfisz was a founding editor of *Conditions* magazine and a contributing editor for the journal *Sinister Wisdom*; Gloria Anzaldúa has fostered the expression and dialogue of women of color in two anthologies she has edited and has served as a contributing editor for *Sinister Wisdom*; June Jordan has written for feminist magazines like *Ikon* and *Sojourner*; Joy Harjo has contributed on numerous occasions to *Sinister Wisdom*; and Minnie Bruce Pratt was a founding editor of and regular contributor to *Feminary*. However, these are just a few examples. The list of the places these poets have published and their interconnections with each other and with other self-identified feminists is extensive.[5]

Another significant characteristic is that feminist poets have continued to expand the earlier visions of feminists in the movement. They have increasingly recognized the range of women's identities and experiences and the fact that gender is variously constructed and, as bell hooks has said, cannot always be considered "the sole determinant of a woman's fate" (1984, 14). In other words, they understand that "Woman" is often too confining a collective identity, and that difference between and within women challenges the assumption that has sometimes structured feminist political organizing and even feminist literary publishing and criticism—that gender can be separated from race, ethnicity, class, and sexuality, and that white middle-class women first and foremost have the tools and the know-how for the enterprise of analyz-ing gendered experience and literary production. A related feature is that this particular group of poets is characterized by the search for difference within their own work. In the tradition of women naming and expressing their experience that was developed by the earliest femi-nist poets, as well as in other political and cultural traditions developed on the margins of dominant American society, they have gone on to explore other cultural axes of identity—race, ethnicity, class, sexual-ity—as well as gender.

One other important feature of the work of these poets is related to their location within the feminist poetry movement and the social/polit-ical women's movement: while not all the poets I examine in this proj-ect identify as either lesbian or bisexual, all the representative poets I have chosen to examine in-depth do. The fact that a large number of feminist poets do identify themselves in one of these ways reflects the dialectics of sexuality and literature developed in the women's move-ment in the 1970s; the movement was profoundly energized by women who already identified as lesbian or bisexual, the movement itself gave many women the freedom to admit/choose nonheterosexual identifica-tion, and many of these women, by virtue of their disinvestment in the dominant culture, have in turn become some of the most vocal and active spokespeople and writers in the feminist poetry movement. In this context, it is especially significant to note that the actual work of these women locates them far from the stereotype of the "man-hating" lesbian feminist separatist propagated in popular culture, especially in the 1980s. They have certainly centrally pursued their ideas of women's, feminist, and lesbian literature, political practice, and community. But they have also consistently offered inclusive visions, in which they have valued difference as a positive and enabling concept, and in which they have addressed the needs of not just their women's, feminist, or lesbian constituencies but also various other communities that include men. Even the very self-consciously lesbian poet Judy Grahn dedicated her first volume of poems in part to "any brothers who want to come along" (1972).

Finally, because of the contributions that self-identified feminists have made to contemporary American poetry as well as to a broadened understanding of the possibilities of a vital social role for the poet, I consider it crucial to reclaim the term "feminist" and to demonstrate that the need for a poetry related to a widespread women's movement is not passé; rather, ongoing gender oppression as well as a continued emphasis on a poetry elite and an overall trend in American poetry toward the idea of the poet as isolated and politically detached mean that a feminist poetry is increasingly rather than decreasingly significant. These feminist poets do place great value on the importance of poetry to American cultural life and thus I have also chosen them because I consider them to be contributing to what Adrienne Rich has said is a new American poetry defined by "the relationship to more than one culture," which is "nonassimilating in spirit and therefore living amid contradictions" and "is a constant act of self-creation" (1993, 130). Thus, even as these poets are forging a revolutionary literary movement of women, they are also participating with other resistant communities in reimagining the cultural function of poetry in the American context.

Reading the Movement

Feminist poetics evolved as the women's movement did. In the "heyday" of the women's movement (1972–1982) (Taylor and Whittier 1993, 534), when feminist organizing fairly exploded and even moved into the mainstream, feminist poetry played a central role in the radical, socialist, and lesbian feminist sectors that flourished outside the dominant culture. In this context, feminists wanted a poetry in which they could name the experiences that societal and poetic taboos had previously kept them from expressing, in which they could make the hidden known. As a result, they turned to more open poetic modes, seeking to strip language and form of excess flourish and meaning and to make it accessible to ordinary women. They also needed to address collective concerns while recognizing difference, and so employed a notion of the poem as tool, as useful, with which they developed a distinctly feminist combination of subjective and collective voice in poetry. In the period of "abeyance" (1983–1991) (Taylor and Whittier 1993, 534) in the women's movement, when merely surviving as a social/ political force was at a premium, feminist poets nevertheless maintained these poetic ideas and practices, as they still do in the 1990s.

Feminist poets have addressed these elements of their poetics in their prose writings and even at times within their poetry, but none of them have developed a comprehensive statement of their approach, and feminist critics by and large have hardly addressed these elements at all. One exception is Lynda Koolish (1981), who brings together a remarkable array of early poems and poets' statements in an effort to ground contemporary women poets' innovative work in their self-conscious struggles with inherited language/poetics, in the self-empowerment of women of color, and in the experience of mothering. Koolish uses the terms "feminist" and "feminist poetry" loosely, however, and her discussions of form emphasize discovering "a specifically female form" (10, 35). Thus, while Koolish's work is helpful for understanding the desires many women poets felt to escape the confines of poetic tradition, it does not explore the practices of a self-conscious and distinctive feminist poetry movement.

Another exception is the poet/critic Jan Clausen, whose essay "A Movement of Poets: Thoughts on Poetry and Feminism" is a thoughtful assessment of feminist poetics as developed in the 1970s (1989). Originally published in 1981, Clausen's essay acknowledges the impulses I have mentioned, including making poetry more accessible, viewing poetry as useful, and developing ways to speak to/for the collective in feminist poetry. However, she relies throughout her account on anecdotal evidence alone, does not explore the roots of feminist poetics in the poetic revolutions occurring in American poetry in the 1960s, and ultimately questions some of the tenets of feminist poetics because she assumes that politics and art are in fact separable and that being too concerned, or even concerned at all, about political and social change will necessarily cripple poetry. While feminist poets consistently maintain that politics and art are inseparable, Clausen relies on the well-worn Western notion that any poetry that addresses politics will ultimately sink into propaganda. In contrast, as I will demonstrate, feminist poets carefully weave together their meditations on personal experience and their desire to speak to collective concerns, so that the result is never simple sloganeering, and indeed they produce poetry that is capable of both performing vital social and political work in society at large and delighting the feminist or nonfeminist reader/listener with its aesthetic play.

The feminist movement was one of the vital countertraditional poetic communities born in the cultural and poetic upheaval of the 1960s, although it was also informed by the groundbreaking work of earlier experimental women poets and faced its own real crucible in the 1970s and 1980s. In chapter 1, I chart the development of feminist poetics in the poetic trends and social/political countercultures of the 1960s and trace its development through the following two decades. This history is central to establishing a sociological understanding of the significance and the actual life of literature, and poetry in particular, in the women's movement, in the feminist poetry movement, and for individual women. Based on this history, I develop the term "coalitional" voice to describe feminist poets' practice of blending subjective and collective voice without eliding difference between women. Finally, I return to the history of feminist criticism of feminist poetry in order to demonstrate that a sociologically based criticism is more suited to addressing the importance of both community and difference in feminist poetry than are older, predominant modes of feminist criticism that focus on developing a comprehensive "women's tradition."

I devote the five remaining chapters to individual feminist poets who have made vital and lasting contributions to the development of feminist poetry in the 1970s and to its survival in the 1980s. I examine Judy Grahn first, not just because she produced significant poetry early in the life of feminist poetry but because she theorized it in some highly influential ways. Through her concept of "commonality," Grahn established a poetics in which the writer/text empowers readers/listeners to discover that which intersects with their own experience and respect the rest. Thus, Grahn illustrated the potential feminist poetry has to unite women in recognition of their common oppressions, even as they recognize and celebrate one another's unique experiences. In three highly popular texts of the early feminist poetry movement—*The Common Woman* (1969), *She Who* (1972), and *A Woman Is Talking to Death* (1974)—Grahn used her poetics of commonality and in the process influenced many emerging or newly feminist poets, including Adrienne Rich.

Like Grahn's, June Jordan's was an important voice in the early feminist poetry movement. But Jordan was speaking not just to/for women but also to/for African Americans, and she developed her particular feminist poetics by integrating the political and poetic sensibilities of the black arts movement of the 1960s and the feminist poetry movement of the 1970s. This synthesis enabled her to write not just against the dominant white culture but against sexism among black men and against racism in the women's movement. By taking from her African-American heritage the emphasis on the positive function of art to build and maintain communal life and combining it with the feminist emphasis on the connections between the personal and political, she was able to combine personal and communal voice that recognizes, respects, and

even relies on difference. Therefore, in chapter 3, I will show how, particularly in her volume *Passion* (1980), Jordan sought to defeat the
"either/or" thinking she says characterizes Western thinking, and in the
process became a central example of both theorizing and practicing
feminist poetics in the 1970s and into the 1980s.

The poets Gloria Anzaldúa and Irena Klepfisz have continued Jordan's work of exploring how gender oppression complicates the relationship of individual women to other women and to their racial/ethnic
communities as well as to the dominant American culture. In chapter
4, I will explore how both have developed a borderlands consciousness
to name a knowing and known self that survives and even thrives in the
margins, and in this project cross and recross poetic genre, form, and
linguistic codes. This kind of innovation has largely been ignored by
feminist critics, and so I will chart very specifically how each of these
poets carry out their work: how Anzaldúa's linguistic and generic challenges turn out to be parts of a reckoning with her feminist, lesbian,
and Chicano/a communities as well as the raw material for constructing
a new home, a new consciousness, as a feminist, and how Klepfisz discovers the intersections between her Jewish, lesbian, and feminist communities by experimenting with lyric voice and historical documents
and by mixing languages.

The question of how both to resolve the conflicts and to establish the
connections between Native American metaphysical beliefs and feminist poetics defines the work of the poet Joy Harjo. In chapter 5, I will
explore Harjo's concept of political empowerment as she has used it to
examine history in the combined lyric and narrative and to integrate
Native American and feminist aesthetic and political interests. This critical exercise is important not least because Harjo is a central example,
together with Anzaldúa and Klepfisz, of how feminist poets of the
1980s journeyed deeply into their own cultural/political histories in
order to survive as their racial/ethnic selves and to contribute to the
survival of their racial/ethnic communities, as well as of how they consistently remained committed to feminist visions and so provided important aesthetic and political ideas from their cultural heritages to the
feminist poetry movement and the women's movement as a whole.

Of the poets I examine, Minnie Bruce Pratt more than any other has
confronted the idea of unity among women. As a lesbian mother separated from her sons because of her sexuality, she came to the painful
realization that new configurations of mother-child relationships have

not yet been thoroughly conceptualized or put into practice by feminists or lesbians. Thus, in detailing her loss in *Crime Against Nature* (1990), Pratt discovers that she cannot rely on any easy notion of women's or lesbian community, nor can she easily move into coalitional voice. Instead, she discovers that she must relate the particulars of her experience in order to confront and transform the underlying assumptions about motherhood and sexuality that circulate in the dominant culture as well as in communities of women, feminists, and lesbians. In chapter 6, then, I will demonstrate how Pratt writes a highly detailed history of her experience in order to resist the cultural and legal dictum that the "unnatural" expression of lesbian desire cannot coincide with the "natural" expression of maternal love, and to build an alternate conception of community among women. This involves exploring how she does what few feminist poets have attempted: she uses nature imagery to overturn definitions of both "woman" and "lesbian" and, out of the "in-between" of natural environments, both challenges ideas of the stable self and offers enlivening ideas of difference to the feminist poetry movement of the late 1980s and early 1990s.

Based on these readings, I will offer a conclusion that measures the developments in feminist poetry overall since 1970 and comments on what the future is likely to hold for feminist poetry and its critics, but finally gives this project back to the poets themselves, for the movement is still evolving.

The Feminist Poetry Movement

One

The Life of the Movement

Feminist poetry has no identifiable birth date, no mythologized beginning to correspond, for instance, to Allen Ginsberg's performance of "Howl" in San Francisco in October 1955, which is hailed as the beginning of the Beat phenomenon. Instead, feminist poetry began in a hundred places at once, in writing workshops and at open readings, on the kitchen tables of self-publishing poet/activists, and in the work of already established women poets who began slowly to transform their ideas about formal strategies and thematic possibilities. It was also less a radical break with the past than a logical expansion of the visions of older women poets, from the activist poets of the 1930s and 1940s to the self-exiled H.D., all the way back to the revolutionary Emily Dickinson in her Victorian secrecy.

But feminist poetry did begin to flower most fully in a single decade, the explosive 1960s, when cultural change and upheaval transformed poetics (and, eventually, vice versa). It was certainly not merely incidental that feminist poetry burgeoned when both self-consciousness and social awareness took a deep hold on the American poetic psyche, in the same way that it was more than incidental that large-scale social/ political women's organizing followed very closely on the civil rights and antiwar movements. Across the country, beginning in the late 1960s, women began to claim control over their own personal and political realities and to challenge gender oppression, and across the country, they wrote poems out of the will to cause these extraordinary changes. In the sea change in post–World War II poetry, feminists found the freedom to innovate, and they in turn contributed to the American poetry scene a distinct and influential body of poetic ideas and practices.

American Poetry in the 60s

A number of the ideas and practices ascendant in the 1960s created an atmosphere of both personal freedom of expression and collective response that accommodated women's needs and aspirations for poetry. Of these, open form, the banishment of persona, and a new emphasis on poetry performance proved to be particularly significant to women poets finding their voices as feminists.

These innovations brewed in the work of the antiestablishment movements of the 1950s—the Black Mountain poets, the Beats, the San Francisco Renaissance, and the New York school—all of which had their roots in the post–World War II trend away from formalism and the attendant conviction that the poet should speak only through a mask. This is not to say that the New Critical style and its proponents in the academy did not still hold sway, especially in the college class-room, but these avant-garde poets fought diligently against what they perceived to be the stultifying influence of modernist excesses. As Leslie Ullman points out, a sure sign of the shifting ground was the battle of the anthologies: *New Poets of England and America* (1958), in which Donald Hall and his co-editors wholly ignored the avant-garde and maintained the English tradition as the ground for American poetry, versus *The New American Poetry, 1945–1960,* Donald Allen's inclusive tribute to the new movements' poetry and their poetic manifestos (Ull-man 1991, 190–91).

Charles Olson's 1950 essay "Projective Verse" was one of these mani-festos; it more than perhaps any other statement of the emerging poet-ics ushered in the age of "open form" and had momentous impact on the course of poetry in the 1960s. Olson found his heritage in the work of the imagist William Carlos Williams (at this point still mostly an outsider to the establishment), for Williams strove to create a poetry of experience, of life in any given moment and immediate contact with one's surroundings. This notion of projective verse, or open form, re-sists any rigidity of either subject or form but rather relies on the fluidity of experience as the basis for both. The poem reflects the writer's move-ment through life and includes observations, feelings, and, above all, attention to the ordinary; as Williams himself stated in the oft-repeated phrase, the poet pursues "no ideas but in things." Born of the poet's attention to bodily experience, the poem itself takes over in the process of its creation. As Kenneth Rexroth puts it, Olson and his contemporar-ies discovered that "the ear, the breath, and the heart were better instru-ments of prosodic analysis than little hooks and lines and the patterns to be found in the back of a rhyming dictionary" (1971, 169).

Denise Levertov, the only woman member of the Black Mountain school, refined Olson's statements in her own views about "organic form." For Levertov, "the metric movement, the measure is the direct expression of the movement of perception." That is, the formal shape of the poem mirrors the shape of the perception itself. This is something more than free verse, which "is written not with any desire to seek a form, indeed perhaps with the longing to avoid form (if that were possible) and to express inchoate emotion as purely as possible" (1973, 11). Poets of the 1960s, whether they sought the inherent style of organic form or the intentional chaos of free verse, found especially appealing this opportunity to unite perception and experience with the poetic vehicle and allow these to direct the poem's form rather than the other way around. This loosening, or reconception, of form deeply affected the work of the Black Mountain poets in the 1950s and of Robert Bly and the Deep Image poets in the 1960s.

While the practitioners of open form naturally found themselves taking their personal experience more seriously, perhaps the so-called Confessionalists did more than any other group of the early 1960s to rupture the boundaries of revelation and release the self in all its unmitigated pain and despair into contemporary American poetry. Robert Lowell and his students, chief among them Anne Sexton and Sylvia Plath, overthrew the smothering burden of the persona in their poems and released the vital energies of relentless introspection and honesty about personal struggles and disappointments. Though this was finally in many ways a tragic genre—in both theme and lived experience, for Sexton, Plath, and John Berryman all committed suicide—it catapulted Williams's focus on the details of ordinary existence into the realm of utter autobiography. This is not to say, of course, that these poets "confessed" anything more than they wished to, but, as Mark Doty so aptly points out, they "created themselves as characters within the poems" (1991, 148). Influenced by the sense of cultural isolation and the widespread emphasis on psychoanalysis that were seemingly endemic to the late 1950s, these poets' depth of self-exploration cast its influence over virtually all the poetry of the 1960s.

The third important development of the decade was the rise of social awareness and a corresponding emphasis on poetry performance. While Ginsberg and the Beats' mystical anarchism was not at least at the outset particularly hopeful, the act of reading publicly for active, involved audiences itself led to a new recognition of the public role poetry could play. As Rexroth says of Ginsberg's celebrated first reading of "Howl," it heralded the return of public poetry, "the return of a tribal, preliterate relationship between poet and audience" (1971, 141). While Rexroth's statement certainly neglects the existence of contemporary oral cultures, it does get to the heart of the difference for American poetry in the 1960s: these poets recognized the power of public performance, not just to involve audiences in the act of making poetry but to inspire audiences to think about, and think differently about, the world in which they were living.

The result, of course, was protest poetry. With public venues provided through antiwar organizing, as well as in the hip counterculture at large, poets began to read their poetic gestures of resistance, not just to militarism and violence but to sexism, racism, and materialism. Ginsberg himself became the ultimate traveling poet, reading from stages around the country, but any number of other poets began to write about their political commitments and to lend their voices to the crescendo. By 1967, the protest had fully erupted. That year, a broad-based group of artists staged the Week of the Angry Arts Against the War in Vietnam, taking poetry caravans through the city streets, with poets reading from a flatbed truck and distributing thousands of poetry booklets. They staged a variety of readings, with women like Adrienne Rich and Muriel Rukeyser taking part. This spawned a series of Angry Arts Weeks in other cities, as well as similar smaller events around the nation ("Angry Arts" 1967).

This emergence of a public, politically visionary poetry certainly reflected the times, but it also testified to the other quite profound currents changing the very course of American poetry in the early 1960s. While projective verse relied on transmission through bodily experience, Robert Bly's Deep Image movement funneled perception through the hitherto unrevealed territories of the psyche. Bly and Denise Levertov, not coincidentally, also became protest poets, for they "forged . . . links between inwardness and the outer world, the explorable self and the collective self, which legitimized 'protest' as a necessary aesthetic in its own right" (Ullman 1991, 206). Parks, streets, coffeehouses, and college campuses became sites of protest, at least in part because the voices of poets—together with those of musicians, artists, and other writers—rose in the cries for change.

All of these developments in the poetry of the 1960s have their historical roots in the transformations that occurred in the repressed 1950s and explosive 1960s. Indeed, this revolution in poetry into more open and energized forms owed as much to the social restlessness of the late 1950s as it did to Olson and Williams, for in this decade the veneer of postwar tranquility gradually began to give way to the social unease that seethed underneath. By the early 1960s, civil rights sit-ins and marches, antiwar demonstrations, Betty Friedan's *The Feminine Mystique,* and the counterculture in all its manifestations had begun to expose the myths of family security and limitless prosperity that had dominated white, middle-class culture.

The Eruption of Feminist Poetry

These changes illuminate the beginnings of the social/political women's movement as well as the beginning of feminist poetry; women found themselves questioning the gendered roles they had been playing in a repressive American culture, and they began searching for an appropriate literary avenue to express this experience. White women found themselves consigned to their suburban homes in the 1950s, while African-American women struggled to fight increasingly virulent racism. Long forgotten or not yet discovered sources of self-knowledge and communal action acted like volcanoes in their lives, out of which erupted both the political analyses and poetic innovations of the 1960s. Women uncovered these possibilities within themselves and adapted them from without; the relationship between women's organizing and writing and the broader cultural shifts was certainly a dialectical one, and women took to both quickly and enthusiastically. There is no simple cause and effect relationship here, for the women's movement produced the need to write lives and to tell them publicly, and these poetic acts in the context of the social/political movement drew more and more women to the act of writing poetry. Nevertheless, the central breakthroughs in American poetry in the 1960s undoubtedly greatly influenced the directions feminist poetry was to take in the latter part of the decade.

The new emphasis on open form profoundly influenced women poets who had previously been careful formalists as well as women who may have never written before but to whom open form itself acted as their invitation to take up the craft of poetry. Adrienne Rich is the prime embodiment of the former: she turned from the prettily distant and formalist poems—highly praised by men critics—of *A Change of World* (1951) and *The Diamond Cutters* (1955) to the increasingly free lines and raw honesty of the new poems in *Snapshots of a Daughter-in-Law* (1963). By the time she published *The Will to Change* in 1971, she had completely shattered the formalist demands she said had kept her, like "asbestos gloves," from her fiery recognition of her own oppression as a woman (Ullman 1991, 216). June Jordan later followed in Rich's footsteps; like many young women receiving their educations in the 1950s, she had been schooled in the rigid forms of older white men poets, and only began to experiment fully with the connections between form and her experience as an African American and a feminist in her second volume of poetry in the early 1970s.

Similarly, women throughout the movement—some who had substantial formal training, many who had none—found this emphasis on open form exhilarating. Women who might *never* have considered a traditionally prosodic poem as a means of expression flocked to poetry when they discovered that it could *emerge* from their experience, that it could reflect the experiences and observations that were emerging in the context of the social/political women's movement. Highly formalist poems would feel like the homes they had been confined to in the 1950s, while the rawness of open form suited the natural expression of their lives in writers' collectives, in consciousness-raising groups, and in the streets. Women recognized in open form a medium they could use to relate the music of the "thing"—their experience as women in an oppressive culture. This focus on experience reflected the spirit of women's movement organizing, as well as the antiwar and civil rights organizing that preceded it, and prompted the drive to encourage any woman who desired expression to become a poet. As feminist writer/activist Margaret Randall has noted of the images of struggle that abounded in the 1960s, "The art rooted in these images, in these events, spurned preciosity and armchair observation—the experience itself was the thing" (1990, 9).

Women concentrated on their personal experience in consciousness-raising groups in particular, and at least in part because of their experience in such groups, feminist poets welcomed the banishment of persona that the Confessionalists had so greatly effected. Especially in the grassroots cells of radical feminism, women gathered in groups to examine their personal experiences and to develop wide-ranging political analyses out of what they discovered; the slogan "the personal as political" became so popular because it so neatly captured the way feminists mined individual experiences in order to understand what was wrong with society at large. Indeed, what was consciousness-raising if not the "confessional" act of admitting to oneself the extent of the anger, despair, and pain that resulted from living in a patriarchal culture? Confessional poetry and its progeny had provided the opportunity for autobiography, for honest and more complete revelation, and feminist poets took up this task without hesitation.

Again, Rich is a good example because she is a "bridge" poet from the 1950s to the 1970s; numerous critic/historians of contemporary poetry have placed Rich with the Confessionalists, for she certainly increasingly viewed and reviewed her own excruciating experience without fear. She was in reality, however, a prototype of the feminist poet, for she engaged in self-revelation not out of despair or some hope that the act of writing itself might lend some meaning to an otherwise pitiful existence, but out of an expansive vision of personal and collective change and renewal. Beginning in the early 1970s, together with other feminist poets, she engaged in radical self-revelation but also pursued a vision of social change that thoroughly challenged the myopic tendencies of Confessionalist poetry.

Rich's example leads to the third influential transformation in 1960s poetry. While the Confessionalists' introspection remained just that, feminist poets' belief in "the personal as political" required that they connect their self-reflections to public life. Thus, feminists joined the Beats and protest poets in their focus on the performance aspects of poetry; as a result, in the ongoing life of the women's social/political movement, poetry became a central feature of cultural and political expression. Performing their works in open coffeehouse and bookstore readings, at women's cultural festivals, and at political rallies of many kinds, poets both evoked in audience members some recognition of their own experiences as individuals and caused them to understand the collective resonances of personal experience, thus encouraging them to give more energy to the movement. Feminist poets fulfilled a functional, cultural, even a vatic, role for the rank and file of feminist organization. This was so much the case that the poet Judy Grahn remarked much later that even though the feminist arts as a whole had flourished in the intervening years, the movement "still keeps one ear to the ground to hear what else its poets may be telling" (1985, xviii). As Sue-Ellen Case put it in 1988, "these authors become characters or *personae* of their community. The readings become communal celebrations and these celebrations help to create . . . 'performance poetry' " (1988, 50).

All of these transformations—open form, the banishment of persona, and the emphasis on poetry performance—had profound effects on the emergence of feminist poetry. But acknowledging this influence requires a strong caveat: any history of feminist poetry must also involve the understanding that at no time did mainstream "establishment" poets simply and benevolently deem it acceptable for more women to turn to poetry or for them to turn to new, challenging forms. When women poets began to write out of their experiences in the women's movement, they not only radically diverged from traditional notions of what women could do in poetry, but they began to create something new and quite apart from what white men poets, and even other women poets, were creating. As Adrienne Rich recalls, "the poetry of women's liberation in the 1970s was *women's* anti-establishment poetry, challenging not just conventional puritanical mores, but the hip 'counterculture' and the male poetry culture itself." Thus, while she says that the work of men poets "doesn't have to be a dead hand in the boat," she also says it cannot substitute for women's own poetic innovations (1993, 168, 159). So while the women's movement certainly took shape as a part of the 1960s milieu, it was also its own literary phenomenon, self-generated and self-sustaining. After all, women found it necessary first of all to present a radical challenge to the poetic tradition in their search for their place within a women's poetic heritage. Thus, before moving on to discuss the details of feminist poetry's innovations, we must examine the way feminist poets sought to understand the past.

Locating a Tradition

Feminist readers, of course, began to search for earlier writers who had forecasted their situation, who could inspire them in their struggle; hence, previously published poems by older or deceased writers were reprinted in small magazines and newspapers across the country. Feminist *poets* began to search out their own precursors not just in an effort to establish themselves apart from the male-dominated tradition, but for the reasons salubrious to any younger generation of writers: they looked for some confirmation of their vision, some clues that the formal and thematic directions they were taking shared a common history. This search for exemplars issued in explorations and tributes by individual women readers and poets (and as women's studies programs took root in the mid to late 1970s, by academic feminist critics), but perhaps the most visible result was the spate of commercial and small press anthologies of American women's poetry that began to appear in the early 1970s.

While many of these anthologies sought to salute inclusively American women's voices in the twentieth century or even since the birth of an American literary tradition, a closer look at the selected poems reveals quite deliberate choices of individual poems that speak most directly of women's gendered experiences. Perhaps the most celebrated of the anthologies, *No More Masks: An Anthology of Poems by Women* attempted to identify a twentieth-century women's poetic tradition and succeeded in building a sense of thematic continuity and substance. As the editors noted, in the beginning they had no "real idea of the number of poets, American women, who had produced good or excellent poetry" in the twentieth century; in the end, they included eighty-seven poets, over fifty of whom were born before 1940 (Howe and Bass 1973, xxvii).[1]

This number of poets also points, however, to the significant difficulties involved in naming a usable past. The enterprise is first of all fraught with the conflicting impulses—to include and exclude—that always plague the task of canon formation. Although the editors of these anthologies sometimes claimed to be recovering a comprehensive tradition, they still made choices about whose work would appear. The politics of publishing and text accessibility also certainly came into play. In the early 1970s, commercial publishers sought to cash in on the rise in feminist sentiment and so published a number of these anthologies. Quite often, in the urgency to publish, editors ignored less accessible (out of print, critically neglected) works by earlier poets. For instance, the work of white activist working-class poets like Lola Ridge and Genevieve Taggard was omitted as was the clear-sighted work of the exiled southern poet Evelyn Scott. Glaring holes also exist with regard to poets of color, for the work of these poets was subject to neglect on a larger cultural scale. African-American women poets are represented in some numbers, but Native American and Asian-American poets were not sought out and included. The contemporary African-American poets Audre Lorde, June Jordan, and Lucille Clifton appear on these pages, but their predecessors Alice Ruth Moore Dunbar-Nelson and Anne Spencer do not. Most of the remaining poets are white and middle class. The editors also do not make visible in any way the lesbians represented in the text. Secondly, this exercise highlights the impossibility of clearly identifying any single set of influences on the women poets coming to their work in the 1960s. Even poets like Louise Bogan, who believed women inherently incapable of important poetry and wanted desperately to dissociate herself from her female contemporaries, certainly made a dent in the male-dominated literary tradition by their very presence on the poetry scene.

Nevertheless, among the earlier twentieth-century poets included in these anthologies, a number of them were especially popular because they were both somewhat acceptable to men poets of their day and resistant to gender roles and the literary establishment in poetry as well as in their own lives; the chief examples among these are Amy Lowell and H.D. As a leader of the Imagists, Amy Lowell was at first hailed by Ezra Pound and others in the movement, and then later criticized as superfluous. She nevertheless never ceased her musings on what it is in women poets that "Singles us out to scribble down, man-wise, / The fragments of ourselves" (1928, 50). She also kept up throughout her entire adult life her overtly lesbian love poems to her longtime lover, Ada Russell. Like the iconoclastic Gertrude Stein, H.D. exiled herself in Europe. As the "ideal" Imagist whose work was both praised and appropriated by Pound, she nevertheless exceeded the bounds of this literary movement to seek a distinctly feminine mythopoesis to counter/ transform the patriarchal world she understood herself to live in. In the gardens and heroine myths of Greece, she pursued a countertradition: "O to blot out this garden / to forget, to find a new beauty / in some terrible / wind-tortured place" (1925, 27).

A constellation of younger, highly anthologized poets was certainly chosen for the ways these women had begun to write in freer, more personal modes and to challenge the tradition. In the confessional style, Sylvia Plath disclosed the long-repressed psychological torment of women and in doing so gave notice that the "private" world of women was *not* all flowers and love, was not what men viewed as "trivial." Her exploration of her victimization dovetailed, however, with her poetic desire to express the depths of her consciousness with precision and tragic effect; her confessional urge led ultimately to isolation rather than transformation. Anne Sexton often exhibited the same nihilist tendencies as Plath, succumbing to the pressures of trying to be both traditional woman and poet. Nevertheless, she gained ground by exploring the psychic boundaries of the existence of a suburban housewife, dealing extensively and honestly with experiences previously examined only rarely by women in poetry: mental illness, surgical operations, child-bearing, and the death of parents. Sexton also certainly exhibited some transformation in her thinking about herself as a woman writer. In a 1959 letter to Carolyn Kizer, she referred to the two of them as part of "a slight, small band of lady poets with guts" (Sexton and Ames 1991, 68); a decade later, not long before her own suicide, she wrote in the feminist magazine *Aphra*, "As long as it can be said about a woman writer, 'She writes like a man' and that woman takes it as a compliment, we are in trouble" (1969, 5).

Two older poets whose style definitely evolved over the tumultuous decade of the 1960s were Denise Levertov and Gwendolyn Brooks, and both were repeatedly anthologized in the wave of collections in the early 1970s. Levertov, Plath, and Sexton all published their first volumes of poetry in 1960, but Levertov's career was to take a decidedly different direction than the two confessionalists'. Out of her commitment to open form and to perceiving experience fully, Levertov gradually blossomed into a protest poet, and in her willingness to express her commitment openly while still remaining faithful to the demands of poems themselves, she served as an inspiration to feminist poets. Her volume of essays *The Poet in the World* (1973) eventually became a much respected treatise on the responsibility of the poet, both to her poems and to political realities. Initially in the condensed, academic style of the 1940s and later in a looser, tougher idiom and freer style that coincided with her involvement in the Black Arts movement of the 1960s, Gwendolyn Brooks provided direct and personal explorations of the ordinary lives of African Americans, and African-American women in particular. Brooks understood the need to explore new forms in light of social change; she said, "I'm not writing sonnets, and I probably won't be, because, as I've said many times, this does not seem to me to be a sonnet time. It seems to be a free verse time, because this is a raw, ragged, uneven time—with rhymes, if there are rhymes, incidental and random" (Brooks 1979, 2).

Though this list of influences is only partial, and itself reflects the inclusive/exclusive work of tradition formation, it nevertheless provides some idea of what women poets/readers, and especially feminist poets/readers, were looking for in the early 1970s; only a full examination of the anthologies would give a complete picture of the diversity of earlier poets being sought out. However, while the anthologies provide an important testament to the developing idea of a women's poetry tradition, in contrast, the central examples for *feminist* poets are identifiable by virtue of the influence they held in the conversations in and about poetry that feminists began having with each other in the 1960s. Emily Dickinson and Muriel Rukeyser represented the ends of the spectrum for feminist poets: the burden of the past for American women who would be poets and the promise of the future based on what women were discovering in a more liberating political and cultural atmosphere.

Dickinson's brilliant range and vision had only become truly visible in 1951, when the complete, unaltered collection of her poems was finally published. While examinations of her enigmatic, punctuated work itself yielded new and evolving insights about her context and poetic goals, for many feminists, Dickinson became *the* symbol of the dilemma of the American woman poet. The editors of the anthology *Psyche: The Feminine Poetic Consciousness* identify Dickinson as the starting point for an American women's tradition precisely because she confronts the terrors of the woman poet: "she articulates the primal concerns which haunt the feminine consciousness: existential isolation, confusion about identity, conflicting realities" (Segnitz and Rainey 1973, 16). Thus, though Dickinson was considered courageous in the very act of writing of these concerns when few or no other American women poets had, she was also the classic embodiment of the "split-self"—split, as Adrienne Rich has said, between "a publicly acceptable persona" and the part of herself that she knew as "the essential, the creative and powerful self, yet also as possibly unacceptable, perhaps even monstrous" (1979, 175).

If Dickinson's work conveyed to feminist poets the classic conflict between one's creative possibilities and the expectation that women be only muses for men poets and never poets themselves, then Muriel Rukeyser's represented a path out of the conflict. In fact, if any one woman could be said to have had the most influence on the feminist poetry movement, it would by a multitude of accounts have to be Rukeyser. Increasingly throughout the 1960s and 1970s, feminist poets began to recognize Rukeyser as a central, or *the* central, prototype of the contemporary feminist poet; Florence Howe and Ellen Bass called her "our first and most persistent rebel" (1973, 7). The reasons for this are twofold: Rukeyser's innovative poetry itself, which spanned over forty years and unfailingly addressed women's experiences, and Rukeyser's actual presence on the poetry scene of the 1960s and 1970s, as a cofounder of Teachers and Writers Collaborative, a teacher of writers' workshops, and as a poet-activist with groups like RESIST and Angry Arts Against the War in Vietnam. The latter is especially significant, for she also very generously made herself available to younger women poets and simultaneously opened up her still evolving poetry into more and more open declarations of women's rights and lives.

Florence Howe remembers when she asked Rukeyser for two poems for *No More Masks*: "But I added we could pay her only $300 for everything . . . The money was not important, she said, and asked about other poets to be included. Could she be helpful in any way?" (1994, 12). Similarly, Adrienne Rich recalls from the times they read together in New York City that "there was an undeniable sense of female power that came onto any platform along with Muriel Rukeyser" (Levi 1994, xv). By the early 1970s, Rukeyser had become in a very real way the physical incarnation of a women's tradition: she lent her aid, she wrote increasingly feminist poems, and she spoke through both her life and her work of the ways a woman can write, as Kate Daniels has put it, in answer to the "poetic imperative" of her own body (1992, xv).

Perhaps the most telling sign that Rukeyser had already become a central influence on feminist poets by the early 1970s is that the line "No more masks!" from her poem "The Poem as Mask" (1968) became a kind of wake-up call to women writers; this line reverberated throughout the feminist political and poetic movements when Howe and Bass chose it as the title for their anthology. As it was anthologized and quoted time and again, the concluding couplet of section three of her long poem "Käthe Kollwitz" (1968) also became a kind of literary anthem for the political women's movement: "What would happen if one woman told the truth about her life? / The world would split open" (Rukeyser 1978, 482).[2] Rukeyser's presence has lingered throughout the years, even though she died in 1980; poets as diverse as Alice Walker and Minnie Bruce Pratt have spoken of her influence, and Marge Piercy dedicated the anthology *Early Ripening: American Women's Poetry Now* to her—naming her "a great poet and a great example"—in 1987 (Walker 1983; Pratt 1991; Piercy 1987).

Rukeyser's unwillingness to bend to the pressures of any male-dominated poetry community had certainly affected her popularity within the establishment, if not her ongoing commitment and unflagging ability to continue writing. In spite of her early explosion onto the poetry scene—she won the Yale Younger Poets Prize for *Theory of Flight* (1935) when she was only twenty-one—Rukeyser's blend of modernist self-reflection and social awareness was thought unacceptable by both the then active Left and "those who maintained (they thought) nonpolitical positions during the fierce politico-literary battles of the 1930s" (Daniels 1992, xi–xii). As her poetry became more and more innovative, she was eventually almost completely "disappeared" by the poetry establishment,[3] precisely because of her deep commitment to social justice—and women's liberation in particular—and her insistence on following her own unique poetic vision rather than the accepted versions of a woman poet's vision. These facts alone make feminist poets' "recovery" of Rukeyser in the 1960s notable; unlike Plath and Sexton, she was not a highly visible, or even token, member of the poetry mainstream.

But feminist poets found much to applaud and emulate in Rukeyser's work. Even in her early career, Rukeyser was never concerned that she did not fit into the romantic/lyric tradition of women's poetry that still dominated in the 1930s and that most men poets thought to be the only vein women could or should write in. By the time *Theory of Flight* appeared, Rukeyser had already developed a highly organic form and a wholly unconventional practice of punctuation, lineation, and spacing in which she could more freely express her own gendered experience and give attention to distinctly woman-identified themes. During the next forty years, Rukeyser went on to articulate very directly her own and other women's experiences. She spoke of her experiences of, for instance, menstruation, orgasm, pregnancy, and nursing; in any number of instances, she was the first American woman to address such experiences in any direct and sustained way in poetry (Daniels 1991).

Rukeyser also became a beacon to feminist poets because she was an avid teacher and theorist of poetics; in fact, her writings about poetics deeply foreshadow those of her feminist descendants. She viewed, for instance, the poem as "a process" (1949, 186), a notion that would be echoed by feminist poets twenty-five years later. Rukeyser believed the poem was made of "change itself," and capable of both being shaped by a woman's voice and transforming the individual reader and society. She always had in mind that the poem would not only reach the reader intimately but would cause change in the reader and thereby, through a ripple effect, change social conditions. She says, "In poetry, the exchange is one of energy. Human energy is transferred, and from the poem it reaches the reader"; this energy "is consciousness, the capacity to produce change in existing conditions." She offers a triadic model of poetic meaning; the poet, the poem, and the "witness" (a term she says

"includes the act of seeing or knowing by personal experience") act together with "responsibility" in the act of writing, reading, and changing
(or acting) (1949, 184–87). The feminist poets of the 1960s began to
echo this emphasis on the social value of poetry in their view of the
relationship between poet and audience as one of active participation
on the part of both writer and reader in the transformation of consciousness, in the construction of an art-generated cultural critique, and
in concerted action to change the conditions of women's lives.

Thus the poet's evocation of experience functions not only to shape
the poem itself (often the terminus of expression in models of organic
writing) but to alter the reader herself and through her, her social/politi-
cal context. Because Rukeyser understood poetry to work in this way,
she interpreted the lack of value placed on poetry in American culture
to indicate individual readers' fear of what poetry would do to them
and require of them. The final stanza of her "Reading Time : 1 Minute
26 Seconds" describes how this fear affects the reading experience:
"They fear it. They turn away, hand up palm out / fending off moment
of proof, the straight look, poem. / The prolonged wound-conscious-
ness after the bullet's shot" (1978, 161–62). Rukeyser understood the
deep, intrinsic connections between poetry and politics: indeed, Rich
has called her "that great poet of inseparables" (1993, 175).

In this attention to politics and her commitment to women's lives,
Rukeyser thus became for many the exemplary feminist poet, while
Dickinson represented for them the rebellion of women trapped between the traditional roles assigned to women and the creative role typically assigned to men. These two poets were never consciously pitted
against each other and no either/or could contain their lives or their
work—indeed, Rukeyser never *called* herself a feminist, and even from
behind her bedroom door, Dickinson certainly rebelled against the
strictures placed upon her. Nevertheless, the two served as distinct sign-
posts of the possibilities, past and future. If Dickinson embodied the
"split-self" women poets had experienced in the past, then Rukeyser
pointed the way to a poetry that encompasses all a woman is and can
be, a poetry rooted in women's lives, both functional in that it provides
maps for viewing and resisting a patriarchal world, and delightful in
that it plays with language and form.

The Feminist Press and Poetry as the Medium of the Movement

While the anthologies established the idea of an American women's
poetry tradition for women readers and even, through the more com-

mercially viable publications, for a mainstream American readership, feminist poetry was emerging in many more published venues than the anthologies of the early 1970s. Perhaps most significantly, not only a select few "successful" poets, but thousands of women of all ages across the country were writing it. As feminists turned away from the mainstream media and commercial presses, they founded their own newspapers, magazines, journals, and small presses, a move that both grew out of and propelled the burgeoning love of poetry in the grassroots women's movement. Newspapers and small magazines published poems by women just finding their way into workshops and writing poetry for the first time as well as by women who, unlike the predecessors who influenced them, found their voices in the weltering 1960s and led the way in developing a distinctly feminist poetic sensibility. Journals were founded for more focused explorations of the literary flourishing (and poetry was the mainstay of many of these), while feminist presses took up the task of publishing the work of mostly young, previously unpublished poets who were writing out of their feminist commitment.

When Andrea Chesman and Polly Joan assessed the role of the arts in the women's movement in the preface to their *Guide to Women's Publishing* (1978), they noted that "poetry was the medium of the movement." Not only this, they asserted, but while "every revolutionary movement has had its poets and its poetry, no other movement has been so grounded in poetry as Feminism" (1978, 3). It is especially appropriate that the editors of a volume on the women's press should make this observation, for the function of poetry in the movement was developed in the matrix of poet (production), poem (performance and distribution), and reader (reception and response). In the political atmosphere of the mass movement, especially in an impressively long list of journals, magazines, and newspapers and at public poetry readings, poetry served as a kind of political clarion call to women to take notice and take action; the consciousness-raising groups and organizing cells of radical feminism proved to be especially fertile grounds for preparing women to hear this call. Poets like Rukeyser, Rich, Grahn, Piercy, and Robin Morgan quickly became some of the movement's most effective and respected spokeswomen, and poetry as a literary practice became a dominant mode of expression for thousands of women across the country.

Practically speaking, poetry was definitely less expensive than fiction to self-publish and share. As Jan Clausen says, the flourishing of feminist poetry grew out of this reality and subsequently mounted an unprecedented challenge to the men-dominated commercial publishing world: "a poet could publish new work in a pamphlet or newspaper days or weeks after writing it. Such poetry satisfied a demand for poems explicitly feminist in their perspective, flourishing in the gap between the explosion of feminist consciousness and the commercial publication of feminist poetry anthologies and individual volumes" (1989, 11). Within the first decade, an impressive number of feminists, many of them feminist poets themselves, began developing alternative publishing venues. Once the groundswell of women's poetry occurred in the early 1970s, the number of women-owned/run magazines, journals, and presses and the number of available chapbooks, broadsides, and books began to proliferate rapidly. By 1970, feminist publishing opportunities in general had opened up across the country; by 1978, when Joan and Chesman published the *Guide,* a phenomenal seventy-three periodicals and sixty-six presses appeared in its pages.[4]

Many of these started as self-publishing ventures, which indicates the strong desire women had to make their work available to women readers; they truly believed, as Out and Out Books' cofounder Joan Larkin put it, that they were "making available to others the books we need for our survival" (Chesman and Joan 1978, 157). In 1970, Elsa Gidlow started Druid Heights Books to bring out her first collection of poetry; she published her fourth by 1976. Lesbian-run Out and Out Books' first run in 1975 included four poetry titles by its founders: Larkin's *Housework,* Jan Clausen's *After Touch,* Irena Klepfisz's *Periods of Stress,* and an anthology of lesbian women's poetry edited by Larkin and Elly Bulkin. Alta established Shameless Hussy Press to publish her own poetry and then brought out the work of Susan Griffin and Lyn Lifshin. As the Women's Press Collective, Judy Grahn, Pat Parker, and Willyce Kim began with only "a mimeograph machine on the kitchen table" and paid for each book based on its own sales (Chesman and Joan 1978, 179). Women's writing workshops proliferated, and many brought forth publishing efforts; for example, the Best Friends Poetry Collective began a small magazine based in Albuquerque, while Embers Publications in Santa Cruz came into being when a workshop published a poetry anthology including the work of all its members (Chesman and Joan 1978).

By the time of the commercial publication of the anthologies in the early 1970s and of Adrienne Rich's *Diving into the Wreck*[5] and Robin

Morgan's *The Monster* in 1972, the feminist poetry community had established itself as a free press force to be reckoned with. Indeed the feminist press was the direct expression of the emphasis on social change in feminist poetics, and constituted both a challenge to the commercial establishment and a clear statement that women were taking their own work seriously. This was not lost even on those poets like Rich who were courted by the mainstream; in 1974, when she was named Prizewinner in Poetry in the National Book Awards, Rich issued a statement with conominees Audre Lorde and Alice Walker: "We . . . together accept this award in the name of all the women whose voices have gone and still go unheard in a patriarchal world, and in the name of those who, like us, have been tolerated as token women in this culture, often at great cost and in great pain" (Olsen 1983, 197–98n).

Publishing conditions for women poets had been, as a matter of course, quite deplorable before the advent of the women's movement. In Mary Biggs's comprehensive study of contemporary poetry publishing, the poet Maxine Kumin notes that prior to the women's movement, "it was commonplace to be told by an editor that he'd like to publish more of my poems, but he'd already published one by a woman that month" (Biggs 1990, 25). Mona Van Duyn and May Swenson both note that women were far less likely than men to be anthologized, while Kumin makes it quite clear that poetry dealing with women's common experiences was especially unacceptable. In Kumin's view, the attitude was that "women are not supposed to have uteruses, especially in poems," and a woman certainly was not supposed to "send 'childbirth poems' to *The New Yorker*" (Biggs 1990, 27). Meanwhile, younger women poets like Ruth Stone and Karen Snow point out that feminism itself was the force that "set their writing free and permitted full artistic development" (Biggs 1990, 30). Stone and Snow echo Robin Morgan, who says that although she was writing before she became a feminist, the women's movement "invited me to find my own voice, to free it from the constraints of 'proper' (patriarchal) subject matter" (1990, 15).

Even though controversy periodically took hold over whether or not women should publish *exclusively* in the women's press, and many poets concluded that they could not pass up the opportunity to publish with the more financially viable commercial presses should the opportunity arise, the prevailing attitude came very close to Susan Griffin's, which she expressed for Jan Clausen's "The Politics of Publishing and the Lesbian Community" (1976): "the fact that I choose to publish two books with a trade house does not change my feeling about Feminist and lesbian presses . . . There is no way, ironically, I could write the book I am writing without their existence, because these presses have made possible the creation of a woman's literature, and it is in the wake of the reverberations of our culture, inside this culture, that I write" (Clausen 1976, 99). Clausen's survey-based article was itself sparked in part by the ongoing argument about radical feminism versus what many termed "cultural separatism," or the belief in women's essential differences from men and in an exclusive women's culture, as well as debates about whether lesbians in particular should publish with self-designated lesbian presses. June Arnold, co-editor of Daughters Press, was considered a central proponent of lesbian-identified cultural separatism. However, an article based on comments she made at a lesbian conference in New York in May 1976 reveals a radical, tactical base to her assertion that women should publish with what she called the "independent women's communications network": "It is vital that we maintain control over our future, that we spend the energy of our imaginations and criticisms building feminist institutions that women will gain from both in money and skills" (1976, 26). In addition, Clausen's survey of lesbian writers clearly indicates that the vast majority of them thought the feminist press was invaluable, even if they themselves felt compelled by the economics of publishing to go with commercial outlets.

The debate between the radical and cultural separatist sectors of the movement in the 1970s occurred simultaneously with increased tensions over difference in the women's movement, which helped lead to another central development, the publishing of women of color. While historian Alice Echols (1989) has argued that the "separatist" impulse originated at least in part as a way to withdraw from the political conflict over racial, class, and sexual diversity, the feminist press reveals that even in the early 1970s, radical feminists were quite concerned about difference, and especially about racism.[6] The commercial publication of the anthology *Black Woman* (Bambara 1970) confirms that the conversation about race was important to even a general readership. It wasn't until the mid 1970s, though, that women of color became a vital force in feminist publishing; previously, poets like Audre Lorde, June Jordan, Joy Harjo, and Wendy Rose had published with commercial or progressive small presses. However, soon after Lorde became editor of Chrysalis in 1976 (with Jordan as contributing editor), a spate of individual volumes appeared from the feminist press, including Willyce Kim's *Eating Artichokes* (Diana Press, 1976), Nellie Wong's *Dreams in Harrison Railroad Park* (Kelsey Street Press, 1977), Mitsuye Yamada's *Camp Notes and Other Poems* (Shameless Hussy, 1976), and Pat Parker's *Movement in Black* (Firebrand, 1978). Lorde and Barbara Smith's formation of Kitchen Table/Women of Color Press in 1980, and its publication of the watershed text *This Bridge Called My Back: Writings by Radical Women of Color* (1983), insured that women of color had fully emerged on the feminist publishing scene and that feminist poets of color played a vital role in the poetry movement.

During the course of the 1970s, the feminist press certainly gave the opportunity to publish to women who would not have had the opportunity before—and not just to women based on their sex or race, but especially to feminists, since the vast majority of those published by the feminist press were active members of the movement and were actively theorizing feminist literature in general and feminist poetry in particular. Almost all of the Women's Liberation Movement's city-based newspapers included poetry by local women from the beginning, and small women's presses around the country printed broadsides, anthologies, single-author volumes—and its products in turn inspired more women to write. Even after the groundswell of women's movement organizing subsided and the majority of feminist newspapers ceased publication by the late 1970s, the emphasis on poetry continued in what had become a stable and increasingly professionalized feminist publishing network. Some self-publishing ventures ended; the Women's Press Collective, for instance, merged in 1977 with Diana Press, which did its own printing and binding. Diana Press itself eventually also closed shop but was replaced by other, larger feminist houses like Spinsters Ink and Firebrand. And, while the 1970s proved to be a time of flourishing, the 1980s became the decade of merely surviving. Under the Reagan administration, feminists faced a dearth of arts funding; Adrienne Rich has noted that during these years, "*human* energies (were) spread thinner" and the movement was "thrown back on old ground again" as it had to fight for political space (Montenegro 1991, 14). The journal *Conditions,* for example, received a substantial grant from the National Endowment for the Arts in 1980 but by 1984 was refused because, according to the NEA panel, it was too focused on lesbian writers and therefore *not* literary.[7] Nevertheless, feminist poets and their poetries continued to be central to a stable women's culture and an ever more diverse feminist arts community. The spadework they had done in the 1970s meant that, even in the repressive atmosphere of the 1980s, feminist poets retained their core aesthetic principles and their deep commitment to the ongoing women's movement.

This leads back to the fundamental question, which still remains to be answered in its details: why poetry? The answers are numerous, and range from the simply pragmatic to the highly aesthetic. Practically speaking, as I have already noted, the conditions for writing poetry made it more accessible as a form of writing both to engage in and to publish. The conditions of women's lives in many ways made poetry a more suitable form; with less requirements for linear narrative and generally produced in shorter units, poetry was easier to write with limited time and money, numerous interruptions, and crude publishing equipment. This is ironic, of course, since beginning in the late eighteenth century, women were considered by the literary establishment much more suited to the prosaic tasks of writing fiction, while the lofty work of seeking inspiration and writing poetry was thought to be the domain of men.[8] However, the revolutions in poetic practice in the 1960s—the conversion to open form, the banishment of persona, and the emphasis on performance—went a long way toward liberating women from these expectations. The revolutions of the 1960s gave feminist poetry its substance as a movement in the 1970s, and insured its endurance as a vital American poetry movement in the 1980s and beyond. But the early 1970s are the crucial years for understanding why women chose poetry, for in these formative years the poetic revolutions of the 1960s coalesced with individual women's own personal and political transformations. To begin with, women began to understand that in poetry they could develop a distinctly personal voice and even relate the most detailed and excruciating facts of individual experience. According to Clausen, "we had an enormous appetite for the *evidence,* for anything that could provide testimony concerning the conditions of women's lives" (1989, 9).

Making the Hidden Known

As I have already pointed out, the banishment of persona, the freedom to equate speaker and subject, profoundly resonated for women beginning to write. The need to call forth what was previously hidden—women's accounts of their everyday, ordinary lives as well as their views on their status in an oppressive society—paralleled the confessional urge that took hold in lyric poetry in the 1950s and issued in the exile of persona in favor of the poet as speaker in the poem. This freedom was so appealing, of course, because it challenged the traditional limitations placed on the woman poet; she could write about her life rather than rewrite her life in order to present the picture of womanhood that the guardians of American poetry expected. But this freedom also completely coincided with one of the goals of the women's movement: to make ways for women to express and explore their experience as a/ the chief avenue toward empowerment and change in women's status. Indeed, honesty and intense self-reflection were increasingly considered a matter of political urgency. As Audre Lorde put it in her highly influential essay "Poetry Is Not a Luxury," "our feelings and the honest exploration of them become sanctuaries and spawning grounds for the most radical and daring of ideas"; the resulting poetry is "the skeleton architecture of our lives" which "lays the foundations for a future of change" (1984, 8).

Writing poetry especially suited the format of the consciousness-raising group, a primary organizing unit of the women's liberation movement. Consciousness-raising was first used by women who had been active in the New Left in the 1960s and involved women coming to understand their own experiences as representative of social problems that result from gender oppression. Hence, a woman would explore her own experience of, say, employment inequalities, and begin to draw connections to this as a problem for many or even all American women. Many women found this process deeply transformative of their self-conceptions and through it formed lasting feminist commitments. In order to facilitate the self-expression necessary to both autobiographical and political discovery, many consciousness-raising groups doubled as writing workshops. The writer and publisher Maureen Brady is typical of this history; she got her start as a writer "around '69 or '70" when she "got involved in a women's writing workshop—which was also a CR group" (Brady and McDaniel 1980, 77). Many women's collectives around the country grew out of "CR" or writing workshops and then themselves sponsored new groups. One prominent example of this phenomenon is the Chicago Women's Liberation Union "rap"/writing group, which formed a collective to publish the magazine *Black Maria* and eventually also conducted writing workshops and workshops on self-publishing (The Black Maria Collective 1983). Jan Clausen's case also illustrates; she wrote in a "poetry support group" with Kathryn McHargue, Mary Patten, and Joan Larkin, and they eventually read their work together publicly ("Poetry Support Group" 1975, 10).

The challenge not just for women poets but for women in general with regard to the details of their everyday lives was how to communicate the previously hidden—the elements of their experience considered taboo in public conversation and writing. Calling the decision to communicate the hidden a "risk" for "hundreds of 'ordinary' women," the writer Donna Ippolito related in 1971 the experiences of women in one of the writing workshops run by the Black Maria Collective in Chicago. The purpose of the workshop, according to Ippolito, was to overturn the hierarchy, in which the written language had been guarded by "an elite group of priests, scribes, aristocrats, or scholars." This belief was quite common especially in the radical feminist sectors of the women's movement: that by revealing the previously veiled details of their lives, women were directly confronting and even stealing power from men-dominated institutions. As Ippolito put it, in the act of conversing with other women in writing, women poets would also be overcoming the old categories for women who tried to find a voice. Women would gather together, she wrote, "through the support of their sisters, to express their dreams as well as their terrors; to dig up herstory, to argue; to analyze; to invent; to sing. In short, startle and overturn the old notions of emptyhead, chatterbox, harpy, gossip, and bitch" (1971, 15).

Women's honesty about the details of their lives was considered quite revolutionary. For readers across the women's movement, Judy Grahn's "The Common Woman" poems felt revolutionary precisely because they delved into the realities—the violence and also the triumph—of "common" women's lives. This series of poems was possible, Grahn says, because "things which had formerly been unspeakable suddenly became vital and desirable things to say" (Grahn 1983, 97). In Grahn's view, "common" also referred to the way art circulated and took on meaning in culture; poetry that revealed women's lives might shock or alienate the poetry establishment, but if she asked for feedback on her poems from women neighbors, she kept her work close to their lives because "real people tell you real things about your work" (97). The final lines of the *Common Woman* series, "Vera, from my childhood," became a much loved sign—showing up in newspapers across the country and reprinted partially on buttons and posters throughout the movement—of the power involved when an ordinary woman told her life: "the common woman is as common as the best of bread / and will rise / and will become strong—I swear it to you / I swear it to you on my own head / I swear it to you on my common / woman's / head" (Grahn 1978b, 73).

The need to move out of silence and into speech, to dispense with the masks women poets had once worn, echoed time and again in the poetries themselves. Indicating that the work of the movement required the oppressed telling their stories, Audre Lorde wrote, "Our labor has become / more important / than our silence." And she made it clear that the very act of speaking was in fact necessary to personal and political perseverance (especially for African-American women): "So it is better to speak / remembering / we were never meant to survive" (1978, 32, 53). In her long poem "Monster," Robin Morgan spoke of the power of bringing the hidden into the open through consciousness-raising: "Those who lie in the arms of the 'individual solution,' / the 'private odyssey,' the 'personal growth,' / are the most conformist of all, / because to admit suffering is to begin / the creation of freedom" (1990, 38). For Adrienne Rich, the bonds between women, and the intimate storytelling they fostered, empowered them to revolutionize their culture; her "fellow-creature, sister" sits across from her, "working like me to pick apart / working with me to remake / this trailing knitted thing, this cloth of darkness, / this woman's garment, trying to save the skein" (1973, 5).

This emphasis on speaking the truth has echoed through the works of feminist poets coming to their writing since the 1970s. Linda McCarriston, for example, after years of believing she could not be a poet because neither her experience nor her formal leanings matched those of her male teachers, finally understood through the example of her feminist predecessors that the purpose of poetry is not simply to *delight* but to *teach,* and at the center of this enterprise is revealing the truth. She discovered that the job of the writer is "to present one world to another world, to present one life to another life, a hidden life to one who would, by and large, prefer not to know it. That which is hidden is hidden for a reason. To reveal it is to make someone uncomfortable—or responsible, let's say" (1993, 69). For McCarriston, in the classic feminist evolution, the move was from "absolute wife-hood" and the conviction through male poets that politics had no place in poetry, to freedom from the constraints of marriage and the " 'formalism of content' "

(1993, 69). This was possible as she became more honest about all the aspects of her experience and changed her expectations for form.

Stripping Down Language and Form

This need to uncover the previously hidden was accompanied by the desire to use more open poetic modes, to strip language and form of superfluous meaning and flourish, and to remove poetry from the realm of the elite—which could twist it to suit its meanings—and place it in the realm of the "common" woman. Charlotte Bunch, the influential feminist publishing figure, remarked in 1977 that "literacy should be a feminist issue," the priority being "teaching women to *read, write, and think*" (1977, 24). The implication, of course, was that artistic expression must necessarily be accessible, readable, for any woman involved in the social/political movement. Thus, the feminist press was founded "as a method of creating new words/new work" (25), and the poetry— seldom the result of formal training, and more often the outcome of women eagerly grasping a new truthfulness and a looser form in poetry—that occupied the pages of the earliest issues of publications from *off our backs* to *The Second Wave* reflected the relevance women found in poetry as a way of expressing themselves to each other. The goal was at least partially, then, to avoid alienating the rank and file of the women's movement through the use of the elite's poetic techniques. But the new freedom of content and form excited feminist poets for another reason as well. Bunch noted that a primary goal of the feminist press was to prevent the cooptation and even destruction of women's writing at the hands of the mainstream, male-dominated press; she said the press grew "as a means of controlling our words and how they are disseminated" (25). The emphasis on open form reflected this desire for feminists to communicate clearly to other feminists and indeed to all women.

Free verse, organic verse, open forms of all kinds—these were emerging modes and available to women who also found in them a viable way to escape older demands that they use highly stylized form and language. Freedom of form (and thus from traditional patterns of rhyme and meter in particular) itself issued in a new freedom of language, which both gave women the sense of escaping ancient, confining demands for poetry and allowed them to play with forms they felt they could at least come closer to identifying as their own. While numerous feminist poets continued to turn to traditional forms—Marge Piercy, for example, wrote in persona, while Marilyn Hacker composed sonnets—almost none wrote in these forms alone. The freer forms seemed essential.

As an Asian-American poet who came to feminist poetry later in her writing career, Mitsuye Yamada reflected on the importance of using direct language and simple form. She remembers that the first awareness she had that "it was okay to express anger, or differentness" came when she read the feminist poets Marge Piercy and Carolyn Kizer in the late 1960s. She began to realize that the poetry establishment thought that women's poetry had "no shape or form" precisely because it had "too much pain attached to it" (Yamada 1987, 102). And yet ironically this was the only way, Yamada began to understand, that women were going to bring their lives into view and confront the oppressive literary establishment that had previously stolen *their* words. In relating this realization, she quotes yet another feminist poet: "I think women started moving away from generalizing, from writing about 'generic' things, almost deliberately. Alta said, 'I'm going to write a poem with no metaphors, because if I write in a metaphor, men misinterpret it. So I'm going to write a kind of poem that they could in no way misinterpret.' She did start doing that: blatant poems that made people uncomfortable" (Yamada 1987, 104). Gloria Anzaldúa observes that this is *not* what the poetry establishment looks for; she says that "they" (including white women) tell Third World women writers that they must "achieve distance in order to win the coveted title 'literary writer,' " that they must above all never be "simple, direct, nor immediate" (1983, 167). In the view of feminist poets, then, the opportunities afforded by the new freedom in choice about form, content, language, and imagery—which generally characterized the avant-garde poetry scene of the 1960s—enabled them to create new routes of open communication and potentially to address issues of literary and political power.

Of course, Alta's comment about metaphor does not mean that feminist poets dispensed with figurative language, or even that they altogether eschewed traditional formal grounding, but that they understood the relevance of using what at that time were considered "freer" forms to convey to women and men an entirely new sense of how women could express their lives truthfully and clearly. McCarriston's recovery of Horace's dual emphasis on delight and the didactic is not accidental. Feminist poets understand that the play of language that brings delight is basic to poetry, and yet they also perceive a truth-telling function in poetry that plays an important role in public life. In her 1982 poem "Aesthetics," Irena Klepfisz begins with the following lines: "No beauty for beauty's sake here. / Life's too lean / a constant 'Let's get down / to brass tacks.' Function and necessity. / Stone and water" (1990b, 161).

Again, another feminist poet's experience illustrates. In New York, Kathleen Fraser found herself pitted against men college teachers who identified her poems as "embarrassing in their directness and not formal enough." She remembers that "there was little encouragement for something more sprawly, risking awkwardness of diction or an unfamiliar and thus uncomfortable rhythmic measure." She found freedom from these restraints first by moving to the open spaces of the West but, more important, by plugging into San Francisco and Berkeley's "surge of women poets, of all ages, tentatively working through their voices, antennae alert, sending and receiving signals" (1977, 154, 157, 159–60). This community—with its workshops, readings, support groups, and classes—provided Fraser the energy to take more risks, to develop the voice she had earlier censored.

The effect of this combination of self-telling and open form has been that feminist poets have largely abandoned the tightly contained and lyrical poem that only thirty years ago was thought to be the only form they were capable of writing in. Largely until the 1960s, women poets were expected to write only of higher, more genteel sentiments, and never of "the more daring and successful flights of the tragic muse" that Hannah More attributed only to men. They were to write quiet and contained lyrics, never tying their exploration of personal feelings to any construction of public identity or commentary on public life. Since the 1960s, however, feminist poets have written, out of their self-telling and a belief in the idea of "the personal as political," a combination of narrative and lyric. As the poet Tess Gallagher has pointed out, the lines between the lyric and the narrative have increasingly blurred in contemporary poetry, while the critic Diane P. Freedman has demonstrated that this form has been especially attractive to women (Gallagher 1986; Freedman 1992). For feminist poets, this form's emphasis on story has meant combining the expressions of personal emotion and observation with the previously hidden narratives of the cultural and political histories from which those expressions arise. This has meant not only that the minute details of any woman's daily life can be explored but that whole histories of women from various submerged cultures come into view. This history-making has direct political implications, as the poem itself becomes a means of confronting the forces that have mandated silence in the past and as it awakens in women readers a recognition of a history, or histories, that provide them a basis for further, more extensive self-exploration. In other words, the need to make history and to express individual lives involves both bringing to light the previously hidden and uncovering and claiming a history or set of histories that create a reading background for more poetry, and by extension, more political involvement together as women, but always as women from different backgrounds.

Looser syntax and a longer line, as well as a heavy emphasis on prose poetry, are related manifestations of this trend. Poets like Janice Mirikitani, Gloria Anzaldúa, and Irena Klepfisz have taken this challenge even further by combining prose poetry with fragments of historical texts and occasionally their own prose. But the evolving form of the lyric-narrative has perhaps become central; poets have increasingly combined expression of their personal feeling with a public voice that documents and interprets history. These poets insist on combining in single poems both searing personal revelations and narratives of the individual lives and broader cultural histories from which they arise. And the free verse that most feminist poets choose to write in accommodates the lyric-narrative, in its attention to detail and precision of feeling, and it has been taken to new stylistic levels in the work of poets from Minnie Bruce Pratt to Lorna Dee Cervantes.

Building the Collective

The third element of feminist poetry that evolved during the late 1960s and early 1970s was the desire to develop a collective voice by defining common concerns and publicly performing poems, which was rooted, at least in part, in the heightened social awareness and increased cultural role of poetry in the Beat and protest movements of the 1960s. The constant round of feminist poetry readings—both organized and open—in the 1970s illustrates the very strong commitment of feminist poets to collective reception and recognition of their poetic message. Poetry collectives and feminist publications across the country sponsored poetry readings. In 1972, for example, the New York Women's

Poetry and Drama Collective began sponsoring ongoing poetry readings as well as a number of poetry marathons, while women's liberation
groups across the country—from Philadelphia to San Diego to Chapel
Hill, North Carolina—sponsored regular open poetry readings beginning in the early 1970s.[9] Open readings were also included at move-
ment-sponsored cultural festivals around the country.[10]

While readings and books by more well-known poets were very popular and indeed inspired the ranks of women writing poetry in the
movement, the common sense was that the writing experience, the *new*
writing experience, of women outside the poetry establishment was central to the feminist poetry movement. When the National Women's
Poetry Festival was held in March 1974 at the University of Massachusetts, Amherst, this consciousness of poetry as every woman's had abro-
gated any notion of a "celebrity" circuit. The organizers said that
"deification" of certain women poets makes other women feel inferior
and disempowered, and that "demystifying them means that what
seemed individual dreams to become artists are in fact, possibilities for
all of us." Therefore, they continued, "By demystifying poets we also
demystify poetry. It can then become an active force in people's lives.
We think that for many women attending the Festival, poetry became
an accessible and vital tool for change" (Le Tourneau and Townley
1974, 8).

Women writing and performing poetry in these settings wove their
personal voice and experience together with distinctly social commitments, for part of the very purpose of the C-R group and of the public
poetry reading was to communicate to other women and to an oppressive society women's realities, needs, and dreams and to create fertile
ground for fruitful political action and ongoing cultural expression in
women's communities. Personal recognition and public unity were indeed central; *Majority Report* said of the poetry marathons running in
New York in 1972, "Feminist poetry evokes more response than other
kinds; people laugh and applaud and understand" ("Poetry Marathon"
1972). Yet, women audience members were not simply in search of
slogans—as one might think when reading the anthologies of the early
1970s, in which the same poems appeared time and again—nor were
they interested primarily in emotionally charged lyrics that provided
some kind of dramatic catharsis. Audiences weren't necessarily looking
for easy or merely pleasurable poems; they sat rapt for Judy Grahn's
readings of her long and complex "A Woman Is Talking to Death"

(1973) in the mid 1970s, while June Jordan's long jazz-inspired "Getting Down to Get Over: Dedicated to My Mother" (1974) was a favorite with audiences. Both of these poems also address racism; indeed, confronting this and other potential obstacles to women's unity was as important as confronting sexism. As Judy Grahn says, one of Pat Parker's gifts as a poet was to bring to the stage what was on the minds of women, and especially women of color: "what white women could not hear at a meeting, we just might hear on a stage, boomed through a microphone. What men would not hold still for on the street, they might listen to in a more formal situation" (Grahn 1978a, 12).

The poet Nellie Wong has written, "I may write by myself in my study at home, on the bus to and from work, or sneak in a poem while I'm at my workplace, but no writing belongs totally to a person herself. Writing is a public act, the pulse and heartbeat of our lives" (1979, 5). Wong is typical of the earliest feminist poets, who fused subjective expression and collective identity. In reclaiming the primary relationship between the individual mind—the locus of poetry in the Western conception of the form—and collective life, they invigorated the cultural role of poetry in ways that demonstrated their debt to the public character of the Beat and protest poetry of the 1960s, as well as to the wellsprings of American "democratic" poetry in Walt Whitman and the Romantics. However, while Whitman understood himself as the representative mind of a nation (and Whitman deeply influenced the poets Hart Crane and Allen Ginsberg, who saw themselves as representatives of generations *against* the nation), feminist poets retreated from any democratic claims that too easily identified speaker with reader/listener. Feminists needed, especially at the outset of the movement, to strive for some collective identity as "Woman," and hence the emphasis on "sisterhood" and, as Marge Piercy put it, "making the revolution out of each other" (1982, 53). But they also have been from the beginning careful to avoid simplistic propaganda that posits a false universal for all women; they are aware that they must carefully attend to their own subjective experience in order to converse with and speak for "Women" while respecting their difference. Again, the belief in "the personal as political" has proven immensely influential. Understanding exactly how feminist poets arrived at their particular task of weaving together subjective and collective voice requires first of all, however, examining what a necessary tool feminist poets have understood poetry to be in the women's movement.

The Poem as Tool

When three poets formed the Milwaukee Women's Poetry Cooperative in 1972 (their call for participants is signed only "Sue, Linda, and Molly"), their statements about what they hoped to accomplish reflected the prevailing aesthetics of poetry within the women's movement. First, they assert that gathering artists as a group—in the consciousness-raising tradition—is essential to their political life: "We believe that a major victory in this revolution is getting ourselves together as women, an oppressed class, defining our thoughts, written and spoken with one another." Second (and echoing the organizers of the National Women's Poetry Festival), they maintain poetry as a "special tool" that "should belong to a community" and "should be tuned to the needs of the people." This assertion dovetails with a distinctly socialist criticism of artistic production in the United States: "Poetry . . . should spread the joys and pains of personal and social growth. But, typically in this capitalist economy, the *content* of most contemporary art strives to make us forget our problems, instead of showing us ways to solve them. No wonder people are confused and unhappy. We, especially as women and artists in struggle, should be leaders in the effort to raise political and cultural consciousness." These poets employ the metaphors of fire and even gunfire to connote the power they believe poetry injects into women's lives and community as well as into the life of the culture at large. To them, poetry is "one of the matches that lights the fuse of revolution" as well as "a trigger finger when the time is right and the people need it" ("Come to the Newly Organized" 1972).

This exuberant and idealistic portrayal of poetry and the masses certainly reverberates with a Marxist belief in the instrumentalism of literature and reveals the roots of the cooperative's founders in the 1960s Left. It is, nevertheless, a splendid example of the enthusiastic belief that women throughout the movement exhibited in poetry's ability to reach *ordinary* and *countless* women and to involve them in revolutionary change. In this way it is a distinctly feminist take on the idea of the "cultural worker," which the feminist poet-activist Margaret Randall traces to Marxist-inspired revolutions in Cuba and later Nicaragua (1990, 9). To follow this line of thinking, if the poet is a cultural worker, producing real changes in society by developing broad-based participation in cultural expression, then art (and poetry was the artistic medium of choice in the women's movement) is a *tool*. In an article entitled "Politics of Women Writing," the feminist poet Karen Brodine says "the poem is surely a tool," and as such is both an extension of the personal life of the writer and a force for expressing the ideas of a movement and fueling resistance. Brodine describes a friend and gardener who says that "only after months of learning to work with tools did she realize they are not foreign objects, but simple extensions of the hand." In the same, way, Brodine says, writing is not a product, but "an extension of our feeling/dream/belief." But the poem also evokes solidarity and action. According to Brodine, no poem by itself will organize women to act on women's issues. However, every experience of organizing inspires new poems, which themselves in turn inspire activists to continue with their activity. She writes: "I see our writing as part of the wave of feminism, not just rising out of, coasting, but diving in, back, causing new currents—not simply a reflection, a result, but part of the moving, creating force . . . New different poems come out of [an] organizing experience. I can give a new poem, copied secretly on the office machine, to my fellow workers. Because the images in it come from us, our anger, our resistance, my co-workers care for the poem, and it becomes a part of the gathering force of our solidarity" (1979, 9).[11] Brodine represents the feminist poet as cultural worker, perhaps (but not always) writing in solitude but relying on a committed band of readers not only to distribute her work but to act on the political vision it contains.

This view of poetry as tool spread not only through the organization of C-R groups and collectives but throughout the feminist press. All the major newspapers that emerged during this period, as well as many of the smaller newspapers and newsletters that followed, listed poetry specifically (and less often other literary forms, or photography and drawings) in their lists of longed-for submissions. This request highlighted the very high premium already placed on poetry as a central mode for self-expression and organizing, and not for a highly select group of readers but for the general readership.

In the emerging literary magazines, in which poetry was in most cases the mainstay, the view of literature as direct political statement or even action appeared in more explicit fashion. The opening editorial of one of the first of these magazines, *Aphra,* spelled out the connections between literature, increased consciousness in readers, and action: "We shall publish what we like and what we respond to, with the idea that we shall be speaking directly to women so that they can say 'There am

I' and feel stronger and more doing" ("Preamble to *Aphra*" 1969). In other words, the editors would choose works based on the ways these works moved them to feel empowered and active, in the belief that these works would have the same effects on readers. Even though the members of the Heresies Collective were very careful to explore their political/artistic differences in the first issue of *Heresies,* they nevertheless stated as a group that they sought "to dissolve the alienation between artist and audience, and to understand the relationship between art and politics, work and workers." One member of the collective, Harmony Hammond, wrote, "My art both is formed by and is a statement of my feminism" (Braderman et al. 1977, 2).

The fundamental tenet of feminist poetry, revealed by the emphasis on poetry as tool, is that *all* poetry, indeed all language, is political. There is, in this view, no such creature as an apolitical poem. Susan Griffin understands it this way: "When I say that no poem is apolitical, I am not implying that poetry *ought* to be political, but that it is political. Political theory cannot possibly teach a poet to be political, because poetry precedes formal political theory in the imagination . . . For this reason, poetry teaches political theory imagination" (1982, 242). As Brodine and Griffin discuss it, this dialectic between writing and action clearly contradicts Jan Clausen's assertion that feminist poets equate poetry with political action itself, which itself neglects the fact that all poems are political. In this view, poetry does have social effects, and feminist poets must always attend to the power of the language and images they use. "The words are maps," as Adrienne Rich puts it in "Diving into the Wreck" (1973, 23); they explore the possible direc-tions, they provide vision even, but they never substitute for actions themselves. Or, to put it another way, they are one *kind* of action among others. This belief among feminist poets in the power of poetry to effect social change has remained through the years; in 1993, the poet Pat Mora wrote, "We raise our voices to be of use. The work of the poet is for the people" (1993, 181).

This idea of the poet and poetry as functional in cultural life is under-scored time and again by the images of healing, prophecy, and vision that show up in the work of feminist poets. These certainly have some roots in American strains of poetry, in, for instance, the Romanticism in Emerson's ideal of the poet as seer and sayer and in the opening lines of Whitman's *Leaves of Grass*: "One's-self I sing, a simple separate person, / Yet utter the word Democratic, the word En-Masse" (1959,

6). The deep concern to speak with and for the masses in the twentieth-century poets Carl Sandburg and Langston Hughes, to name but two examples, echoes this belief. But the predominant view in the American tradition has been that the poet is a genius who works in isolation from society at large and who relates to a tradition defined by the avant-garde; perhaps the most influential statement of this notion is T.S. Eliot's "Tradition and the Individual Talent" (1965). Feminist poets, in contrast, hold together spheres that have been radically separated in American literary thought, and in doing so often employ views arising from their "minority" or even non-Western cultural backgrounds.

These poets understand that the notion of poetry as self-expression, even as part of a process of self-healing, does not necessitate the idea of the poet as an isolated creator. For Gloria Anzaldúa, the poet is the soul of a people and integrates all facets of life. She turns to her (pre-Conquest) Mexican Indian heritage: "In the ethno-poetics and performance of the shaman, my people, the Indians, did not split the artistic from the functional, the sacred from the secular, art from everyday life. The religious, social and aesthetic purposes of art were all intertwined" (1987, 66). In terms of the role of the poet in contemporary American society, Anzaldúa says that the oppression of women of color "takes the form of metaphors" and the shamanic/poetic "cure" involves removing the deadening metaphors and/or adding what is lacking, "restoring the balance and strengthening the physical, mental, and emotional states of the person" (1990b, 99). In her perspective, the power of the metaphor extends to social and political change through the reader. Thus, she provides an interesting contrast to Alta's perspective on metaphor as obfuscating, as she draws on the shamanic tradition to create a Chicana/feminist poetics that parallels Rukeyser's model of connection between the poet, the poem, and the reader: "We preserve ourselves through metaphor . . . And most importantly, we can *share* ourselves through metaphor—attempt to put, in words, the flow of some of our internal pictures, sounds, sensations, and feelings and hope that as the reader reads the pages these 'metaphors' would be 'activated' and live in her" (1990b, 100). And for Judy Grahn, poetry affects the reader by actually calling out forces of nature; in her words, an image or metaphor uses "the geometry of language to capture the power of some force in the natural world to materialize the thought-form of the poem" (1990, 102).

The feminist poet, then, understands herself to be tending to the survival and flourishing of her culture by relying on commonly held, functionalist elements of art. The poem is a "tool" with very real effects, and the group takes precedence over the individual, that is, art plays a larger cultural role than simply to satisfy the aspirations of an individual talent.

Blending the Subjective and Collective: Coalitional Voice

The key to the definition of the poem as tool, and to poetry as a functional element of cultural life, is the relationship between the poet and her readers/listeners. In this view, a poem cannot exist as a poem without the author's vision, disciplined practice, and skill. Neither can a poem exist, however, without the reader/listener, who completes the artistic act by reading or hearing the poem and responding in some way to it. Susan Sherman, longtime poet-activist and the editor of the journal *Ikon* in both its early leftist and later feminist incarnations, has reflected extensively on this relationship. In the position statement for the feminist version of *Ikon,* entitled "Freeing the Balance: Activism and Art," she writes: "The question is not 'art for art's sake' versus 'political art.' In fact, the discoveries of the work of art cannot exist without the understanding of relationship that is an integral part of social interaction." Sherman decries the idea of art as purely utilitarian (as propaganda, a charge often enough leveled at feminist poets) as well as the idea of art as its own end (which she calls "the most accepted and *acceptable* critical view in the United States," and which is the ground for critics' charges of propaganda in feminist poetry). Instead, Sherman says that poetry occurs somewhere in the relationship between self and other, poem and world: "The poem, if allowed to sing freely through us, can teach us how to reach beyond imposed limitations—as can any free action or thought which manages somehow to escape the rigid self-censorship we impose on each other and on our world. . . . Unlike the poet, whose existence as a living being is constant, the poem is actualized only upon being written or read. As the poet finishes the poem, readers seize and interpret it, live it, according to their own individual experiences and needs" (1982–1983, 2-3). This echoes Rukeyser's belief that the reader/listener (or "witness") receives a transfer of human energy in the poem, and thereby increases her "consciousness" or her "capacity to produce change in existing conditions" (1949, 187).

But the central question yet to be answered here is, how can the poet speak to the collective concerns of women—how can she speak for

"Woman"—while also attending to the difference inherent in "women"? How can she speak to and even for her readers/listeners without either universalizing her own experience or descending into mere sloganeering? The answer is multilayered. It involves a high level of intertextuality among feminist poets and a variety of formal innovations, but it is centrally grounded in the relationship between the poet and the collective that feminist poets construct through what I call *coalitional voice*. Here I borrow a term widely used in feminist politics, the coalition being a temporary, or at least an always potentially shifting, association of various women and/or women's groups. A coalition adheres for the purpose of accomplishing a particular cultural or political goal or set of goals, and the relationship between the individual and the group always requires a recognition of difference. According to this idea, it is only in speaking out of the integrity of her own personal experience that the feminist poet establishes her relationship to the community. She cannot simply assume a common identity, for difference abounds. However, she can with integrity find a way or ways to speak to and for the community, or coalition, by very carefully charting her own experience within a complicated nexus of identities (that includes not just gender, but race, ethnicity, class, age, and sexuality) and perspectives on political theory/strategy and even aesthetics. Again, the idea of "the personal as political" plays a key role, for it is only in relating and understanding her own location in relation to both systems of oppression and feminists themselves that the feminist poet can begin to achieve coalitional voice.

The prose writings of a number of other feminist poets are helpful in understanding the basis and practice of coalitional voice. In "Blood, Bread, and Poetry: The Location of the Poet," Adrienne Rich says that at the heart of her task as a lesbian-feminist poet is understanding how her location in the United States, with its racism and its belief in the transcendence of art, shapes her experience. She has to link the political world "out there" to her location as an individual in order to avoid the shallow collective voice she saw in, for instance, much of the poetry written against the Vietnam War; in this poetry, she says, "there was little location of the self, the poet's own identity as a man or woman" (1986, 181). Elsewhere, she makes clear that the "out there" also includes readers/listeners themselves, and the women's movement itself, when she says that poetry cannot be written "with propaganda as an aim, to persuade others 'out there' of some atrocity or injustice." Poetry

can arise, she asserts, only out of the poet's "need to identify her relationship to atrocities and injustice, the sources of her pain, fear, and
anger, the meaning of her resistance" (1978, 12). Rich's poetry illustrates; in the mid 1970s, she was writing poems like "Hunger," in
which she attempts to come to terms with her "Western skin" and then
says to another woman that the oppression will not stop until they act
and act together. The final line reads, "Until we find each other, we are
alone" (1984, 230, 232). And Rich has continued this task of locating
herself and yet speaking "coalitionally" in all her subsequent works. In
the series of poems "Atlas of the Difficult World," she again writes of
her identity as an American, based on her observations of violence
against women, and acknowledges the sameness and difference of herself and her readers: "I promised to show you a map you say but this is
a mural / then yes let it be these are small distinctions / where do we
see it from is the question" (1991, 6).

Judy Grahn also speaks quite extensively of the dialectic that exists
between the aims of the writer and the needs of the collective. While
she wishes to be "everybody's poet," Grahn says that she doesn't speak
for anyone but herself, and yet wants to "speak about and to a large
number of people." The key to this process is to be most fully herself
(especially as a lesbian) in her work: "My intention is to write poetry
for everyone, and, given that, I have to do it as me. So first I have to
establish that everyone can see me as who I am and take that for
granted, and then we can go on to what comes next" (1983, 99). The
key to a publicly relevant poetry, then, is not a strict political agenda
but an individual and culturally specific voice speaking to collective concerns. According to Grahn, the feminist poet's work, "in locating itself
so specifically socially and historically, takes on a power it cannot have if
she chooses, instead, to speak anonymously, 'universally' " (1985, 58).
Grahn chooses the term "commonality," in which every element of the
poem, and by extension every member of the writing and reading community, "equally matters and is centered in itself and in addition is in
continual overlapping relation to every other element" (1989, 8).
Grahn was a pioneer feminist poet in developing coalitional voice in the
early to mid 1970s. Her long poem "A Woman Is Talking to Death"
(1973) is especially effective in weaving together Grahn's explorations
of her own experience of oppression, how her oppression intersects
with that of others, and how the oppressed ("we") can face and defeat
oppression: "wherever our meat hangs on our own bones / for our own

use, your pot is so empty / death, ho death / you shall be poor" (1978b, 131).

Other poets echo this belief, and relate how they had first to learn that purely "collective" poetry ultimately betrayed the impulse to write on behalf of the community. In the 1960s, June Jordan says, she aspired to a collective voice, "to speak as a community to a community." She found in the 1970s, however, that the matter of poetic identity was more complicated, that while the poets she knew may have been working on a common project, they could only fully participate by beginning with their experience as individual human beings: "it did seem to me that we were all of us working on the same poem of a life of perpetual, difficult birth and that, therefore, I should trust myself in this way: that if I could truthfully attend to my own perpetual birth, if I could trace the provocations for my own voice and then trace its reverberations through love, alaska, whatever, that then I could hope to count upon myself to be serving a positive and collective function, without pretending to be more than the one Black woman poet I am, as a matter of fact" (1977, 107–8). Jordan's volume *Passion* strongly indicates this development in her poetry; in "Poem About My Rights," for example, she writes of the intersection of multiple oppressions and of the reader/listener's responsibility to recognize these as well, but this emerges only out of describing her "personal and idiosyncratic / and indisputably single and singular heart" (1980, 89).

Gloria Anzaldúa writes that the specifics of women's lives ground poetry and give it its power. To arrive at this belief, she first indicts the literary establishment: "*they lied, there is no separation between life and writing.*" In fact, she says, the real danger is in "not fusing our personal experience and world view with the social reality we live in, with our inner life, our history, our economics, and our vision" (1983, 164). For Anzaldúa, the task is to develop a coalitional voice precisely because as a Third World feminist writer, she has been excluded from the poetry establishment even more radically than white feminists have. She needs to speak out of what she finds all women have in common, but more especially to the racism and classism that continually threaten to make her an outsider in the women's movement itself. Thus, in *Borderlands/La Frontera,* Anzaldúa weaves highly lyrical assertions of her cultural identity as a Chicana, and then effects coalitional voice by both asserting her feminism and challenging (feminist) readers' cultural assumptions with her bilingual poetry.

Coalitional Voice and Difference

As more and more women of color have found the means to publish their feminist poetry, the dimensions of coalitional voice have increased, for indeed the ability to confront blind spots in the women's movement is itself essential to expanding its vision and working toward new successes. As poets like Jordan, Anzaldúa, Pat Parker, Chrystos, and Audre Lorde have bravely spoken out of their personal experiences in order to battle especially racism in the movement, they have expanded the sense that this is indeed the empowering route to collective identity, for their writings have deeply influenced feminist poets and white and nonwhite feminist readerships to build and maintain feminist coalitions across identities. While they acknowledge their debts to each other, to other feminist poets, and to the unifying and necessary idea of a feminist literary community, these poets also initiate and sustain a conversation, often confrontational, about the censures and erasures they have experienced because the idea of community often masks difference. This conversation goes on through the use of coalitional voice in poetry itself, but much of it also occurs in essays, creating a substantial degree of intertextuality that itself illustrates that these poets are self-consciously feminists and feminist poets and that they consider themselves invested in a community they want to maintain.

For Irena Klepfisz, the notion of community was complicated early on. She very quickly lost her original idealism about the solidarity of women across different groups, because of anti-Semitism and homophobia: "As a lesbian, I felt alienated from the community of my roots. The original Jewish impulse behind my early poetry was still there, but it suddenly seemed out of place. I did not feel comfortable presenting my Holocaust poems in the lesbian community, and I felt to some degree unwelcome in the Jewish community" (1990a, 169). During this time, Klepfisz recalls, she felt so confused that she wrote very little. But she points out that both the lesbian and the Jewish communities have undergone significant shifts toward recognizing and understanding difference since that time, and she has moved to a place where she can integrate her cultural histories, as well as formal preferences related to these, into her work (1990a).

For Gloria Anzaldúa, confronting the literary establishment at times coincides with challenging white feminists; in 1981, she wrote that the "woman of color is invisible both in the white male mainstream world and in the white women's feminist world, though in the latter this is gradually changing." Her words echo pre- and early feminist poets who understood themselves to be "split-selves," defined by the establishment as monstrous in their difference: "We speak in tongues like the outcast and the insane" (1983, 165). Mitsuye Yamada echoes Anzaldúa's assertion that women of color have gone unheard, even in the women's movement and by feminist poets; she says Asian-American women in particular must remember that "one of the most insidious ways of keeping women and minorities powerless is to let them only talk about harmless and inconsequential subjects, or let them speak freely and not listen to them with serious intent" (1979, 4).

Poem after poem indicates how women of color especially have confronted the silences that surround feminists' lack of attention to difference in the women's movement. June Jordan was one of the earliest feminist poets to issue direct challenges to the racism and general dichotomous thought she saw as characterizing movement organizing. In her "A Short Note to My Very Critical and Well-Beloved Friends and Comrades," she parodies the tendency toward exclusiveness in social movements: "Make up you mind? They said. Are you militant / or sweet? Are you vegetarian or meat? Are you straight / or are you gay? / And I said, Hey! It's not about my mind" (1980, 78). Meanwhile, her poem "Meta-Rhetoric" calls for an end to this kind of ideological blindness; she writes, "My hope is that our lives will declare / this / meeting / open" (1989, 31). In "The Bridge Poem," Donna Kate Rushin is even more straightforward, using second person. She says she is tired of being "the sole Black friend to 34 individual white people," and declares to the reader, "Find another connection to the rest of the world / find something else to make you legitimate / Find some other way to be political and hip" (Anzaldúa and Moraga 1983, xxi).

For these poets, coalitional voice involves a return to the personal; in other words, they begin with self-assertion in order to challenge the collective, and then in response to exclusive practices in the movement return to the personal to assert their identities even more strongly. In "Give Me Back," for instance, Chrystos ends with a manifesto of self-empowerment in the image of taking back the skeleton of her oppressed self: "I crack out / arrange my bones in their naming places / I take what I want / shaking my sacred hair / dancing out taboo / I mark out the space I am / with knives" (Anzaldúa and Moraga 1983, 197). Rushin takes a similar journey in "The Bridge Poem," ending with the stanza: "I must be the bridge to nowhere / But my true self / And then / I will be useful" (Anzaldúa and Moraga 1983, xxii). In "Poem About My Rights," Jordan prefaces her final challenge to racism among her readers with "My name is my own my own my own" (1980, 89). But the dialectic continues, for this poetry is also always hopeful, as Nellie Wong's poem about the women's movement, "Toward the Rainbow," indicates:

> And to you who are provoked by our words,
> will you walk toward the rainbow,
> will you believe that feminism doesn't mean
> you must continually starve
> on the other side of the tracks?
>
> (Wong, Woo, and Yamada 1979, 1)

The feminist poetry by women of color has demonstrated its impact in the work of feminist poets. Audre Lorde and Adrienne Rich's 1979 dialogue about difference in the women's movement provides an important example; Rich shares her pain at realizing just how divergent the perceptions of white women and women of color can be, and Lorde responds with a line from her poem "Need: A Coral of Black Women's Voices": "How much of this truth can I bear to see / and still live / unblinded? / How much of this pain / can I use?" (Lorde 1982, 115; Lorde 1984, 105–6).

Similarly, Minnie Bruce Pratt attempts to come to terms with the ways poetic voice itself may elide rather than celebrate difference. She realizes that she writes of her life, and especially her lesbianism, only because "we have created a circle of women to speak within," but she struggles to maintain boundaries between herself and the women she believes she is writing for and about. She asks: "When are my words an opening of myself to a new place? When are they the appropriation of another's life? . . . I have struggled over how to use words to search out a connection between me and others, the way lightning from the ground meets lightning in the air, a fiery spirit that calls but does not command another" (1991, 131, 134). She says she is interested in developing "power with" rather than "power over," so that developing her own power through her writing "doesn't mean draining it away from the community or using it in opposition to others but rather using

[it] collectively with others to build a transformative future" (1992, 36).

Intertextuality

Other kinds of intertextuality, whether in mentioning each other in the dedications of poems or volumes of poems, or in poems themselves, illustrate that the use of coalitional voice occurs with the sense that feminist poets are an ongoing, interactive community that discusses difference but also celebrates feminist poets' connections to each other. Indeed, Lorde and Rich at times echo each other; each wrote a poem entitled "Power," and Rich uses the language of Lorde's version in several poems in *A Wild Patience Has Taken Me This Far* (Lorde 1978; Rich 1981). Joy Harjo and June Jordan are just two examples of feminist poets who have acknowledged their debt to Lorde and Rich; they have also acknowledged each other. Harjo quotes June Jordan in the preface to *In Mad Love and War* and addresses her poem "Hieroglyphic" to Jordan (1990). She also dedicates her poem "Anchorage" to Lorde. The final line of this poem ("Because who would believe / the fantastic and terrible story of all of our survival / those who were never meant / to survive?") echoes Lorde's "A Litany for Survival" ("So it is better to speak / remembering / we were never meant to survive") (Harjo 1983, 14–15; Lorde 1978, 31). Harjo has stated very directly her debt to Lorde: "Lorde's work has been a tremendous influence on my work and the work of many other writers, especially Third World women. She, like many of us, has been the embodiment of other people's fears" (1984, 158). Jordan dedicates her collection of poems, *Naming Our Destiny,* in part to Adrienne Rich and also includes a piece entitled "Poem for Joy," written as a letter to Harjo and dedicated to the "Creek Tribe of North America" (1989).

In other instances, Gloria Anzaldúa thanks Irena Klepfisz in the preface to *Borderlands* and dedicates the poem "Poets have strange eating habits" to her ("Irenita") (1987). In turn, Klepfisz acknowledges Anzaldúa's help in both *Dreams of an Insomniac* (1990) and *A Few Words in the Mother Tongue* (1990), and includes references to their conversations in her essays. Throughout her essays in *Rebellion* (1991), Minnie Bruce Pratt refers to the works and words of other feminist poets, among them Anzaldúa, Klepfisz, Harjo, Lorde, and Rich. Judy Grahn says that the work of Pat Parker and Alta strengthened her to be more and more truthful in her poetry, a process that yielded "A Woman Is Talking to Death" (1978b, 112), while Parker in turn wrote another long poem, entitled "Womanslaughter," after being inspired by this "marathon" of Grahn's (Grahn 1978a, 13). For her discussion of lesbian poetry in *The Highest Apple* (1985), Grahn reads the work of her feminist contemporaries Rich, Lorde, Olga Broumas, and Paula Gunn Allen. These instances of intertextuality reverberate throughout the work of this particular group of poets as well as among other feminist poets, who expand in connection to one another like a series of ripples out across the women's movement.

Formal Strategies and the Collective

Like intertextuality, formal strategies that promote performance and group reception are deeply related to the impulse toward community that gave rise to coalitional voice in feminist poets. In fact, when these strategies are used, they almost always coincide with the use of coalitional voice. Repetition, refrain, and rhyme in particular characterize poems especially geared to performance; these elements give an oral dimension to the reading of a poem, inviting the audience to participate in the poem both by anticipating key words as the poem goes on and by following the poet easily because of the resultant regular (or most often semiregular) beat. These elements create a unity of theme and form in a poem, without resorting to traditional rhyme and meter patterns, and thereby give listeners a sense of the poet's presence and message. A number of examples from the early 1970s illustrate. In "I Like to Think of Harriet Tubman," Susan Griffin uses both repetition and refrain; she repeats phrases as they occur in this long poem ("and she lived / and she lived to redress her grievances, / and she lived in swamps"), while the refrain "I like" that structures the first half of the poem becomes "I want" as she imagines the future in the latter half (1982, 263–65). In "An Answer to a Man's Question, 'What Can I Do about Women's Liberation?' " (1976), Griffin uses both simple repetition and the repetition of anaphora to illustrate the layers upon layers of women's oppression (Howe 1993, 363–64). Pat Parker uses the refrains "there is a woman in this town" and "Is she our sister?" for similar effect in her poem about the connections between diverse women's lives; in the last two sections, she uses repetition of the phrase "a dream" to indicate that in fact women can be "sisters," can act as a community (1983, 154–57).

These and other poems ask questions about how to struggle for women's liberation, so in theme as well they are geared toward the group. Judy Grahn's "The Common Woman" series and June Jordan's "Getting Down to Get Over" share these concerns, and yet are more celebratory of women's lives and therefore especially fit for public readings. Grahn uses repetition and refrain, but also rhyme, to develop a cohesive picture of each woman's life, to connect the seven portraits of women to each other, and to indicate to the audience these connections. The refrain "The common woman is as common as . . ." is especially important, for it establishes that these women have much in common while also indicating their differences in the rhyme that completes the refrain at the end of each poem (1978b, 61–73). Jordan uses repetition together with a very short line (often just one word) throughout "Getting Down," and as a result develops a seamless picture of the African-American woman ("MOMMA") while propelling her listeners toward a hopeful ending ("momma / help me / turn the face of history / *to your face*") (1974, 118–28).

Judy Grahn indicates that a profusion of detail is typical of working-class writing, her own included, and Jordan's poem is clearly influenced by jazz techniques. This brings up a related point with regard to performance. The 1960s poetry scene valued open form, and simultaneously feminist and African-American poets began to turn to forms derived from their own cultural histories; these groups were joined or followed by Chicano/as, Native Americans, Asian Americans, and Jewish Americans, who fused their cultures' ancient understandings of the poet as public voice and of poetry as performing a valuable, ongoing public function with contemporary Western poetic forms. The result is often performance poetry. As feminist poets use cultural forms from their diverse backgrounds—women's work songs, folk songs, the blues, jazz, and oral storytelling practices, among others—they create a vital, engaging, collective-oriented poetry.

All of this is not to say, however, that coalitional voice only exists in performance poetry. Indeed, the most prevalent form of feminist poetry, the lyric-narrative, is more often than not quiet, even prosaic, in its details and form, and yet in the majority of cases combines personal reflection and expression of feeling with contemplation of collective concerns. In the midst of the details of her life—which quite often are woven together in free verse with a minimum of stylistic patterns—the poet draws out the connection between personal experience and political realities. Hence, when a poet like Minnie Bruce Pratt relates her ex-husband's violence in excruciating detail ("one minute I was in my own body, the next, / outside myself, displaced, while he took control"), she also moves outward to understand her experience in the context of a women's community:

> We locate forbidden places, the kind marked *dangerous*
> *swamp, unknown territory* on the old charts.
> We plot change. We love one another.
> Our bodies become lodestones to the future . . .
>
> (1985, 9)

Feminist Poets and Feminist Criticism

As a feminist poet of the 1980s and 1990s, Pratt represents the ways that feminist poets have maintained their desires for change in women's lives and in culture at large. Indeed, though their formal strategies have evolved over the years, and though the women's movement has gone through distinct stages of heated organizing and mere survival, feminist poets' vision of social change has remained constant: they imagine a society in which women freely and equally participate, in which the arts (and poetry in particular) enliven grassroots cultural expression, and in which women are empowered to be some of the most creative and daring of cultural workers. Charting the roads individual feminist poets took beginning roughly in 1970, and are taking in the 1990s, is essential to understanding this vision. The remaining chapters of this book are dedicated to reading in detail the works of individual feminist poets who have made vital contributions to the poetry movement and the social/political movement, both established but both still evolving.

However, these readings first require some additional history, that is, a reevaluation of the history of feminist criticism of poetry itself. This is necessary since the prevailing criticisms offered to date have not thoroughly explored the ways that feminist poetics has addressed the tension between the need to suspend difference in the interest of the notion of "Woman" and the need to recognize differences between and within women. This is also necessary in order to develop a critical approach that can accommodate conflicting ideas about the function of criticism itself and also attend to the particulars of who feminist poets are and how they function in interaction with other women and with dominant American culture and other nondominant cultures.

This first requires looking closely at how feminist criticism has evolved. In her provocative "Toward a More Feminist Criticism," Rich proposes that the survival of the women's movement depends on its "communications network," one aspect of which is an ongoing critical dialogue about the forms of literary expression inspired by and in turn inspiring the movement. Rich maintains that two kinds of self-defined feminist criticism have been conducted since the inception of the contemporary women's movement in the 1960s. The first is rooted in academic communities and focuses on past works that can be easily "canonized" or on contemporary works produced by commercial presses. This kind of criticism, according to Rich, has typically not paid attention to what she identifies as the second, the criticism done in the larger feminist community, which displays an "increasing consciousness of diversity," looks at commercial and small press texts, and is published in feminist political and literary magazines and journals (1986, 85–86).

The effects of this split have often been devastating for feminist poets. As Rich points out, a principled, well-trained criticism that is highly conscious of what is going on in the wider feminist movement could help eliminate the "applause and accolade" that is often uncritically offered up by nonacademic critics to the feminist poets who are considered the spokeswomen of the movement (1986, 90). Analyzing poets' work with honesty while at the same time acknowledging both the ongoing need for some sense of unity and the multiplicity that teems in and invigorates feminist poetry requires a principled criticism that simultaneously addresses what is happening in the women's movement and deals with the ideological demands and effects of literary and cultural institutions. This critical model must reflect on both the oppositional function of women's literature and the difference that abounds within it. The central question of such a model focuses on gender oppression and yet recognizes it as only one axis of identity; therefore, an understanding of the female writing subject is essential. How does she understand her subjective location as writer? What is her relationship to the feminist collective? What are her relationships to various groups of feminists who identify differently by race, sexuality, class, and so forth? How do the demands of the public versus the private mediate the value of her writing for both the American literary and academic marketplace and the political "world" of the contemporary feminist movement?

Early critics and even feminist poets themselves fostered an anticritical attitude from the first days of the movement, however, both because of the mass-based nature of women's poetry and because they considered criticism coming from the male poetry and academic elites highly suspect. As Clausen and Irena Klepfisz understand it, this attitude also resulted from the need for political—and all too often, financial—survival, which deepened rather than decreased in the 1980s (Clausen 1989; Klepfisz 1979). As Klepfisz puts it, "the feminist and lesbian/feminist literary movement has been too busy simply surviving and existing" (1979, 29). In this vein, grassroots criticism has relied on an aesthetics of crisis and community, necessitated both by the economic and practical considerations of marketplace demands and by the political questions raised in the ideological fray of the movement, which since 1980 have increasingly been concerned with the relation of gender to other elements of identity.

Unfortunately, the intent of feminist criticism done within what Rich calls the "liberal supermarket of the intellect" has all too often been to stay within the strict parameters of academic study as defined by men, and thus to focus on critically establishing the reasons that women poets are worthy of inclusion in the American canon (1986, 88). This was particularly true of women's studies in the beginning; as Andrea Chesman and Polly Joan noted in 1978, they first turned to feminist criticism, but found it "not helpful—too concerned with justifying the very existence of feminist criticism . . . to the male scholarly world" (1978, 10). In the initial academic feminist criticism produced on women's literature, when the tendency was to universalize women's experience and women's literary goals in the interest of creating a "women's tradition" that was legitimate and worthy of recognition by the white, male poetry establishment, women poets were defined almost solely in terms of sexual difference.

The majority of the general body of feminist criticism of women's poetry written since 1970 has stayed in this vein, concentrating on healing the split between "woman" and "poet" (DeShazer 1986, Juhasz 1976, Ostriker 1986, Pope 1984). These criticisms consider gender the central site of oppression and consider all women to have a core experience of this oppression. As I have already discussed, this was initially a preoccupation of feminist poets themselves, but early on they enlarged their consciousness to explore multiplicity of relationships between men and women and in fact between woman and women. The views of feminist critics of women's poetry, however, have not evolved so quickly. Margaret Homans said in 1980 that because the literary tradition identifies "the figure of the poet as masculine, and voice as a masculine property," women writers "must take part in a self-definition by contraries" (3). Nevertheless, ten years later, Joanne Fiet Diehl still identified the central question to be how woman, "that perpetual 'other' of male consciousness," can find a linguistic and social location from which to become "the predominant, shaping consciousness" of poetic texts (1990, 143).

These criticisms suggest that the central act of women's self-representation is to integrate the private and the public, that is, to overcome the dyadic construction of gender in which "private" matters (woman, the emotional, the trivial, literary inspiration) and "public" concerns (man, the rational, the universal, literary agency) have remained separate and women's lives have been viewed as irrelevant to poetic expression except as written ideally or mythically by men poets. This has been extremely valuable for understanding poetry as a vehicle for women's experience. However, the danger involved is that a conflation of the private and public, in which experience is asserted unself-consciously, may merely repeat the traditional authorial pattern of asserting "private" experience as universal. The modern writing subject remains central and intact, an authorial pattern that directly contradicts the idea of the feminist writer committed to the concerns of a feminist collective and yet always mindful of difference. Thus, the concern with healing the "split-self" at least in part through unmediated self-expression is ultimately a recapitulation to the division between public and private that has structured American poetry and criticism overall.

The only collective apparent in the work of the critic Alicia Ostriker (1986), for example, is "Woman" as this totality relates to the totality of "Man." In Western culture, according to Ostriker, women privately experience themselves as marginal or inferior, as alternately invisible, mute, deformed, and dissolving. Their aims are to reveal their private horrors of incompleteness, thereby merging the private and the public, and thus to participate in the publicly sanctioned "completeness" of the male writing subject. Ostriker assumes that a coherent, autonomous subjectivity is the only lived and poetic goal of women and that the end of the search for this subject position is the discovery of a single authentic femaleness that corresponds to an authentic maleness. She ignores, however, the way that such an authentic femaleness is located in binary hierarchical oppositions that determine gender opposition as well as race, class, and other differences, and neglects to identify how the notion of gender opposition itself in the West has largely been defined based on the experience of one group of women (white, middle class, heterosexual).

While Ostriker and other critics like her consider this to be progress toward equality, I side with those critics who recognize differences among women and perceive feminist forms of liberal humanism as just additional acts of erasure of women for whom gender could never be considered the only condition of oppression and ultimately an empty challenge to Western notions of subjectivity. As Norma Alarcón has said, the "most popular subject of Anglo-American feminism is an autonomous, self-making, self-determining subject who first proceeds according to the *logic of identification* with regard to the subject of consciousness, a notion usually viewed as the purview of man, but claimed for women" (1990, 357). This model of consciousness results in losing sight of the "complex and multiple ways in which the subject and object of possible experience are constituted," especially because the pole of opposition is not only male, but white (361).

In addition, the familial model—women as literary "sisters," united by some biological bond that precedes any historical conflict—is based on the establishing idea of the patriarch women must oppose, and potentially serves to maintain the dyadic construction of father/son/ brother/husband versus mother/daughter/sister/wife and the public/private split on which it relies. Some feminist critics' emphasis on mutuality and nurturing as the primary forms of interaction between literary sisters, as Betsy Erkkila has so aptly noted, has "tended to naturalize and indeed heroize the separate sexual space of women's historical colonization" as well as "to mask, silence, or write over women's culture as a site of historical struggle and difference among women themselves" (1992, 7). It also denies the complex relations of "sororophobia," a term Helena Michie uses to describe the "negotiation of sameness and difference, identity and separation, between women of the same generation" (1992, 3, 14). Indeed, familial metaphors elide the real discontinuity and dissension among women in general, and among women poets, and do not provide an accurate model for exploring a feminist community that relentlessly recognizes and explores the multiple other axes of identity that women occupy within the cultural field and the personal and collective conflicts these cause.

The role of feminist poetry in the women's movement, as well as the particularities of the poetics involved (and most specifically the attention to collectivity), mean that a different understanding of the relationship between private and public is necessary. This understanding must be grounded in a sociohistorical approach to the women's movement—to its numerous players, to evolutions in its direction(s), and to different claims for its value. While the tendency in many feminist criticisms has been to continue to identify women with the private only in opposition to the public, the practices of feminist poets call for an alternate model, like Rita Felski's of the feminist public sphere and counter-public sphere. In Felski's definition, in the feminist public sphere, women explore the private in order both to counter patriarchal omissions and to establish bonds with other women, and in this process the private becomes public. But this public community is also a "counter-public sphere," which retains its oppositional stance toward a culture that oppresses based on gender and establishes its own values for reading, its own interpretative communities and its own literary standards. In Felski's conception of the relationship between the individual and the collective, the "individual subject is viewed in relation to and as a representative of a gendered collective which self-consciously defines itself against society as a whole." Thus, says Felski, feminist literature, like other counter-public spheres that have emerged since the social upheavals of the 1960s, "reappropriates some of the concerns first addressed by bourgeois subjectivity while rejecting both its individualism and its belief in the universality of male bourgeois experience" (1989, 155). In contrast to the idea of universality that dominates in the increasingly bureaucratic and commodified public sphere, these counter-public spheres rely on specificity and location as central precepts; they affirm specificity in relation to gender, race, ethnicity, age, sexual orientation, and so on (166).

While the women's movement as one of these contemporary counter-public spheres relies to some extent on a solidarity grounded in collective gender identity, and thereby often engages in a suspension of forms of difference other than gender, it also relies on the notion of equality, which allows for conflicting ideologies among women involved in the movement. The movement relies on a universal understanding of the oppression involved in sexism and yet is comprised of multiple internal groups; Felski suggests the term "coalitions of overlapping subcom-munities" (166), and indeed "coalition" is the term I have found most helpful in charting the ways feminist poets have negotiated the relation-ships between self and other, and between various groups of women, in their writing.

This approach helps to elucidate the ways women have sought to understand themselves as subjects of their own poetic practice as well as members of a feminist community. This is a practice characterized simultaneously by a recognition of the common elements in women's gendered experience—by an allegiance to "Woman"—and by a com-plexity of vision that arises from the multiple and varied experiences of individual woman and the subcommunities with which they align themselves. The subject of this practice is complex and ambiguous. As Alarcón has said of the subject of the groundbreaking anthology of writings by women of color, *This Bridge Called My Back,* she "is and has been constructed in a crisis of meaning situation which includes racial and cultural divisions and conflicts" (1990, 359). The notion of difference in this criticism is one of ambiguity rather than conflict; as Trinh T. Minh-ha has phrased it, difference should replace conflict, so that it is "not opposed to sameness, nor synonymous with separateness" (1990a, 372). The result is that the subject position of "Woman" is not represented by the simple opposition of "insider" and "outsider," the "split-self" who must ultimately become one or the other, but who is both.

The result is a multiple subject, not in the postmodernist sense of fragmentation and ever-elusive coherence, but in that any woman may never understand herself or be understood through gender oppression alone. Her identity is shifting, made up of multiple cultural locations. Gloria Anzaldúa has posited this self in her *Borderlands/La Frontera,* in which she says that the self adds a third element and strives for a new synthesis when it is torn in two in this pattern of gender. In Anzaldúa's words, "That third element is a new consciousness—a mestiza con-sciousness—and though it is a source of intense pain, its energy comes from continual creative motion that keeps breaking down the unitary aspect of each new paradigm" (1987, 79–80).

Therefore, feminist community is only possible in terms of the multi-ple locations the individual woman inhabits, for the relations within a woman are mirrored in her conversational and contentious relationship with other women. My critical approach, then, is grounded in the desire to understand difference as the destabilizing effect on oppositional terms—gender, but also race, class, ethnicity, and sexuality—that in turn produces fruitful interactions between individual voice and collective concerns in the work of feminist poets. In the spirit of these poets themselves, I examine how their work is addressed to "the central paradox of feminism: it does its work even as it recognizes the instability and potential impossibility of its subject" (Erkkila 1992, 4). My analysis of feminist poetry—which involves my own crossing and recrossing different communities within the feminist community, communities in which I am alternately insider and outsider—will repeat the central aspiration of feminist poetry itself: to be one voice in the continuing conversation between women and to be echoed, answered, and challenged by others.

Two

Judy Grahn's Poetics of Commonality

When she composed the series of seven poems she calls *The Common Woman* (1969), Judy Grahn wanted to create images of "regular, everyday women without making us look either superhuman or pathetic" (1978b, 60).[1] She wanted both to pinpoint the common or ordinary aspects of a group of women's lives and to celebrate, by weaving these accounts together, what these women have in common. Out of this writing experience, Grahn also formulated the central tenet of her poetics: the concept of "commonality," in which the writer writes so that readers/listeners seek "what overlaps with ourselves, then learn what we can from the remainder and leave it alone with respect as a whole that belongs to, that is, is centered in someone else, not 'us'" (1989, 8). With these poems, Grahn made a central contribution to feminist poetry, for she demonstrated how poetry can unify women as they celebrate each others' lives and identify their common oppressions, and yet at the same time she offered a poetics in which difference figures as a central operating principle.

But Grahn's poetry was "common" in another sense as well: it was radically antiestablishment in its working-class roots and straightforward lesbian orientation, a fact that placed Grahn squarely outside the commercial literary realm, and even resulted in her exclusion from academic feminist conversations. Fully understanding the significance of *The Common Woman* and the poems Grahn went on to write in the course of the 1970s, then, first requires highlighting the historical context of their production and critical reception.

The 1970s and *The Common Woman*

The Common Woman poems were immensely and virtually immediately popular. By Grahn's own account, these poems traveled the country, even the globe, without a commercial publisher, and fragments of them filtered out throughout the women's movement to be used in myriad ways. She says they "were reprinted hundreds of thousands of times, were put to music, danced, used to name various women's projects, quoted and then misquoted in a watered-down fashion for use on posters and T-shirts" (1978b, 60). In 1978, the feminist writer/activist Elly Bulkin echoed Grahn's own assessment when she noted that, in the course of that decade, the *Common Woman* series had "lent its title to bookstores, restaurants, and periodicals, and its poetry to posters, flyers, and brochures" (1978, 115). Excerpts of *The Common Woman* were used time and again, especially the last lines of the seventh and final poem:

> the common woman is as common as the best of bread
> and will rise
> and will become strong—I swear it to you
> I swear it to you on my own head
> I swear it to you on my common
> woman's
> head
>
> (1978b, 73)

Published by Grahn's own Women's Press Collective, the poems were advertised by word of mouth in women's liberation movement meetings, and initially distributed chiefly via mail. They were also advertised in the feminist press; a flyer insert in the Spring 1972 issue of *Mother Lode* listed Grahn's own address in San Francisco as the source for *Edward the Dyke and Other Poems,* "including the Common Woman / a portrait of seven women."[2] But perhaps it was Grahn's performance of these poems and her later series *She Who* (1972) and long poem *A Woman Is Talking to Death* (1973) that spread the power of her poetry most quickly. As Adrienne Rich recalls of Grahn's reading of *A Woman Is Talking to Death* in New York City in 1974, "I have never heard a poem encompassing so much violence, grief, anger, compassion, read so quietly. There was absolutely no false performance" (1978, 10).

The poetic direction that Grahn established with *The Common Woman* and developed in her subsequent work during the 1970s, together with the enthusiastic response her poetry received, indicate that Grahn was getting to the political and aesthetic heart of the matter for feminist poets and their readers/listeners alike when she began publishing in 1971. Indeed, both Grahn's poetic practice and prose elaboration of her poetics signal her as a central figure in the early development of feminist poetry. Most significantly, she notes that her struggle to be an "everybody's poet," to speak to/for the collective, means that she must begin with her own experience. She says her "intention is to write poetry for everyone, and, given that, I have to do it as me." This means, she says, that "first I have to establish that everyone can see me as who I am and take that for granted, and then we can go on to what comes next" (1983, 99). She states this idea of a coalitional voice even more succinctly in the following: "The decision an artist makes, to speak for women and to speak as a woman . . . is probably the most powerful decision she will make. For in making it, she chooses autonomy, she chooses to stand somewhere in particular to speak out to her society. Her work, in locating itself so specifically socially and historically takes on a power it cannot have if she chooses, instead, to speak anonymously, 'universally' " (1985, 58). This notion of coalitional voice coalesces with Grahn's emphasis on ritual and performance and her idea of poetry as a tool, both of which came to be typical of feminist poets. Poetry, in Grahn's definition, "repeats and recreates the ceremonial myths which give human lives their meaning." It connects individuals "to a universe that has a place for us" (11). Feminist poetry in particular invites its readers/listeners into a "dream/vision" that has real social consequences: "In defining the precise dimensions of that dream, by attempting to live it, and by helping each other to see and feel and express it, we will affect the world, by changing its mind" (38).[3]

The story of how Grahn arrived at poetry is also in many ways typical (or perhaps prototypical, considering how early she became involved in the women's movement) of feminist poets. She became a member of the Gay Women's Liberation Group, the first lesbian feminist collective on the West Coast, when it was founded in 1969. A year later, the collective started the bookstore A Woman's Place in Berkeley, and Grahn and two other poets launched one of the first all-women presses in the United States, the Women's Press Collective. Grahn started with a mimeograph machine in her basement; working with the visual artist Wendy Cadden, and later with writers Willyce Kim and Pat Parker, Grahn eventually published works using this equipment (Case 1988, 49; Joan and Chesman, 179–80). When Grahn wrote *The Common Woman* in 1969, she did so because of her experience in this nexus of women's movement activities: "I had just joined a women's consciousness-raising group . . . and I suddenly wanted something to read about women, but I couldn't find anything" (1983, 94). Thus, she says, the poems played a functional and celebratory role in her evolution as a feminist; as she says, "their origin was completely practical" (1978b, 60). Grahn's poetic flourishing, then, began in the same way that many women's did within the social/political women's movement; she wrote poetry out of the desire to find/found a literary representation of women's lives that in turn would be useful to women trying to figure out how to live their lives and to resist oppression.

Grahn is also a pivotal example of how feminist poets during the early 1970s were taking their own work seriously enough to find unconventional ways of distributing it to readers. Indeed, the Women's Press Collective demonstrated how successful this endeavor could be. Grahn wrote "Edward the Dyke," a prose satire on psychological definitions and treatments of lesbianism, in 1965 but hid it away because at that time she could foresee absolutely no context in which it could be published; by 1978, the collective had sold six thousand copies of *Edward the Dyke and Other Poems*. They also released *The Common Woman* (1971) and *She Who* (1972) as short books of poetry. The title of the first of these indicates Grahn's resistant stance to traditional notions of what poetry could be and do; by indirectly indicating that "Edward the Dyke" is a poem, she effectively questions inherited generic designations. She took a similarly rebellious position regarding the possibility that publishing could be noncommercial and movement-based; as she has said, "we shifted the basis of poetry, coming out of what the beatniks had been trying to do, but they had stayed a little exclusive, and I think the women's movement and the black arts movement also shifted the basis for art and infused it with a new set of ideas and a new lifefulness. Our publishing simply magnified that" (1983, 97).

Grahn was very conscious of how necessary it was to leave behind eastern centers of artistic production and publication. For this reason, the openness of California—both geographically and culturally— especially suited her purposes; in this way, she did resemble others like Allen Ginsberg who had moved west and helped found an innovative poetry front. But she was above all interested in becoming an "everybody's poet." She wanted to throw open the gates to the world of poetry writing and criticism, and in this way reflected, or influenced, feminist poets' emphasis on the importance of poetry to people's daily lives and certainly to any possibility of social change. Grahn put this into practice not just in her publishing practices, but also in the kinds of criticism she sought out; in fact, her writing process itself was deeply affected by the criticisms offered her, not even by a women's writing collective but by her women "neighbors": "I took [my poems] to my neighbors and asked them what they thought of them. I did not say that I had written them. Sometimes I just said, 'Someone gave me these poems. What do you think of them?' to get female feedback. I was very courageous in those days because real people tell you real things about your work" (97). This grassroots criticism itself was the source, according to Grahn, of the feminist impulses to reveal the previously hidden and to get poetry into as many hands possible. "It established," says Grahn, "a new basis for women's art—things which had formerly been unspeakable suddenly became vital and desirable things to say, and *The Common Woman* poems spread all by themselves without any help from any New York publication of any kind" (97).

This last assertion of Grahn's also illustrates, however, just how audacious this kind of poetry production by necessity had to be. In a publishing climate that by tradition did not receive women's work warmly, Grahn understood how assertive she and her cohorts had to be about the kind of work they were doing, and that they would likely be perceived as grandstanding and even narcissistic women poets in the minds of the commercial press and the poetry establishment. Of women's publishing in the early 1970s, she said, "To publish your own poetry is not vanity, it's aggression" (quoted in Arnold 1976, 24).

Grassroots Popularity, Critical Neglect

This narrative of Grahn's early career demonstrates that she certainly was a central figure in the nascent feminist poetry movement, and begins to illustrate how, perhaps more than any other poet at that time, she was able to create coalitional voice as a concept and practice. As it continued to grow during the 1970s, Grahn's immense popularity within the women's movement certainly attested to this fact, and her popularity has been sustained among feminist poets themselves and at the grassroots level since then. But her reputation and influence among academic and establishment critics has been mediated by these very same facts, and the reasons for this phenomenon are complex. First of all, as she was founding one of the first and most illustrious examples of feminist self-publishing, Grahn also became an outspoken proponent for developing and sustaining a women's communications network that would circumvent the traditional, men-dominated publishing outlets entirely. The aim was, as Grahn's close colleague June Arnold of Daughters Press spelled it out, to share knowledge and thereby to understand "the ubiquity and interdependence of our oppression," to develop "an analysis by arguing back and forth in print across the nation," and to "deepen and broaden our grasp of female life by reading autobiographies, novels, stories, poetry by women talking only to women" (1976, 18). To achieve these goals, Arnold recommended that feminists publish only with women's presses and withhold support from any women who choose to publish with what she called the "finishing press"—"because it is our movement they intend to finish" (1976, 19)—which she said publishes feminists only when feminism is in style. Arnold and Grahn were joined in this approach by, among others, Coletta Reid of Diana Press, which was to merge with the Women's Press Collective in 1977.

This perspective on the commercial press caused a good deal of controversy after Arnold, together with Parke Bowman of Daughters Press and Bertha Harris, argued for it adamantly at the 1976 New York City Lesbian Conference's panel discussion/workshop on lesbian publishing. Subsequently, Arnold and the others have often been labeled "separatist," a term that has a long, complex history within the women's movement and certainly in the academic discourse on the movement. The controversy has been over whether strategies like Arnold's constitute a tactical radical feminism or a separatist cultural feminism; the debate from the mid 1970s certainly caused factions to develop within the rank and file of the predominantly white, middle-class movement, and set up a basic opposition between institution-oriented academic feminists and the more activist feminist literary and publishing community. In addition, separatism as a strategy in the women's movement has also long been associated with the wave of lesbian feminism that in many ways defined the women's movement in the mid 1970s (and with which Grahn readily and consistently identifies herself), so that no small amount of homophobia has contributed to the neglect of the so-called separatists of that decade.[4]

Practically speaking, among many feminist critics the terms "separatist" and "lesbian" have relegated Grahn and the others to a particular niche within the history of the women's movement: their work has not been used in women's studies courses as often as have books by women who publish with more "mainstream" presses,[5] and their work has in general been subject to critical neglect or even dismissal by feminist critics based in the academy. (The exception is Adrienne Rich.) This neglect has also resulted because Grahn positioned herself deliberately outside eastern centers of publishing and reception, and certainly outside the main channels of conversation and exchange within the poetry establishment. She and other West Coast feminist poets may have become enormously popular with a feminist readership, but not with establishment critics or the mainstream media, which catapulted, for example, the San Francisco-based Beats (all male) into the national spotlight in the late 1950s.

In addition, because Grahn has always refused to give credence to any poetics that smacks in the least of elitism, Grahn has in many ways been relegated by feminist critics to the category of *popular* (read "not serious") poet. Adrienne Rich, in contrast, is received critically in exactly the opposite way, although she herself was so affected by Grahn, and in fact wrote the introduction to Grahn's collected work in 1978. Since the advent of women's studies, Rich has been the subject of countless academic explorations, while Grahn's work has received attention in only a handful of articles (Avi-ram 1987; Backus 1993; Carruthers 1983; Case 1988; and Montefiore 1987–1988). While most of the authors of these articles view Grahn's work positively, or even count her as a central contemporary figure, one contrasts Grahn, Rich, and Denise Levertov's debt to H.D.'s visionary poetics and says that Grahn's vision is "as politicized as Rich's but considerably simpler" ("too simple," she says later on). In the view of this critic, Grahn's reading of H.D. clearly helps her interpret H.D. as Rich and Levertov do, "but in a less sophisticated way" (Montefiore 1987–1988, 187).

I suggest that the general critical neglect of Grahn and a critic's choice of words like "too simple" and "less sophisticated" to discount Grahn's poetics indicate an irony: that precisely one of the poets who pioneered feminist poetics in the most innovative and daring ways has been marginalized in the very name of critical appraisal of feminist poetry. Grahn's commitment to writing for "common women" rather than an elite group of establishment poets or feminist poets who had training in/connections to establishment poetics and politics—together with the fact that her poetry circulated on its own merits rather than on a wave of critical notices—may have in fact diluted her appeal to critics. Perhaps she became too "common," in the negative sense of the word, in their eyes. Indeed, even Elly Bulkin approaches this attitude, citing Grahn's very commitment to performance and wide distribution as the reason for being disappointed in *She Who* when the series was published as a "graphic book" in 1977: "*She Who* suffers from the five-year gap between Grahn's writing them and their publication in book form. In those five years, they have been doled out at Grahn's readings, in women's publications . . . and, most recently, on the record *Where Would I Be Without You*" (1978, 115). In these intervening years, says Bulkin, *The Common Woman* and *A Woman Is Talking to Death* had also "settled quickly into a kind of informal canon of lesbian-feminist poetry," so that "hardly any book could withstand the resultant burden of expectation on *She Who*" (115). According to this view, Grahn's poetics and popularity themselves, rather than the politics of literary publishing and approval, are the roots of a not altogether favorable review of her poetry.

The central irony here lies in the fact that Grahn's poetics, and especially her ideas about form, audience, and difference, are formally complex in addition to being profoundly egalitarian. Like other feminist poets, Grahn believes that understanding and developing one's personal identity is essential to being able to make larger political observations and to speak to/for a larger community. Indeed, her desire to be an "everybody's poet" is grounded in this belief, and certainly does not betray any "separatist" ambitions. But this belief is also grounded in an intricate poetics. Grahn is centrally influenced by the work of none other than the singular—and many would say "elite"—Gertrude Stein. In fact, Grahn's work is an effort to understand the deeply democratic goals at the heart of Stein's complex works, and to adapt formal principles derived from Stein's work to the political context of her own writing, namely, the women's movement.

It is in Grahn's aspirations to develop a coalitional voice, to express "commonality," that her integration of these egalitarian and formal strategies is most evident. Understanding the ways Grahn achieves this synthesis first requires elucidating the details of her Stein-influenced poetics and, second, reading for "commonality" in each of the three major works she produced by 1975—*The Common Woman* series, in which she first uses coalitional voice and in which she begins to develop the concept of commonality through experimentation with rhyme and rhythm; the *She Who* series, in which she most elaborately works toward community identity and commonality through performance-oriented strategies; and the long poem *A Woman Is Talking to Death,* in which she achieves her most complex development of coalitional voice as she explores commonalities among not just women but all victims of patriarchal oppression. This understanding of her work is necessary to override the critical neglect she has suffered over the years and to place Grahn justly at the center of the feminist poetry movement as it began to develop in the late 1960s and early 1970s.

Steinian Equality and the Idea of Commonality

Each of the seven poems in *The Common Woman* series pays tribute to an individual woman, a "common" woman in the details, from the joyous to the tragic, of her life. And Grahn certainly intends each of these as a "common" woman, in the sense that each represents ordinary women rather than "exceptional" historical or contemporary figures. As Grahn remembers, she "wrote those seven poems to ordinary women I had known" (1983, 94). But the word "common" also carries multiple other meanings for Grahn. She has in mind converting the word "common" in its most colloquial, derogatory sense (base, familiar, even sexually impure, as in "common slut") into a positive modifier for women's lives; by reclaiming the word, she can defuse its power to harm women in description, and invest it with other, more affirming meanings. She says the word "common" also makes her think of "the commons of England and of Boston where people could meet together and assert themselves," and thus indicates "what we have in common, which is a cross-connection between us all" (94). The very word, then, carries many connotations, all interacting together to convey some sense of women—all women—as special in their very "commonness" and as connected to each other. This sense of "common" powerfully contradicts a culture that prizes individual achievement and especially genius, and exposes as suspect even feminist attempts to commemorate exceptional women figures. Grahn's definition of the word is a potent expression of the powerful impulse toward community in feminist poetry in the early 1970s, for she wanted to recognize women's subjective experience and at the same time link it to collective life and concerns.

Out of the experience of writing *The Common Woman,* Grahn also settled on "common" as the central concept in her poetics. While these poems provide the first example of Grahn's use of "commonality" in her poetry, she elucidates this concept most clearly in her writings on the work of Gertrude Stein. She identifies in Stein's poetry, fiction, drama, and essays the quality of "equality," in which Stein used "the entire text as a field in which every element mattered as much as any other, every part of speech, every word and, good poet that she was, every space and punctuation mark" (1989, 8). According to Grahn, the result in Stein's work is that every element of a sentence is equal to every other, so that the reader is required to enter the text on this leveled plane as well, and "life is perceived as a dance in which every element contributes to every other" (11).

Grahn's definition of commonality is related to Stein's of equality, and yet she develops additional nuances; she more directly draws out the social and political implications of such a practice. When universality is the rule in the act of reading, says Grahn, readers look in an author's work for the parts with which they can identify, and then dismiss the rest as irrelevant (8). Unlike "universality," which relies on a single center, commonality has "infinite numbers of changeable centers." With commonality as the guiding principle, readers seek what they can clearly identify with, and respect the remainder (8). While Grahn sees Stein's practice of textual equality as subversive in its potential to teach readers about social relationships as they experience complete equality in the text, she herself understands commonality to be both subjective and objective, operating both on the page and in social relationships. "Using the idea of commonality," she says, "means standing exactly where you and/or your group (of whatever current definition) are, and noticing what part of you overlaps with others who are standing exactly where they are" (8). In a "many-centered multiverse," according to Grahn, difference itself is so "essentially common" that "duplication . . . is the oddity." Ultimately, this process becomes a "matter of perspective, of metaphor": readers look not for the "universal," but rather seek what is "common," "what overlaps with others without losing its center" (145).

Thus, in her development of the concept of commonality, Grahn combines the discrete individual and the messy collective. Therefore, when Grahn says that she wants to be "everybody's poet" and that she has to become most herself in order for people to see her and hear what she is saying, she is calling directly on this idea. She will become a poet of the people only as readers/listeners hear the elements of her life, understand the events and identities they have in common with her, and respect the rest. She cannot simply speak for the people—her own perspective posited as the universal perspective—but she must be her most individual, identifying and celebrating her own "center" (or herself as center), in order to speak as one of and for the people, out of the "cross-connections" of the collective. Concentrating on one's own experience is never sufficient, either, and in fact may merely repeat the tendency to universalize. Grahn says that the woman poet, upon deciding to explore her personal experience, then "faces another danger, for if she addresses only members of her special groups, her work will have limited power, and limited integrity." Instead, poets must recognize and include "*all* our selves" in order to understand that life consists of "many expanding, multicultural worlds in which everyone is ultimately included (as well as excluded)" (1985, 58).

This *is* indeed an anti-intellectual poetics, though not simplistic in concept or practice. In its goal of using poetry as a medium for constructive political and cultural dialogue, it counters the dominant notion of poetry as an elite art, removed from public life and accessible only to those with training and talent enough to understand and interpret it. Out of both her feminist/lesbian and working-class orientations, Grahn resists the idea of poetry as aesthetic artifact or commodity rather than functional, mass-based cultural practice. She also effectively erodes the notion of the artist as an exception, the one above or outside society, who requires isolation and specialized training in order to funnel artistic products into the free market. In Grahn, the emphasis on the details of real life in working-class poetry is complemented by the emphasis on the connections between the personal and the political in feminist poetry.

In this vein, Grahn has from the beginning viewed her poetry as useful. Grahn says that *The Common Woman* even exceeded her expectations about poetry as a cultural tool. She says they "more than fulfilled my idealistic expectations of art as a useful subject—of art as a doer, rather than a passive object to be admired" (1978b, 60). In her introduction to *The Work of a Common Woman*, Adrienne Rich shares this view; she notes that Grahn's work is not about an outdated, less than useful "revolution"—which in many ways, because of its metaphorical connotations as well as its historical uses, is a static concept—but rather about "transformation," or the "vision of a process which will leave neither surfaces nor depths unchanged, which enters society at the most essential level of the subjugation of women and nature by men" (1978, 8).

In theorizing the idea of transformation, Grahn again turns to Stein, whose writing she says was transformative because her vision was deeply scientific and methodical and never condescending. Rather, says Grahn, Stein's work was "integrative" and "central to itself and to its own principles" (1989, 21). Consequently, it does not require "understanding" so much as "interstanding." The reader is not required to interpret her way to some deeper, universal meaning behind the words on the page but rather is to interact with the words themselves, with the ways they play with each other in the text. By escaping, for instance, the linear plots that have empowered Western, patriarchal culture, Stein employs equality to the extent that the text has no beginning or ending but continually repeats relationships between the elements within it. This destroys, Grahn says, the hierarchies that uphold our society, "postulating a field in which everything is equal" and flying "in the face of every functional social moment we experience outside the experience of reading" Stein's text (22). This once again brings Grahn around to the concept of commonality and its feminist underpinnings: the interaction between writer and reader/listener is profoundly capable of changing both of them as well as the larger culture.

The Common Woman

Like many other women poets who wrote poetry before the advent of the women's movement and the development of feminist poetry, Grahn herself may or may not be, and in fact is quite often distant from, the speaker in her earliest poems. In many of the earlier pieces included in *Edward the Dyke and Other Poems,* Grahn often writes in third person, and even uses persona (as in "Vietnamese woman speaking to an American soldier").

The Common Woman was Grahn's breakthrough poetry; with this series, she established herself as a presence in the poems and illustrated, especially as she used rhythm and rhyme, her notion of commonality, of equality and interaction between multiple centers within a poem.[6] The effect is a blending of subjective and collective presence as well as a truth-telling about women's lives that use old formal traits in innovative ways: she calls these poems "flexible, self-defining sonnets," pieces that redefine/resist the older, stricter prosodic forms in the leveling and enlivening action of her "common" writing (1978b, 60).

Grahn explores the common life details of seven ordinary women, and she develops commonality between herself and these women by creating a nontraditional equality between elements of the text. The latter involves a series of formal techniques that frees each poem from rigid form and yet establishes some patterns to create a sense of ritual, celebration, and shared identity. She resists strict, traditional prosody by dispersing rhyme—full rhyme, near rhyme, broken rhyme— throughout the poem, sometimes along a regular beat pattern, some- times not. She also employs assonance and consonance as well as alliteration to help establish this pattern, without resorting to any com- pletely consistent use of any of these throughout the poems. All of these strategies lend a sense of pattern to the poem without falling back on the rigid, hierarchical structure of traditional rhyme and meter patterns. Instead, these sound and cadence effects relate to each other playfully across the poem, rather than defining the poem in a clearly identifiable and limited way. The undulating relationship of rhyme, rhythm, and line thus functions both to establish the fluidity and dynamism of indi- vidual women's lives and to demonstrate the similarities and differences that define their relationships with one another. At the same time, it builds an incantatory feeling in the poems that adds a level of ritual celebration of women's lives, for the individual reader but especially for public performance.

The first poem in the series, "Helen, at 9 a.m., at noon, at 5:15," indicates how serious Grahn is about dealing with the actual details of ordinary womens' lives: it deals with a corporate drone rather than the empowered feminist that feminist readers/listeners, in the ideological fever of women's movement organizing, might easily expect. Grahn im- mediately employs textual "equality"—dispersing rhyme and rhythm within lines and layering the details of Helen's everyday experience—in her pursuit of the "common" experience and the individuality of this woman. Simultaneously, the rhyme and rhythm, together with conso- nance, lends some pattern to the poem, and provides it its ritual/celebra- tory effect. Lines 6-11 illustrate:

> Wearing trim suits and spike heels,
> she says "bust" instead of breast;
> somewhere underneath she
> misses love and trust, but she feels
> that spite and malice are the
> prices of success . . .

> (1978b, 61)

The consonance of "s" threads through this passage and is grounded in the word "success," the "center" of this woman's experience. The rhyme of "bust" and "trust" and "heels" and "feels," internal to the lines, adds beat to the poem as does the consonance. The word "success" is repeated in line 12, adding another layer of rhythm and emphasis.

Similarly, the next section of the poem, in lines 14–18, relies on the same strategies: "After a while she'll be a real / killer, bitter and more wily, better at / pitting the men against each other / and getting the other women fired. / She constantly conspires" (61). The double "t" sounds in "bitter," "better," "pitting," and "getting" provide the consonantal beat, while the rhyme of "while" and "wily," "fired" and "conspired," deepens the effect. Helen is a sad and bitter person: the softness of "s" sounds hint at her tentative, cheerless inner life while the toughness of "b" and "t" sounds iterate her hard, even brutal edge. The conclusion of the poem is that "the common woman is as common / as the common crow." By entering Helen's experience through dispersed rhyme and rhythm, both the potential tragic and the potential comic effects of strict rhyme and meter patterns have been eliminated, while the chantlike effect of the dispersed rhyme still adds a performative dimension to the poem and thereby invites readers/listeners into the poem to identify with this woman where they can. Helen is a "crow"— forbidding, solitary—but "common" to be sure.[7] She is a woman like many others, but also different, and therefore to be recognized in her similarity and respected in her difference. She is both representative and individual.

The next common woman—poem two is entitled "Ella, in a square apron, along Highway 80"—is, like Helen, sad and oppressed by the role she must play in a man's world, but she is also empowered, angry, and, like a snake, ready to strike. The consonantal sounds, indicating hardness of character and purpose, inform the poem's opening lines: "She's a copperheaded waitress, / tired and sharp-worded, she hides / her bad brown tooth behind a wicked / smile . . ." The reference to a fanglike tooth and a "wicked" smile reinforces the snake metaphor. In lines 4–6, repetition and rhyme also occur, building the incantatory effect within the poem and further layering the snake imagery; Ella here seems like a rattlesnake as she ". . . flicks her ass, / out of habit, to fend off the pass / that passes for affection" (63). The rhyme of "ass" and "pass," and the subsequent repetition together with the hard "f" sounds also combine to develop in the reader/listener a ritual identification with

Ella; the harmony they develop invites the reader/listener to see both individuality and pattern, both difference and sameness, in this woman.

As in the first poem, the rhyming within lines continues throughout this poem, only to culminate in a final rhyme which involves the last word of the poem. In lines 7-10, Ella "keeps her mind the way men / keep a knife—keen to strip the game / down to her size. She has a thin spine, / swallows her eggs cold, and tells lies." And in lines 18–23: ". . . Like some isolated lake, / her flat blue eyes take care of their own stark / bottom. Her hands are nervous, curled, ready / to scrape. / The common woman is as common / as a rattlesnake" (63). The consistent figurative reference here is to the snake; Ella, who is "copperheaded," is thin, swallows eggs, and has hands curled and ready to strike. The rhyme in the final line contributes to the celebration of what these women have in common; indeed, each of the seven poems ends with the same pattern of a rhyme that culminates in the final word. The rhyme in each instance is different, thus maintaining the individuality of each woman, while the refrain "the common woman is as common as . . ." remains the same, which establishes the connections between these women.

This portrait is also obviously quite different from the first poem's, however. While Helen is a victim in some ways, she is also by class, education, and professional status a privileged person. In contrast, Ella is quite clearly without class privilege; she resorts to violence against a lover who abuses her child, winds up in jail, and finds when she is released that the courts have taken her child away. While Helen is bitter, Ella is angry. In their details, then, these first two poems represent Grahn's overt effort to compare and contrast, to unify and differentiate between women.

The other five poems continue this portrait-weaving enterprise, and Grahn also continues the more complex work of developing textual and social commonality within the economy of the poem itself. In the third poem, the single mother Nadine sustains life in the inner-city: "She's made of grease / and metal, with a hard head / that makes the men around her seem frail. / The common woman is as common as / a nail" (65). In the fourth poem, the lesbian Carol ". . . makes her own / bets, and fixes her own car, with her friend. / She goes as far / as women can go without protection / from men"; she carries "angry energy inside a passive form. / The common woman is as common / as a thunderstorm" (67). The hitchhiker Annie, in poem five, is an alcoholic who finds her only emotional release in drifting: "She leaves the taste of salt and iron / under your tongue, but you don't mind / The common woman is as common / as the reddest wine" (69). In poem six, Margaret is called a "big baboon" by her husband but explodes his description in her inner life of revenge and vision: "Lusting for changes, she laughs through her / teeth, and wanders from room to room. / The common woman is as solemn as a monkey / or a new moon" (71).

In poem four, Grahn clearly indicates that she views traditional prosody as oppressive when she uses end rhyme and regular meter—for the only time in this series of poems—to state the view of the dominant society toward Carol's lesbianism:

> She has taken a woman lover
> whatever shall we do
> she has taken a woman lover
> how lucky it wasn't you
>
> (67)

The clear pattern of rhyme and meter here marks this passage (the first four lines of the poem, which establish the tenor of the society in which Carol lives) as clearly different from the rest of the *Common Woman* poems, with their dispersed design of sound and motion. But the voice of establishment poetry and, by implication, of society in general is not unquestioned here and thereby left in a simple oppositional relationship with Grahn's alternative techniques. Rather, this is a parody, and with a quatrain of trimeter lines, reads more like light than serious verse. In other words, Grahn clearly identifies rigid prosodic practices with an oppressive society/tradition and pokes fun of them rather than accepting them as inevitable.

The final poem in the *Common Woman* series is entitled "Vera, from my childhood" and concerns an old woman who has faced trauma after trauma—a "bastard boss" as well as a "fine husband" broken by liquor—and yet retained extreme dignity (her religion insists that people "are beautiful golden birds and must be preserved"). Vera is last in the series by virtue of age and experience, and therefore represents what is possible for the six other women represented. She maintains a sense of self and self-respect that sustains her through oppressive conditions: "the common woman is as common / as good bread / as common as when you couldn't go on / but did." As a result, she is full of promise, in spite of the fact that she is merely a castoff in a society that values beauty and obedience in women. She is in fact full of revolutionary potential and indicates what woman have "in common": "For all the world we didn't know we held in common / all along / the common woman is as common as the best of bread / and will rise / and will become strong . . ." (73).

In poem seven, Grahn finally enters the poem in its final five lines—the final lines of the entire series—to "swear" that the revolutionary, "rising" potential of women's lives will "become strong": ". . . I swear it to you / I swear it to you on my own head / I swear it to you on my common / woman's head" (73). The poet herself only becomes an actor in the poem in response to what she—and her readers—have discovered about common women's lives: that they are "common" in the sense of solidarity but also "common" and celebratable in their very ordinary differences, in their multiple centers of identity and experience. Thus the poet acts not as protagonist, extrapolating universal characteristics from her own experience, but as chronicler, discovering similarities and differences in the accumulating details of women's lives and then making a commitment—"swearing" or pledging—to take strength from these women and follow through on this strength's potential effect in other women's lives and in the life of the society. These final five lines, because of their repetition, because of the sudden and startling appearance of the "I," and because of the two final short and stressed lines, feel confrontive and very confident in resisting both poetic and societal oppression. As it coalesces with the practice of commonality in this series of poems, this is an example of coalitional voice. The poet roots her observations in her own experience as a woman. The poet's basic task, however, remains to preserve and celebrate the lives of the common women she describes; except for the final five lines of the seventh and final poem of the series, all the poems are written in third person, with the figurative energy residing in lean metaphors and the formal impetus in irregular rhyme and rhythm, rather than in extended lyrical analogies or explanations.

Grahn's evolution of voice and theme extends from *The Common Woman* through the two other major pieces she wrote by 1973. In *She Who* (1972), Grahn mixes first person and third person within poems as well as writes individual poems in each so that the collective and the subjective mix freely and fluidly and a complex blend of coalitional voice and celebratory performance results. The result is a multifaceted meditation on the nature of power and the power of woman/women. It is only later in *A Woman Is Talking to Death* (1973) that Grahn writes completely in first person, but it is in this poem that she in fact achieves her most complex weaving of the subjective and collective, as she contemplates the intricate nexus of oppressions that affect her companion citizens by virtue of their gender, sexuality, race, and class.

She Who: Mythology as Political Practice

Grahn's interest in mythopoesis is reflected in her writings on the self-exiled goddess-seeking poet, H.D., and especially in Grahn's later books of poetry, *The Queen of Wands* (1986) and *The Queen of Swords* (1987), in which she extensively rewrites the story of Helen of Troy. Grahn's move in this direction begins in the series of poems entitled *She Who*. However, the primary effect of *She Who* is to indicate that, in fact, Grahn doesn't understand the mythologies she engages/rewrites to be timeless or essential; rather, she understands Western myths like that of Helen to convey deeply held assumptions in Western culture, assumptions that can have various effects and that can be overcome or, more important, transformed into empowering ones. Grahn has used the term "mythic realism" to describe her task in this regard. The point, she says, is to use "female subjects portrayed realistically on one level, yet with deep connections to a communally held myth at the same time" (1985, 87). This work is always grounded in the needs of actual women, and particularly in the need for a sense of community and even unity. Indeed, Grahn wrote *She Who* out of a functional impulse just as she did *The Common Woman*; she was living communally with a group of lesbians during the nine-month period in which she wrote these poems, and she understood that these women were trying to invent a woman-based culture and in this process needed "to concretize the bonding of women into a group identity" (74–75).

The ways Grahn uses both form and theme in *She Who* iterate this fundamental fact about her search for the mythological roots of oppression, for She Who is both mythological presence and the presence of real women in real time. As Grahn constructs coalitional voice and employs formal strategies—anaphora, listing, repetition, word play—

which promote performance and collective identification with her subject matter, she forwards the project of commonality she began in *The Common Woman*. The theme of women's oppression and the way rituals and story itself can overcome it is coterminous with her voice and style and also parallels that of *The Common Woman*. Here, woman (She Who) is a suppressed and yet unified and resistant power in the Western world, while as *women*, "she" is diverse and celebrates differ- ence. Once again, the effect is to bring readers/listeners together as a community while encouraging recognition of each other as individual women. She Who is the communal celebration of unity among women, but she is also each woman in her diversity; She Who is both stable and shifting center, inviting individual reader/listeners to find both them- selves and each other in the poems. And, in the vein of coalitional voice, Grahn begins with her own experience.

The autobiographical instance of the "I" in this series is "plainsong from a younger woman to an older woman," which Grahn wrote for performance at the funeral of her "first lover and longtime friend," Yvonne Mary Robinson (1978b, 103). Because Grahn indicates that this poem is for ritual use only, I will not parse it too extensively, except to demonstrate the way it grounds the entire series in Grahn's experi- ence of the bonds between women. As in *The Common Woman*, Grahn's personal entry into the poems occurs quite late; this plainsong is one of a pair that shows up near the end of the series of twenty-one poems.

The very term "plainsong" indicates multiple voices in unison or two contrapuntal melodies sung together; in either sense, the idea is of a gathering of voices. The first plainsong is clearly from Grahn to her departed companion, and the "group" here is both the two of them in their love for each other and all women who participate in the ritual creation of community this poem enacts. (The contrapuntal potential is also extended in the second of the songs, "Slowly: a plainsong from an older woman to a younger woman," which provides the other half of the dialogue implied in the first plainsong) (104). Through a chaining effect ("i am your best, i am your kind / kind of my kind, i am your wish / wish of my wish . . ."), Grahn both pledges to her friend the ways she will continue living on her behalf and creates a strong portrait of all the ways women can do this for one another. She writes, "i will be your heart now, to do your loving / love belongs to those who do the feeling" (101). As in *The Common Woman*, out of her personal experience Grahn makes a *pledge* to another woman/to women. The final lines of "Vera, from my childhood" are echoed throughout this plainsong; "I swear to you" becomes "i will." Though the tone of this plainsong is ultimately more commemorative and less defiant than that of "Vera," the promise that women together can/will have revolutionary impact remains: "i will be your fight now, to do your winning / as the bond between women is beginning" (102).[8]

However, though Grahn does use first person here, though she clearly records and makes sense of her personal experience in this poem, the effect is finally only a heavily ritualized coalitional voice: Grahn uses only an uncapitalized "i," she relies on incantation through chaining and repetition, and she forgoes prosaic detail (unlike in *The Common Woman*) in favor of the future-oriented pledge itself. In other words, while this plainsong grounds *She Who* in Grahn's own life, this personal experience remains almost secondary, for the poem simultaneously promotes the series' theme: the ongoing power of women to transform the future. Grahn understands and uses coalitional voice, and yet she longs deeply to speak to and for a community/set of communities that must piece together a common history in order to imagine a common future.

Grahn does use "I" in various other poems in the series, but these are either clearly representative of any woman's life or, once again, so highly ritualized that they have this effect as well. In the sixth poem of the series (untitled), for example, she writes, "I shall grow another breast / in the middle of my chest / what shall it be" (83). The additional breast is clearly impossible in the literal sense and achieves its strength as a metaphor for women claiming their own power. The impetus of the poem resides in the beginning couplet ("She Who increases / what can be done") and the poem's final three lines, which echoes it ("Now I have a longer tongue / and three good breasts, and some have none. / what can be done") (83). Grahn's word play with the question "what can be done?" indicates that She Who increases women's power; that as She Who increases, the question becomes more insistent; and that the fact that "I" has been empowered but other women have not increases the question. And the question itself is obviously precisely how to empower other women through the knowledge of She Who.

She Who, then, is the personal and collective energy that enlivens this series of poems. The very first poem (untitled) demonstrates the function that She Who is to fulfill. In repetition and word dispersal reminiscent of Stein, Grahn poses the existence, the question, the over-

whelming power of She Who: "She. who—WHO, she WHO. She
WHO—who SHE? / who she SHE, who SHE she, SHE—who
WHO—" (77). As she repeats the words over and over, as she punctu-
ates and capitalizes them variously, and as she combines and recombines
them, she creates equality in the text. She also establishes the performance dimension of the series, because the punctuation and capitalization
in this poem provide further cues for public reading (unlike, for instance, unusual spatial arrangement would). These formal traits illustrate the unity and separateness that infuse the presence of woman/
women in She Who; all at once "she" is mythological power, historical
figure(s), individual women, and women together. No hierarchy exists
in She Who; this is not the "source of life" or primal goddess but the
power of women alone and together, throughout history and in the
present context.

While the play in this first poem has all these effects, the very determination of a single name, She Who, displays the drive toward collectivity,
or at least coalition. At the very least, though, this is an active body of
agents, rather than a static essence. "She," after all, is followed by the
pronoun "who," which in its placement after another pronoun indicates
some action to follow. Indeed, this is precisely how Grahn conveys the
diverse women who make up She Who. In the second poem (untitled),
she repeats the actions themselves and conducts word play on various
verbs that complete "She Who," demonstrating that She Who is simultaneously without beginning or end and expressed in multifarious ways.
The combination of "She" and "Who" implies both "She Who" as the
name of an ongoing female presence, and "She" and "Who" as pro-
nouns, which in a series indicates both a list of women and a list of
diverse acts:

> She Who marks her own way, gathering.
> She Who makes her own difference.
> She Who differs, gathering her own events.
> She Who gathers, gaining
> She Who carries her own ways.
>
> (78)

Later in the poem, Grahn states She Who as plural: "for She Who gathers her own ways, / carrying / the names of She Who gather and
gain . . ." (78). Of course, the anaphora Grahn uses here also increases

the performance potential of this poem, while She Who is both stable and shifting center, both the point of unity for women across their identities and women in their diversity.

She Who also takes on her central unifying power precisely because of women's oppression; poem seven, entitled "The enemies of She Who call her various names," is a barrage of names given to her by her enemies. Significantly, the formal pattern here is provided only through listing and repetition of the most widely used labels; the point, in this case, is certainly not celebration but rather to resist the power these names have held over women's lives by bringing them into the open, by having women speak them instead of men. The entire poem, in fact, is a catalog of names, all of which denigrate women based on their sex ("a whore, a whore, / a fishwife a cunt a harlot a harlot a pussy") (84). The list also reveals how oppressors intertwine sexism and racism; the list includes "you black bitch—you white bitch—you brown bitch—you / yellow bitch . . ." (84).

While poem seven indicates that sexism knows no color lines, the final poem in the series (untitled) celebrates the fact that She Who is made up of difference and of different women. The poem consists of nine long, irregular stanzas, a tercet, and a couplet. The stanzas all use the anaphoric "the woman," with each line naming a different woman with the pronoun "who" or the possessive pronoun "whose." In the first two stanzas, these women are marked by their different physical characteristics (from "the woman with too many fingers" to "the woman with broad shoulders"), while the remaining stanzas in largest part name their actions ("the woman who gathers peaches / the woman who carries jars on her head / the woman who howls") (107–8). The anaphora creates an incantatory feel, while the actual phrase "the woman who/whose" resonates because the name/action "She Who" has structured the body of poems until this point, thereby deepening the effect of naming individual women in this final poem. The anaphora does not, however, drive the chant to an ending; instead, Grahn uses a longer, somewhat regular line to establish a beat, and avoids rhyme, assonance, and consonance. The result is a cyclical feel, as if the chant could go on forever, encompassing all women in their individuality. Nevertheless, the poem does have a structured ending, which focuses on and values the variety:

> the woman whose children are all different   colors
> singing   i am the will of the woman

> the woman
> my will is unbending
> when She-Who-moves-the-earth will turn over
> when She Who moves, the earth will turn over.

(109)

Grahn returns to She Who at the poem's (and series') end, only to indicate again both that She Who is powerful and active and that her powerful resistance will transform the world. She is only capable of this transformation, however, because of the song sung by the diverse children of diverse women.

These are the central poems in the series, all dealing directly with the named She Who. They structure the entire series; most important, they provide the central thematic emphases and the formal qualities that give the series its performance dimensions. The series does include, however, a secondary strain of She Who poems, which further expand the idea of women taking action by focusing on women's "work." Just after "The enemies of She Who" comes a poem about She Who in the labor of giving birth (poem eight, untitled). Here, She Who ". . . carries and bears / and raises and rears is the first labor, / there is not other first labor" (85). In contrast to the very real instances of sexist oppression that women face through language and labeling, She Who is an ordinary, originating presence, who is enduring and generative. In poem 10 (untitled), the image of birth appears again, only it is She Who herself who is born; She Who ". . . carries herself in a bowl of blood," and though she shakes the bowl and loses some teeth and bone, the last two lines reveal that this suffering leads to birth: "She shook it in the third season and some body was born, She Who" (87). Similarly, in "She Who sits making a first fire while the goat watches," She Who is not even named outside the title, but her actions (grinding, slaughtering a goat) signal her as the woman who works to provide for and sustain others.

Grahn achieves commonality in the above poems, then, by grounding her observations in her own experience of bonding between women; by positing She Who as woman and women through the use of word play and anaphoric listing; and by offering a variety of poems like multiple doorways into the theme of women's power. The latter is especially significant because on first glance, this variety of poems seems to indicate a loosening of form in comparison to *The Common Woman*. Closer examination reveals, however, that the She Who poems provide the framework for a unified theme in the entire series, and that the non–She Who poems reiterate this theme while repeating forms among themselves. While the She Who poems occur regularly throughout the series, interjected between them are the plainsongs, parables in both prose and poetry, short poems that read like ritual fragments, and one portrait, of "Carol," which is reminiscent of *The Common Woman*. The She Who poems are heavily geared toward developing a sense of community in a performance setting, while the non–She Who poems don't universally contain formal strategies that lend themselves to performance. Thus, while the end result is decidedly performance-based, for this collection can be read publicly as a whole or it can be used in its parts as they are appropriate, the non–She Who poems further extend the commonality that Grahn pursued in *The Common Woman,* because they create other diverse and less heavily ritualized avenues into the multiple meanings that She Who carries. In *The Common Woman,* Grahn develops seven individual portraits linked by a common refrain and rooted in the poet's pledge to resist oppression; in *She Who,* Grahn expands this project by once again making her own pledge and then weaving together a core of performance-based poems with a group of less formally structured and more various poems. The impulse toward community drives both coalitional voice and commonality as they operate in *She Who,* but the emphasis on difference and the lives of individual women is never lost; indeed, Grahn bases all the qualities she assigns to She Who in the lives of actual women she has known (76).

A Woman Is Talking to Death

That Grahn calls herself a "witness" in the long poem *A Woman Is Talking to Death* is no accident; unlike both *The Common Woman* and *She Who,* this poem is rooted in Grahn's "testimony," her detailed, even graphic, account of her own personal experience. While the first two series of poems offer the potential for celebration in their empowering portraits of women, *A Woman Is Talking to Death* is wrenchingly painful in spite of its defiant attitude toward "Death." As Grahn bears witness to the struggle of "lovers" (literal lovers, but more generally anyone who opposes oppression and seeks to survive it), she searches for ways to counter "Death" (patriarchy or any social forces that inhibit or destroy life) and to be generative both politically and culturally. Those who side with Death have "no child in them" (129), while "lovers" search for a way to give birth to a different order.

Grahn develops commonality in this poem by demonstrating through repetition and refrain the overlap between different kinds of oppression, among them racism, homophobia, and sexism. The "centers" at stake here are both the inside and the outside of dominant society and its oppressive practices, and Grahn's goal is both to reclaim power from the oppressors and demonstrate that any one of us—any reader/listener—is indeed both inside and outside. Amitai F. Avi-ram has very well demonstrated the ways that Grahn uses these strategies to name and transform oppressive practices; as she says, "the refrains and repetitions bring about a new relation to prejudice and violence, as they work to release us from the oppressions we use against each other and which continually divide us" (1987, 38). But this is thoroughly effective in this long poem precisely because Grahn relies so heavily on coalitional voice, weaving her own experience with her experience of others and also with fragments of written accounts of historical oppressions. As she understands herself as both victim and oppressor—as caught up in the astoundingly complex web of oppressive practices supported by patriarchy—Grahn makes contact with the reader/listener, asking that she/he achieve this same realization. Finally, a single ritualized section (number four) of the poem establishes the more formally crafted performance aspect of the piece and grounds the poem for public recitation.

Compared with her earlier works, this long poem does indeed read as if Grahn had to dispense with formal techniques like rhyme, anaphora, and word play precisely because she chose to delve so deeply into her personal experience that the unadorned "facts" required straightforward statement. Grahn uses the phrase "that's a fact" throughout the poem, seemingly to emphasize the painful necessity of getting it right, although she also uses this phrase to demonstrate the limitations of the possible in an oppressive society; when she imagines a general emptying hospitalized soldiers' bedpans, she declares "that's a fantasy" (1978b, 121). Thus, the formal patterns that Grahn used so creatively to establish commonality in *A Common Woman* and *She Who* won't work so well here.

As she grounds her observations in her own experience, Grahn grounds her pursuit of commonality in the related experience of others. Returning to a single refrain, which sums up the power of those who fight back, throughout the poem, she also repeats details of oppression from one person to the next. The refrain is in fact Grahn's point of departure; it constitutes the first two lines of the poem's first section: "my lovers teeth are white geese flying above me / my lovers muscles are rope ladders under my hands" (113). Grahn has noted that "geese" is another word for gay (as in the old expression, "gay as a goose"), but also that the combined imagery of ladders and flying "conjures a ship's sails and a ship's ladders, not a modern ship but an old fashioned vessel, perhaps going to an ancient land." To Grahn's mind, the refrain images "two lovers together, now one flying above and now the other," which "constitute the ship" (1985, 33). These lines interject a meditation on the transformative power of love into a narrative dealing with the destructive effects wrought by a nexus of oppressions. They appear at the outset of the poem, and in sections five and nine, when the poet is standing her ground in her conversation with death.

Avi-ram (1987) and Margot Gayle Backus (1993) have both pointed out the repetition of detail that ties together Grahn's characters in this poem. In the central narrative of the poem, which is set forth in the first section, a man who has parked his motorcycle in the middle of San Francisco's Bay Bridge is struck and killed by an unwitting African-American man; in the wake of this accident, the poet is forced to make a decision about whether to stay and bear witness to the innocence of the driver or to escape in order to protect herself and her lesbian lover from the scrutiny of the police. Within the course of this narrative, Grahn layers details among the characters. The man who is killed is wearing a peacoat and Levis, and so is the poet. Both the driver and the poet's lover have faces grey with shock and fear. The poet leaves because she has "a woman waiting"; when she later phones the driver's home to find out what happened to him, she discovers that "he had a woman waiting for him" as well (1978b, 116). Grahn also repeats details from this section in later sections of the poem. "Six big policeman" beat the driver and trump up evidence against him; Grahn uses the same designation for the officers who laugh at her report of gay-bashing and those who come to pick up a raped and abandoned Asian woman that the poet and her friends attempt to help. As these repetitions accrue, the poet develops commonality among all these characters—she defines multiple, moving "centers"—demonstrating that they are all both inside an oppressive order and capable of moving outside it.

The other way Grahn establishes connections between these characters is by designating them all as her "lovers." When she leaves the African-American man on the bridge to face the police alone, she leaves him, she writes, "as I have left so many of my lovers" (116). When she relates how the police took the driver to four hospitals in order to get a drunken driving test to suit their case, she repeats this point about betrayal: "how many lovers have we left" (118). She names as lovers the women she implicated when she confessed her lesbianism in the military, but she also calls her friends "lovers" and ponders their actions when they turn the Asian woman over to the police: "we left, as we have left all of our lovers / as all lovers leave all lovers / much too soon to get the real loving done" (129). Again, it is death that is at fault: "death wastes our time with drunkenness / and depression / death, who keeps us from our / lovers" (116). The point, of course, is that love is opposed to death, and that a "lover" is any other person one can empower by participating in commonality through appreciating each other in solidarity and at the same time recognizing and respecting difference. The point is also that all of us, and not just men in powerful positions, have betrayed lovers, even as we have the power to defy Death. The "real loving" is denied because all victims of oppression either give in to it or even perpetuate it at one time or another, and yet "lovers" everywhere have the capacity to "talk" to Death.

Grahn illustrates this last point in all the personal narratives she includes in this poem, in which she is victimized but is also potentially extending the effects of oppression. In the main narrative, of the accident on the bridge, she concludes that her betrayal of her "lover" the driver illustrates how difficult it is for anyone to escape this pattern: "there are as many contradictions to the game, / as there are players, / a woman is talking to death, / though talk is cheap, and life takes a long time / to make / right . . ." (118). When she relates her experience of being discharged from the military, Grahn illustrates this complexity: "I drowned, I took 3 or 4 others down / when I signed the confession of what we / had done   together" (121). When a young man calls her names in Spanish and then hits her, she discovers that no one will call the police for her; the next day she goes to the police station only to have "six big policemen" laugh at her. As a result, she fantasizes revenge, in which she smashes the young man's head with a chair, kill-

ing him: ". . . I called him a spic, and / killed him. My face healed. his
didn't / no child *in* me" (127). This is perhaps the most startling revelation of the individual's potential for taking part in death, for the poet
has indicated that she is very aware of and angry about oppression in
the abstract, and yet when she is confronted with it in her own life, she
wants to partake in death's practices and simply strike back.

This sense of the individual's capacity to betray love/lovers deeply
informs the ritual core of the poem, in section four. Interestingly, this
is also the section in which the poet straightforwardly proffers herself
as a witness, who can speak authoritatively on behalf of herself and
other women. (Of course, the entire poem is a piece of testimony; the
poet's very act of writing is an act of bearing witness.) When the interrogator (Death) wants to pinpoint and condemn her lesbianism, Death
asks if she has ever held hands with a woman; the poet answers with a
list of women in various stages of health, sadness, and fulfillment. This
section is highly reminiscent of *She Who* and allows the poet to establish
her central solidarity with women, *all* women. However, though Grahn
uses listing to establish a pattern here, she still writes in prose poetry,
in keeping with the intimate details of the coalitional voice she uses
throughout this poem: she writes that she has held hands with "women
who had been run over, beaten up, deserted, starved, women who had
been bitten by rats; and women who were happy, who were celebrating . . ." (123). Similarly, when the interrogator asks if she has kissed
women, she offers a list of women who are hurt and need assistance, as
well as women who, like her, hope and work for a different, liberated
world. However, when the interrogator asks about "indecent acts" she
has committed with women, she responds that she is guilty of not establishing relationships of solidarity with as many women as she could: "I
am guilty of not loving her who needed me; I regret all the women I
have not slept with or comforted, who pulled themselves away from me
for lack of something I had not the courage to fight for, for us, our life,
our planet, our city, our meat and potatoes, our love" (125).

The way that Grahn most fully develops coalitional voice in *A
Woman Is Talking to Death,* however, occurs in her actual conversation
with Death itself. The title of the poem itself overturns the stereotype
of the woman who chatters on and on, and empowers the poet, who
resists death by talking directly, forcefully, and defiantly to it. This is a
confrontation rather than an interrogation; the latter implies a power
relationship, and is the mode in which Death questions the poet in

section four and the Asian woman in section eight. When Grahn confronts Death, she taunts it and rebels against it. Grahn hints that the force of her stories of her own and others' experience is leading to this confrontation in a couple of places earlier in the poem (sections three and five), but it is in the poem's ninth and final section that she directly ties the power she experiences with her "lovers" with her ability to resist the power of Death. Most significantly, however, Grahn switches from first person to third person here; the goal of her use of coalitional voice has been achieved. She has spoken of the most profound levels of her own experience, and has thus established the ground out of which she can speak for others when she addresses death:

> Hey you death
>
> ho and ho poor death
> our lovers teeth are white geese flying above us
> our lovers muscles are rope ladders under our hands
>
> (130)

Integrated into this collective response to death, however, is Grahn's personal pledge, which is the touchstone instance of coalitional voice in all the three series of poems under discussion here. She declares, "to my lovers I bequeath / the rest of my life" (130). Out of this commitment, she is able to offer the final gesture of defiance, that the "lovers" will find their purpose in each other and will ignore death until it withers away:

> wherever our meat hangs on our own bones
> for our own use
> your pot is so empty death, ho death
> you shall be poor
>
> (131)

Commonality and the Early Movement

As I have already pointed out, Grahn's work in the 1980s delves more deeply into mythopoesis, which produces its own various effects on form and certainly on theme. However, as a central figure in the feminist poetry movement of the 1970s, Grahn exemplifies the very strong current of communally oriented, performance-based poetry that developed during that time. More important, though, she provides a lasting legacy to feminist poetry in her concept of "commonality," for it so effectively captures the desire to express self, find unity in community, and recognize difference that fueled the movement from its earliest days. If Rukeyser was women poets' "most persistent rebel" (Howe and Bass 1973, 7), then Grahn was feminist poets' most daring one: as she carved out alternative publishing routes and performance venues, as she relentlessly pursued her own poetic vision even before the tradition of the older poets had become widely known, and as she brought the "common" into view in order to unite women even in their difference, she moved feminist poetry forward as practically no one had until that time and as few have since.

Three

Feminist and Black Arts Strategies in the Poetry of June Jordan

Like Judy Grahn, June Jordan strives to be a "people's poet," who wishes to speak not only *of* her own experience but also *for* her communities and *to* readers who have the potential to act constructively in both a cultural and a political capacity. More specifically, and also like Grahn, she speaks of and for women by exploring the highly charged intersections of her personal experience and the experiences of other women. But Jordan also speaks of and for African Americans, a reality that has deeply influenced the development of her particular feminist poetics, and vice versa. In fact, Jordan's inclusive vision so profoundly synthesizes the central political and poetic sensibilities of the black arts movement of the 1960s and the feminist poetry movement of the 1970s and beyond that she is hard to "classify," and hence has received little substantive critical attention from either camp. The feminist poet/critic Sara Miles speculates that feminist critics have been reluctant to address Jordan's vision precisely because it encompasses so many connections (1981, 87). African-American critics have given her a bit more attention, but in this field, too, she seems something of an anomaly because she is so expressly feminist.

It is precisely Jordan's integration of black arts and feminist aesthetics, however, that enables her to write so effectively not just in resistance to the dominant white culture but against sexism among black men and against racism in the women's movement. She discovers the elements of her African-American heritage that value the positive function of art to build and maintain communal life and combines them with the feminist emphasis on the connections between the personal and political, and as a result joins contemporary feminist poets like Grahn in emphasizing the enabling dialectic between particularity and difference (or emphasizing, as Jordan might put it, the self as the democratic representative of the whole). By skillfully combining personal and communal voice, she builds a sense of an integrated and deeply rooted political project that nevertheless recognizes, respects, and even relies on difference. Her project, as she puts it, is to overcome "either/or" thinking, the "fundamental habit of Western thought," by acting out of what she calls "love" (1981b, 90). The result is a poetry both deeply personal and resoundingly communal, both profoundly angry and definitively affirmative.

Jordan's refusal to engage in dichotomous political thought—focusing only on the plight of women as an oppressed group or only on the problems faced by African Americans—is well illustrated in two political essays she wrote during the 1970s. In "Declaration of an Independence I Would Just as Soon Not Have" (1976), originally published in *Ms.,* Jordan confronts the civil rights movement, the women's movement, and what she calls the "Third World Movement." She has discovered, she writes, that each follows "a ranking of priorities, a peculiarity of perspective, that conflicts with the other two, in an apparently irreconcilable manner" (1981a, 117). Of the civil rights movement, she asks why it continues to be the case that "when our ostensible leadership talks about the 'liberation of the Black man' that is precisely, and only, what they mean" (118). Of the Third World Movement, she wonders why class divisions and sexism continue to plague this movement in its various manifestations throughout the "underdeveloped" world. And in the women's movement, she says, she finds narrowness of vision—a focus on sexism that nevertheless fails to give attention to the problems of working-class or poor women, and fails to realize, just as the male-dominated movements do, that "you cannot aid half a people" (120).

In "Where is the Love?" (1978), presented at a seminar entitled "Feminism and the Black Woman Writer" at the National Black Writers Conference at Howard University, Jordan explains her feminist commitment in a similarly synthesizing fashion: "I am a feminist, and what that means to me is much the same as the meaning of the fact that I am Black: it means that I must undertake to love myself and to respect myself as though my very life depends upon self-love and self-respect" (1981a, 142). She also makes clear that the root of her approach is respecting difference. For her, self-love is basic and yet is only verifiable in the ways one acts toward those different from oneself: "How do I reach out to the people I would like to call my sisters and my brothers and my children and my lovers and my friends?" (143). The answer Jordan finds for herself is that, as a "Black feminist serious in the undertaking of self-love," her self-love leads to love and respect for other women. But the answer is also that she "cannot be expected to respect what somebody else calls self-love if that concept of self-love requires my suicide to any degree" (144). In this way, she calls on African-American men to recognize the problems confronting African-American women and to join with her in ending violence against women and poverty, as well as to "exhume" the works of African-American women writers (145).

Jordan remained committed to this stance even after she began to realize that both African-American men and feminists often found it difficult to swallow. When she published her selected poems as *Things That I Do in the Dark* in 1977, only the *New York Times* and one African-American periodical reviewed it, while no feminist periodicals reviewed it. Jordan later said that since she was contributing editor for *Chrysalis* as well as the African-American journals *First World* and *Hoo-Doo,* she felt compelled to reexamine her ideas about writing out of her concern for these collectives. The result was the manifesto "Thinking about My Poetry" (1977), originally printed in *Chrysalis,* in which Jordan clearly maps out her poetic journey toward a combined black arts and feminist aesthetic, the center of which is a commitment to tell her own life as a way of understanding, communicating with, and representing the collectives to which she belongs. In this essay, she says that the work of feminist poets and writers "occupies a first place of influence," while she maintains her commitment to "Black English" as central to expressing her African-American experience. The result is the distinctive blending of personal and political so characteristic of feminist poets from the early 1970s on; she writes, "if I could truthfully attend to my own perpetual birth, if I could trace the provocations for my own voice and then trace its reverberations through love, Alaska, whatever, . . . then I could hope to count upon myself to be serving a positive and collective function, without pretending to be more than the one Black woman poet I am, as a matter of fact" (1981a, 126). Thus Jordan arrived at an understanding of the relationship between "self-love" and difference, between subjective and coalitional voice, that establishes the course by which to read her poetry as it evolved from the late 1960s into the 1980s.

Establishing an African-American Identity

With her arrival at a feminist position/poetics, Jordan charted a feminist course she has never abandoned, and which sets her apart from many other African-American women writers; indeed, among African-American women writers, she has been more adamant and outspoken in her feminist commitment than all but perhaps Audre Lorde and Pat Parker.[1] However, when her first volume of poetry, *Who Look At Me?*, appeared in 1969, she was still primarily concerned with developing an African-American identity. Like Judy Grahn, Jordan was searching for literary representations that would confirm her own reality, and decided to write them herself. Jordan's central question in these first poems was not Grahn's, however; she longed to see realistic portrayals of her *race,* while Grahn yearned to see "common women" on the page. In the title poem of *Who Look At Me?* Jordan explores black-white relations using metaphors of sight, blindness, and invisibility. By emphasizing outdated and new modes of perception, Jordan uncovers and overturns stereotypes. Jordan's insistent, challenging voice is also already present here, especially in the abrupt confrontation of "Although the world / forgets me / I will say yes / AND NO . . ." (1977, 4). However, Jordan does not complicate her understanding of racial constructions by acknowledging the effect of gender constructions: "look close / and see me black man mouth / for breathing (North and South) / A MAN / I am black alive and looking back at you" (4). Though she addresses the complex circumstances of racial oppression in the United States, in this poem Jordan is not yet writing out of a distinctly feminist consciousness. Jordan's awareness of her oppression as an African American was forged instead in the heat of the civil rights movement of the 1960s, and in her ongoing work as a poetry workshop leader and as a city planner in New York.

In Jordan's second volume *Some Changes* (1971), she extends the project of *Who Look at Me?* by focusing on the power of self-naming to build African-American identity. In *Some Changes,* she writes a few painfully personal revelations, primarily about family ("For My Mother" and "For Christopher," about her son), as well as communal meditations like the commemorative "In Memoriam: Martin Luther King, Jr." She also writes narrative poems—slices of African-American life—like "The Reception": "Doretha in her short blue dress / and Roosevelt waiting for his chance: / a true gut-funky blues to make her really dance" (1971, 7). Peter B. Erickson has said of these poems that her "efforts to create space for her personal liberation serve as a microcosm and model for a general ideal of black community" (1985, 147). Jordan herself stated at roughly the same time that the poetic struggle "to determine and then preserve a particular, human voice is closely related to the historic struggling of black life in America" (quoted in Erickson 1985, 151). In other words, even in her earliest works, Jordan understands that exploring her personal struggle toward identity is central to speaking in any way on behalf of the community. Therefore, although she attempts at times to write out of a distinctly communal voice in which the "I" is completely suppressed in favor of the "we," she often writes in purely subjective lyric or persona. Nevertheless, this struggle toward self-affirmation is still incomplete; her voice remains rather distant, even melancholy, as the last lines (which in her later poetry so often carry the thrust of her message) of several of these early poems clearly demonstrate. In the despairing "I Live in Subtraction," she writes ten lines, all beginning with "I," but ends with the following lines: "I forgive my mind its dream. / I can end a dream with death" (1971, 26). In "Whereas," the final lines read "Whereas / Judas hung himself / I find no rope as strong" (1971, 33).

Not coincidentally, this distance corresponds with her early focus on poetic forms in the Western tradition. For three years as an adolescent, Jordan studied at the Northfield School for Girls in Massachusetts, where her interest in writing poetry was affirmed but where, as a matter of course, she studied only white male poets. She said later that precisely because of racism she worked very hard to master the variety of techniques she encountered in this poetry: "I wanted to say, 'Listen, I can alliterate for hours . . . I can do an iambic pentameter number that will never stop' . . . what I was trying to say was 'Don't say she's a good poet because she's Black and she's not doing so badly.' Say, 'She can do anything we can do and she can do something we can't do.' This was my goal, and it's related to what my father and mother always used to say to me: 'You're Black and so that means you can't be a good student. You've got to be twice as good a student as anyone else' " (1981a, 93). Jordan understands that this virtuosity could merely result in a "pyrotechnical ecstasy which is quite irrelevant to statement" (93), but even in her earliest poetry, she attempts to use these techniques to her own ends. Hence, in "Let Me Live with Marriage," she stages her own rewrite of Shakespeare's Sonnet 116, and produces a meditation on race and love that mixes iambic pentameter with irregular line lengths/meters but retains Shakespeare's play on words and the final couplet, which points out the paradox inherent in the fact of her writing: "If this be baffling then the error's proved / To love so long and leave my love unmoved" (1971, 35).

Likewise, in "If You Saw a Negro Lady," Jordan draws on the style of T. S. Eliot for her portrait of an African-American domestic worker out for a holiday; tersely observing social mores, she creates a somber but almost comical scene in which the woman cocks her "little finger broad and stiff / in heavy emulation of a cockney / mannerism." Jordan does write in second person here and does finally address the reader ("would you turn her treat / into surprise by / observing / happy birthday") (17); this is notable since she writes many of her later poems in second person in order to acknowledge a bond of solidarity with the reader or to implicate the reader in systems of oppression. However, in "If You Saw," Jordan does not address the very real violence done to this woman's life by the brutal forces of racism, nor does she reflect in any sustained way on the particular plight of female domestics. These early poems illustrate that Jordan struggled with the influence of the male-dominated tradition and thereby postponed discovering a personal style rooted in her own cultural traditions and political concerns. This influence, she has said, "crippled my trust in my own sensibilities, coerced me into eclectic compulsions I had to struggle against, later, and generally delayed my creative embracing of my own, known life as the very stuff of my art" (1981a, 127).

By 1979, Jordan was calling Eliot "that consummate Anglophile whose name I can never remember," indicating her increasing distance from the Euro-American tradition (1980, x). Indeed, a few poems in *Some Changes* hint at the future emergence of this "creative embracing." While in many instances in this volume, Jordan uses stark, fragmentary phrases and no capitalization—reminiscent of Eliot and other modernists like e. e. cummings—in other places, she begins to experiment with distinctly African-American rhythms. She was later to remark that she had begun to understand the need to combine what she called "rhythm as vertical event"—listing single words or only a few words on each line—with political sensibility, and that "In Memoriam" was perhaps her first attempt at such a combination (1981a, 124–25). In this poem, she certainly seems on the verge of vertical movement when she describes "America":

> tomorrow yesterday rip rape
> exacerbate despoil disfigure

crazy running threat the
deadly thrall
appall belief dispel

(1971, 15)

Here the layering of individual words is irregular but certainly the
shorter lines create a sense of motion, inviting the reader/listener to
anger and even making the reader/listener want to move.[2] The words
also function to resist or even invert commonly held patriotic notions
of the nation.

Similarly, Jordan begins to hint at her future synthesis of personal
reflection and collective statement when she makes emphatic political
statements of self, especially in the final lines, of some of these poems.
In "Poem for My Family: Hazel Griffin and Victor Hernandez Cruz,"
Jordan again deals with perception but notes her own awakening to the
violence of slavery/racism, and this time ends a four section poem with
a vital self-affirmation in the final lines: "I see. / I see my self / Alive / *A
life*" (1971, 56). Similarly, in "Poem to the Mass Communications
Media," she ends with "I will to be / I have begun / I am speaking for /
my self" (81).

Vertical Rhythm and Feminist Voice

It is in her third volume, *New Days,* that Jordan's integration of black
arts and feminist consciousness begins to influence her work heavily and
to result in the playful and yet angry, the personal and yet deeply ritualistic, the informative and yet confrontive style she maintained through
the following two decades. Almost all of the poems in this volume indicate a real transformation from her earlier style. Jordan leaves behind
the fragmentary phrases and short sentences for longer sentences but
not a longer line. Rather, she carries longer thoughts through shorter,
enjambed lines, establishing a cadence and an element of performance
missing in her earlier poems. She also gives increased attention to spatial
arrangement, more often indenting or even skipping lines to correspond to natural pauses or even to create longer pauses. All of these
changes are consistent with the revolution in American poetry going on
during the 1960s, which indicates Jordan freeing herself from her former influences. However, one poem in this volume indicates that in fact

something more is happening; in "Getting Down to Get Over," Jordan's African-American and feminist aesthetics fully begin to fuse.

Written in 1973 for an African-American women writers conference at Radcliffe, "Getting Down to Get Over" originated as a performance piece and as a conscious attempt to represent the realities of African-American women's lives. Thus in its very function it called for something new in Jordan's work, for while she had written about African-American identity, she had not done so specifically from the point of view of oppressed women. In other words, it is the first of her poems in which sexism is *the topic,* and therefore it is especially interesting that this poem more than any other written in the early 1970s heralds the blend of African-American speech and music patterns and feminist voice that shape Jordan's later works. The most salient point here is that with "Getting Down" Jordan did not simply append feminist consciousness to a black arts aesthetic. Rather, because of the intersections between the poetic concerns of the black arts movement and the feminist poetry movement, elements of Jordan's poetic sensibility converge in this poem: her desire to develop an affirmative African-American presence in poetry, her desire to develop a feminist consciousness for herself personally and for women and African-American women in general, and her deft craft in both Western poetic forms and African-American and feminist innovations.

Because "Getting Down to Get Over" combines distinctly African/African-American elements with an emerging feminist recognition of how necessary it is for the poet to address her personal experience in order to achieve collective voice, it constitutes a definitive achievement in Jordan's poetics, combining her already evolving understanding and use of jazz and vernacular rhythms with the vertical rhythm and arresting final line that later became so common in her work. In this long poem, Jordan fulfills both ritual and didactic functions by celebrating African-American women's strength ("Consider the Queen / a full/ Black/glorious/a purple rose"), their oppression ("WHO'S THE MOTHAFUCKA / FUCKED MY MOMMA"), and their responsibility ("teach me to survive my / momma") (1974, 118, 128).

The very title "Getting Down to Get Over" indicates this poem's spirit and goal; it is about "getting down," celebrating and/or dealing with the truth, in order to "get over," to survive and move beyond the effects of violence in the lives of African-American women. The title also hints at the power of inverting structures of oppression like language. According to the rules of Black English as Jordan has elaborated them, "down" illustrates the general rule that "if you wish to say something really positive, try to formulate the idea using emphatic negative structure" (1986, 130). Moreover, Jordan creates the collective sense in this poem through the effects of the *naming* process, which is based in the West African concept of giving life through the word (*nommo*). She also uses jazz and blues techniques, as well as other instances of Black English, which establish the performance and hence communal tone of the piece as well as provide rich references to the sustaining social and political function of these music and language forms in African-American and American culture.

This emphasis on performance, on the gathering of the people, is central to African-American cultural forms. The repetition and refrains of the blues (as well as gospel and the spiritual), the improvisational rhythms of jazz, and the oral qualities of Black English all arise from the nontextual, communal, performance-based nature of these modes of expression. According to Rita Dove and Marilyn Nelson Waniek, African-American poets are continuing the work of the African griot: "The older tradition of the griot, or storyteller, has been kept very much alive by poets who perform their works on street-corners, at political gatherings, and anywhere they can find an audience willing to listen" (quoted in Jones 1992, 156). And this oral storytelling tradition has also been carried forward in the variety of cultural forms—from slave narratives to later forms like jazz—from which contemporary African-American poetry draws. Black English is a prime, or perhaps the primary, example; as Jordan says, "Black English is, preeminently, an oral/spoken means of communication" and an "irreplaceable system of community intelligence" (1986, 128, 123). This emphasis on orality is certainly echoed, if not matched, in feminist poetics. As women in the early 1970s yearned to recognize in/with each other the possibilities for struggling against oppression, they came together for various kinds of cultural expression, and particularly poetry readings. Thus, feminist poets in turn molded formal qualities like rhyme and rhythm to the collective experience, to call forth and affirm women's experiences and aspirations. In doing so, many feminist poets—and Jordan is a chief example—used elements of other, older oral traditions in conjunction with their feminist aims. "Getting Down" embodies this confluence of political/cultural work.

In the first section of the poem, Jordan lists names given to African-

American women, terms that have been used in callous or even brutal disregard as well as in loving intimacy:

> MOMMA MOMMA MOMMA
> momma momma
> *mammy*
> nanny
> granny
> woman
> mistress
> sista
>
> (1974, 118)

As she employs vertical rhythm, the list right away becomes both an incantatory naming and a jazzlike improvisation on the original note "MOMMA" and establishes itself first and foremost as a performance piece. The act of calling out the names repeats the historical acts of the people engaged in this naming process—other African-American women and children, to be sure, but also African-American men. The subsequent call to "*Black* Momma / *Black* bitch / *Black* pussy" reveals the violent nature of naming; the italicized references to color indicate the racialized nature of violence against African-American women, as well as the move among African-American men to the purportedly empowering self-designation "Black" in the context of the 1960s (118). Jordan indicates very clearly that "*Black* pussy / piecea tail / *nice* piecea ass" are heard from African-American men by following these lines directly with the friendly monikers of the time: "hey daddy! hey / bro!" (118). Here Jordan is not just inverting—by reusing the names herself—white stereotypes of African-Americans, which William J. Harris has identified as one of the chief characteristics of jazz as practiced by musicians like John Coltrane and as transformed into poetics by Amiri Baraka (1985, 91–98). She is also inverting—or restructuring as oppressive—the naming processes engaged in by African-American men. Thus, the poet's act of naming—or *renaming*—is also an act of recovery, so that the list begins to read as a *healing* incantation; as Jordan defiantly repeats these names, they ironically empower African-American women in spite of the words' historical usages. Here she engages in the same feminist project that Grahn does when she attempts to recover the meanings of "common" as a demeaning term for women, or that Minnie Bruce Pratt does when she uses the image of the snake to counter popular, oppressive images of the lesbian. This renaming as a healing process is not unusual in oppressed groups trying to achieve self-definition, but it was widespread and ongoing in much of feminist poetry written in the 1970s and 1980s.

In lines 25–35 of this first section, Jordan proceeds from a history of names to the contemporary scene and gives an Afrocentric turn on naming when she transforms the names of popular African-American women artists (Nina Simone, nikki giovanni) through the term "nommo" into "Momma": "nina nikki nonni nommo nommo / momma Black / Momma" (1974, 119). African-American writers/critics as diverse as Angela Davis, Molefi Kete Asante, and Barbara Marshall have discussed the West African concept of *Nommo,* which roughly translated means "the power of the word" (Davis 1990, 4–7; Asante 1987, 17, 49; Marshall 1992, 91–102). According to this metaphysical idea, "the life force is actualized by the power of the word" (Davis 1990, 6). In traditional African practice, *Nommo* endowed humans with the power to direct their existence and to harness the powers of the universe. But *Nommo* is not a phenomenon within/for the individual; instead, it is functional and communal, and this is best illustrated in the fact that song is its best expression, and song is not separated from the everyday language of the people. In other words, in this African tradition, the *word* is instrumental in the daily survival/flourishing of the human collective. Thus, in Jordan's "Getting Down," the act of *Nommo* is very specifically an act of naming, but it also embodies the African-American cultural environment, in which the word has generative power and works communally. This makes her reference, later in section one, to the absence of men in the everyday lives of African-American women even more poignant: "no / big Black burly hand / no nommo / no Black prince / come riding from the darkness" (1974, 121). While the concept of *Nommo* was central to Afrocentric, even cultural nationalist, approaches developed in the late 1960s and 1970s, the power of *Nommo* is undermined, as Jordan describes in this passage, as the community is fragmented by the actions and/or the absence of African-American men.

Angela Davis notes that "the structural emphasis on rhythm" in African as opposed to European music "derives from its part in the process of *naming,* of imbuing things with the life force, in short of humanizing the environment" (Davis 1990, 6). Jordan's use of vertical rhythm to establish a distinctive and regular beat throughout the poem is strikingly new in this first section of "Getting Down," and corresponds to her focus on *nommo,* and to the emphasis on rhythm that has been the heritage of African-American women, as Davis points out, in slave songs, lullabies, the blues, and jazz. Thus, Jordan ends section one of the poem with two stanzas that move from naming and inversion/renaming to jazz and blues rhythms. She acknowledges the common history of African-American women and African-American men even as she maintains a focus on transgressions against African-American women: "hey daddy / what they been and done to you / and what you been and done / to me / to momma" (1974, 121). She follows this with a long string of single words, with the effect of a lively jazz score ("deep / tall / bad / buck / jive / cold / strut . . ."), and then a narrative in Black English and all caps that is distinctly reminiscent of the tales of sexual woes so common in the blues songs of Ma Rainey and others:

> sweet SWEET DADDY
> WHERE YOU BEEN AND
> WHEN YOU COMIN BACK TO ME
> HEY
> WHEN YOU COMIN BACK
> TO MOMMA.
>
> (122)

The repetition and refrain as well as the tone of longing and lament here create layers of association with the blues and, perhaps most notably, echo the political overtones of such lyrics. As Davis has pointed out, most of Ma Rainey's blues focused on problems in personal relationships, one of the only areas of life about which African-Americans at that time could freely express themselves. These songs also therefore became the repository of messages of resistance, messages about remaining strong enough to face larger political and cultural struggles; thus the language of Ma Rainey's blues "metaphorically reveals and expresses a range of economic, social, and psychological difficulties which Black people suffered during the post-Civil War era" (Davis 1990, 13–14). Similarly, James Cone explains blues songs about sexuality by saying that because African-Americans "expressed their most intimate and precious feelings openly, they were able to survive as a community amid very difficult circumstances" (1972, 132). Certainly it is this spirit of community that Jordan strives for—even in the knowledge of what needs fixing in the community—as she completes the "song" in the final stanza of the section: "AND SUPPOSE HE FINALLY SAY / 'LOOK, BABY. / I LOVES ME SOME / EVERYTHING ABOUT YOU.' " Returning to standard capitalization in the next line, the speaker leaves the "song," but explains its sustaining relevance: "That reach around the hurtin / like a dream" (122).

In section two of the poem, Jordan continues the process of naming using vertical rhythm but this time structures a longer reflection on a single image of African-American women by using the refrain "Consider the Queen." This reflection naturally emerges from the first section, however, and consists of wresting an image from the hands of both white American and male-dominated African-American political groups. In section one, the attitudes of modern Americans are represented by the bureaucratic terms "Female Head of Household / Black Matriarchal Matriarchy" and the patronizing "Black Woman / Black / Hallelujah Saintly . . . given thanks / for / Annual Reports and / Monthly Dole" (1974, 119). But she is also questioning, or at least revising, the very notion of the African-American woman as an African queen that took shape within the cultural nationalist segments of African-American arts and organizing, exemplified in poems like nikki giovanni's "ego-tripping" (1970) and Sonia Sánchez's untitled assertion ". . . i will be called / QUEEN. & / walk/move in / blk/queenly/ways" (1970, 6). In Jordan's version, the queen is alive and American; she is a worker in the fields and responsible for the household at the same time, a nurturing but too often sad mother, a domestic or factory worker who gets a little wild and ends up in jail. In addition to the refrain and vertical rhythm, Jordan also uses alliteration ("steamy under the pale/sly / suffocatin sun" and "soft/Black/swollen momma breast") and periodic repetition ("the beaten beaten beaten / weary heart beats" and "but she works when she works / in the laundry in jail / she works when she works"). The end result is the same as in section one: she creates an incantatory, communal feel to these lines, calling out the queen to reclaim her and make her representative of African-American women's realities. But Jordan also ends this section in the same future-oriented way that she does section one; she concludes with an idealized portrait of the Queen that closely resembles the cultural nationalist version but nevertheless maintains both her centrality to African-American everyday survival and her oppression:

Consider the Queen
a full/Black/glorious/a purple rose
* * * * * * * *
a hungry one feedin the folk . . .

(1974, 125)

While Jordan certainly orients her African influences to women's experiences specifically, the influence of feminist poetics shows up most
obviously in this poem in the ways that Jordan mixes the first person
with her more communally oriented voice. As we have seen, in her
earlier poetry, she wrote individual poems either all in third or all in
first person, and thus maintained subjective distance from the more
public pieces. Here, however, Jordan begins to integrate her personal
voice with the collective and to work toward coalitional voice, just as
Judy Grahn does in the *Common Woman* poems: she deals with the
realities of African-American women's lives, periodically threading in
comments about her own mother, and ending with a vow to use her
own strength and the strength of the women she is writing about to
cause change. It is clear from the outset of this poem that Jordan is
interweaving details for her own experience; she dedicates the poem to
her mother and thus gives her every use of "MOMMA" or "momma"
the connotation of both all African-American women and her mother
in particular. In section one, she culminates the long list of names with
an explosive reference to her and her mother's experience. This is the
first substantial sign in Jordan's poetry of the confrontive power produced by the confluence of the highly personal and the deeply collective
tone, for the reader/listener is both at the center of the "performance"
of the poem and yet thrust out of it by the poet's personal anger. The
reader/listener is both at the heart of and outside of the center of the
poem, which forces a recognition of both common identity and difference. Jordan writes:

WHO'S THE MOTHAFUCKA
FUCKED MY MOMMA
messed yours over
and right now
be trippin on my starveblack female soul.

(120)

In these six lines, Jordan unites herself, her mother, and the mothers of all who read/hear these lines. She continues with a rhyming takeoff on the "hip" word "dig," which highlights the contemporary and yet ancient ("primordial") nature of sexism: "a macktruck / mothafuck / the first primordial / the paradig/digmatic / dogmatistic mothafucka who / is he?" (120).

Based on this angry precedent, Jordan in the final section relates the state of America and the struggles of African-American men once again to the plight of African-American women. She begins the section with yet another list, which starts with "MOMMA MOMMA" and goes on to string together affirming titles. In the stanza on ongoing racism in the United States, she begins to speak directly to her mother: "hey / turn / my mother / the face of history / to your own." In the stanza on African-American men, she speaks directly to "my Daddy / my Blackman," saying "you take my body in / your arms. . . ." But it is in the final stanza that her most important personal and communal goal becomes clear, as she speaks directly to her mother again, asking for help. She asks both that her mother help her rewrite history and that she help her survive (even to survive "momma" herself, to survive both the ravages of her mother's history and the defeat of her mother's own individual life). The externalized anger becomes a loving appeal for survival: "teach me to survive my / momma / teach me how to hold a new life." In the final four lines, the exorcism gives way to healing didacticism: "momma / help me / turn the face of history / *to your face*" (128).

This instance of italics is one of the first examples of Jordan's use of momentum through vertical rhythm and a mix of personal and collective voice to explode in a new realization or challenge in the last line of the poem. Here, as the rhythmic, even musical buildup of the poem climaxes, Jordan simultaneously invokes her own power as well as her mother's and demands social recognition of and restitution for the realities of African-American women. The result is dramatic: when Jordan the poet ritualizes her connections to the community and then invites the community into Jordan the woman's individual experience, the poem's political vision unites the community of women and the struggles of the individual woman without erasing difference.

Since the final line carries so much import in Jordan's later work, it is important to note how it operates throughout *New Days*. While the final line of "Getting Down" is lovingly directed to the community, invoking the strength of African-American women to rewrite history for themselves, another poem in *New Days* ends in angry confrontation. In "Memo to Daniel Pretty Moynihan," Jordan speaks very forthrightly to the object of her anger, decrying the bureaucratic rhetoric used by the U.S. government to categorize African-American women's lives (which she also incorporates in the naming process in "Getting Down"). She identifies this rhetoric in Senator Moynihan's highly controversial report on the state of African-American womanhood/motherhood in the United States,[3] and claims for herself what Moynihan has defined as disease: "Don't you liberate me / from my female black pathology" (1974, 6). After asserting she is satisfied with her own identity and lifestyle ("And when I vine / I know I'm fine"), she clearly points to Moynihan as the object of her anger and frustration: "But you been screwing me so long / I got a idea something's wrong / with you . . ." (6). In the last line, she breaks the regular rhyme, mostly in couplets, that she has used throughout the poem, and with a short phrase indicts her target. The result is like a finger pointing in blame: "Clean your own house, babyface" (6).

Jordan directs this anger outward, clarifying who the oppressor is and what he has done. In this way, this final line resembles those of her later works like "Poem about my Rights" (1980, 86–89). But Jordan writes in collective voice in "Memo" (the "I" clearly representing African-American women as a group), even though the voice becomes so strident in tone by the end of the poem that it begins to take on a distinctly individual edge. Jordan here has not yet thoroughly integrated the personal and the political, subjective and collective voice, to achieve the most complete effects with her political meditation and anger. It is only with her continuing work through the 1970s, leading up to the breakthrough volume *Passion* (1980), that Jordan fully achieves the blend of personal and political so characteristic of feminist poetics.

Through the 1970s: Maintaining the Connections

Several poems from the years (1974–1980) between *New Days* and *Passion* demonstrate that this process of development was indeed gradual and that it coincided with Jordan's increasing involvement in what was by anyone's definition the most turbulent years of feminist self-definition and activism. In this explosive decade for women's movement organizing, Jordan found herself attempting to develop an orientation not only to feminism as a social/political movement but also to the still evolving civil rights front and the leftist arena of Third World organizing. In this regard, she was like other feminist poets of the 1970s like Pat Parker and Irena Klepfisz, who found themselves to be outsiders in one or even all of the movements to which their emerging self-definitions compelled them to give their energies. Jordan's struggle, however, as the essay "Declaration of an Independence I Would Just as Soon Not Have" (1976) demonstrates, was always to combine her very real commitment to each of these movements with her unfailing, ongoing indictment of the blind spots of each. Simultaneously, she solidified her commitment to self-love and to feminism, steadfastly maintaining the term "feminist" for herself within the African-American community ("Where Is the Love?" 1978). Jordan refused to retreat from the tension between her love for the community and her need to maintain self-love in the midst of incomplete (even "either/or") political visions. Thus, while she increasingly moved toward a synthesis of the personal and political, her poetics during this period demonstrates that this movement was often difficult.

Among the previously unpublished poems included in Jordan's first volume of collected poems, *Things That I Do in the Dark* (1977), two poems that integrate concerns for women's rights with concerns for African-American and Third World struggles hint at this ongoing transformation. Dedicated to the president of Angola, "I Must Become a Menace to My Enemies" is layered with nationalist sentiments but, most important, is a powerful statement of self-assertion. The "I" in this three-part poem at times seems to represent any individual involved in the struggle for African/African-American self-determination, and yet the details of the speaker's life are often so specific that the "I" certainly seems to be the poet herself. "I will no longer lightly walk behind / a one of you who fear me," the first section begins; it ends with the powerful statement of agency, "I must become the action of my fate" (1977, 144–45). This declaration of self continues the project Jordan began in her first three volumes, with poems like "Who Look at Me?" and "Poem for My Family." This is indicated in the play on the word "become" in the poem's final couplet: "I must become / I must become a menace to my enemies" (146). However, the word "menace" and the threatening tone of much of this poem indicate a new level of angry confrontation.

In "From The Talking Back of Miss Valentine Jones," Jordan again writes of Third World struggles, this time in Southeast Asia. Rather than speaking in first person, however, she uses both third person and persona, and with the latter speaks, or "talks back," to the dominant culture, through the African-American woman Valentine. She also writes a long poem, employing alternately Black English, a pseudojournalistic tone, blues lyrics, and a pastiche of a variety of voices on the American political scene. The result is, once again, an attempt to draw the connections among racism, classism, and sexism, with Valentine's as the central, even the most truthful, voice. Valentine asserts with the rhyme and refrain of the blues,

> The streets is mean
> (the streets is mean)
> An' my ship ain' nowhere
> to be seen
> The war's not hardly over

> (153)

But this voice is superseded in the final section of the poem by the observer/narrator's voice, which notes that in the struggling independent nations of Africa, a young militant woman "straps the baby to her back / and / she carries her rifle . . . for the love / for the life / of us all" (154). In the end, this curious mix of voice creates a sense of distance from the issues; even though Jordan has developed a consciousness of gender constructions at this point, she has not fully integrated her personal voice with her collective concerns as practiced in feminist poetics. "From The Talking Back" works as an attempt to achieve collective perspective on international revolutions, much like Jordan's similar attempt with regard to race relations in "In Memoriam." It also grows centrally out of a concern for women's struggles, as does "Getting Down." But in this poem, she doesn't yet achieve the emphatic blend of subjective and collective voice, of the personal and political, that she reaches in later poems in *Passion*.

In contrast, the most successful attempt at synthesizing collective and personal concerns in *Things That I Do in the Dark* is a statement made by the poet about her life and directly to the object(s) of her confrontation. In "Metarhetoric," she develops her oppositional stance within the movements in which she is active; she is attending a "meeting," a code word for the endless rounds of discussions and strategy-planning sessions that abounded in 1970s political organizing. The "metarhetoric" that informs these meetings is set up in the first four lines of the poem, which consist of single, determining ideological terms. Jordan italicizes these terms to illustrate the ways they circulate as words of importance, as well as to emphasize their abstract nature: "*Homophobia / racism / self-definition / revolutionary struggle*" (84). Jordan attempts to cut through the rhetoric of revolution that dominates this meeting by asserting the importance of another kind of more intimate relating: "the subject to-night for / public discussion is / our love" (84). The actual discussion in the meeting covers theory, the history of struggle, and statistics, but the poet is concerned instead about the love—both in self-celebration and relationships between individuals and within groups—the discussion is not addressing: "Can you give me the statistical dimensions / of your mouth on my mouth / your breast resting on my own?" (85) The arrangement of the final three lines conveys the speaker's desire that the closed borders of conversation be overcome by the action implied in her use of the word "love": "My hope is that our lives will declare / this meeting / open" (85).

"Metarhetoric" involves more personal detail than "Memo," so that the dialectic between individual speaker and collective concerns/voice comes to the forefront. In this way, "Metarhetoric" foreshadows the later poem, published in *Passion,* "A Short Note to My Very Critical and Well-Beloved Friends and Comrades." In the latter, Jordan resists either/or formulations and speaks in a confrontational but playful style to those she identifies as upholding those formulations. Most important, however, Jordan uses anaphora and internal rhyme, which develops a performance feel in the poem, and indicates her desire for communal response. She also uses turnabout in the final lines to provide a climax for her teasing anger and to indict the reader/listener abruptly and forcefully: "Make up your mind! They said. Are you militant / or sweet? Are you vegetarian or meat? Are you straight / or are you gay? // And I said, Hey! It's not about *my* mind" (1980, 78). The "they" in this poem are "friends and comrades" in the movements in which she is active. Jordan thus reiterates her resistance to dualistic oppositional strategies by refusing even to play identity politics in the movements she is most involved in, including the women's movement, and simultaneously hits upon the mix of subjective voice and collective concern that she fully develops in *Passion*.

Passion: Fully Developing Feminist Voice

In the strongest group of poems in *Passion,* Jordan's "self-love" fully emerges as she finally and substantially brings the most intimate details of her own personal oppression as an African-American woman, as a *woman,* into focus. As the poet explores her own experience, she writes to/for the collective not as distant spokesperson but as a fully involved/ implicated member of the complex struggle for change. The result is a feminist voice at its most angry and affirmative: she both indicts the reader/listener as a possible oppressor and asks the reader/listener to transform the conditions that lead to oppression. As in her earlier poetry, Jordan also expresses her experience using elements of her African-American heritage—jazz improvisation, the blues, Black English— and in the traditional African tradition of *nommo*/storytelling as integral to the community's well-being. Thus she most successfully combines her feminist and her African-American aesthetics, and achieves a bombastic and yet loving style.

Jordan certainly continues many of her earlier practices in this collection; she writes persona parodies of whites' skewed views ("Letter to the Local Police," "Memo:") and playful but acerbic renderings of racist/imperialist pieces of popular culture ("TV Is Easy Next to Life," "Found Poem"). She also includes "1977: Poem for Mrs. Fannie Lou Hamer," which celebrates the civil rights activist in much the same terms that "Getting Down to Get Over" celebrated African-American women in general; written mostly in Black English, this poem honors Hamer as "one full Black lily / luminescent / in a homemade field / of love" (P 41). "Poem about Police Violence" is also written mostly in Black English. A very angry speaker asks if police violence might not decrease if African-Americans killed a cop every time a cop killed a young African-American man; the voice is still rather distant, though it does use a refrain to establish the message/rhythm of the poem.

However, in this volume, two shorter, highly personal pieces and two performance-driven long poems most fully illustrate Jordan's innovative mix of feminist and African-American aesthetics. Her reflections on politics in these four poems concentrate on her own experience of rape, the particular act of violence that most consistently affects women, whether as threat or reality. Indeed, Jordan's quieter, more lyrical meditations on her personal experience of rape ("Case in Point," "Rape Is Not a Poem") both show a considerable deepening of self-reflection over earlier poems and provide the base for her long poems on the same topic ("Poem about My Rights," "A Poem About Vieques, Puerto Rico").

Based on her own ordeals, Jordan's depictions of rape scenes are graphic and filled with pain, in contrast to some feminist poets' more abstract, more figurative poems about rape that do not rely on active anger or grief (see Rich 1973, 44; Piercy 1982, 164–65). In the poem "Case in Point," Jordan is in fact most concerned with plainly and straightforwardly relating the circumstances of her violations, which exceed any racial boundaries:

> 2 weeks ago I was raped for the second
> time in my life the first occasion
> being a whiteman and the most recent
> situation being a blackman actually
> head of the local NAACP
>
> (1980, 13)

The tone here is merely informative, flat even. While punctuation is minimal in this poem, the lines are longer and the syntax less fragmentary than most of Jordan's earlier meditations on her own experience; she needs simply to tell the story. But her declarative tone serves another purpose, for she is commenting more broadly on the plight of women.

Jordan begins the poem by describing a friend who tells her, in her belief that women's oppression is in quality no different from any other kind, that "there is no silence peculiar / to the female." Jordan's response is to say something "about female silence: so to speak / these are my 2c on the subject" (13). She goes on to describe her own experience of rape and thereby ironically to make the point that though she has a voice (and will use it to tell her story), the violence of rape is capable of drowning women's speech, and indeed has drowned her own. Vividly recounting her own experience, she illustrates: ". . . he rammed / what he described as his quote big dick / unquote into my mouth / and shouted out: 'D'ya want to swallow / my big dick; well do ya?' " (13) The very violence of this imagery is highlighted by the simple manner in which Jordan relates it; though she could not speak at the time of her rape, she can speak in a poem and does, to demonstrate that women in sexually threatening/violent cultures *are* limited in their ability to participate in the power of language. As the victim of sexual violence, women are literally and symbolically silenced: "He was being rhetorical. / My silence was peculiar / to the female" (13).

In an interesting twist that illustrates Jordan's ongoing concern with difference, Jordan both asserts her personal experience of this phenomenon and rebuts another woman who believes differently based on her own experience, or her lack of experience of sexual violence. Jordan is talking back to the man who raped her, but she is simultaneously talking to the woman who could be her "sister" and yet who differently conceives of women's vulnerability as sexual beings. The subjective and the collective are in dialogue in this most personal of Jordan's poems; she relies more heavily than before on autobiographical detail but emphasizes more strongly that personal experience is inherently connected to political conversations and realities. Perhaps most significantly, she highlights difference between women even as she asserts that all women have at least one common experience.

In "Rape Is Not a Poem," Jordan makes another series of personal and political connections based on another highly detailed account of one of her rapes. But the experience women have in common in this poem is not social (or physical) silence, but an identification by patriarchy with the earth. Jordan's concerns for the environment in fact thread through many of even her earliest poems; indeed, as this poem illustrates, she views environmental degradation as one in a series of linked oppressions. In section one of this poem, she speaks in third person of a woman who sees others ("they," presumably men) coming into a garden and trampling flowers because "They were asking for it." The implication, of course, is that the flowers themselves are responsible for their own ravaging because they are so boldly and unabashedly beautiful. In section three, the poet asks her rapist: "Is this what you call / Only Natural?" (80), while in section four, she says he should learn a lesson from another "lesser" creature, the dog, who cherishes whatever he finds on the ground: "a big dog / (licking at the tiny water) / delicate as he is / elsewhere / fierce" (81). Here, Jordan's reflection on her own experience of violence extends into a lyrical meditation on the roots of this violence and on the possibilities for change.

Jordan's long "A Poem About Vieques, Puerto Rico" uses rape as reality and metaphor. She does relate her own experience of sexual violence (this time, sexual harassment on the beach), and thereby retains the integral focus on the connections between the personal and political.

However, her voice here is more garrulous, her own experience informs but does not ground the poem, and she actually invites other voices into the poem. She pieces her observations about the connectedness of oppressions together in a more fragmentary way, reminiscent of her earlier poems. She observes and connects abuses at the hands of American military and tourists, while using as her central narrative event the rape of a woman; in fact, the central metaphor is one of rape, and the tone of this poem is much more controlled, the language more dense and the goal to contrast and connect oppressions through personal observation and narrative rather than to describe her own condition as a marginalized subject (63).

The headiest mix of anger and self-celebration, of African-American influence and feminist voice, occurs in Jordan's long poem about how rape is connected to other forms of social domination. "Poem about My Rights" starts with the fact of Jordan's literal rape and then uses rape as a metaphor for imperialist expansion, government crackdowns, and racism in the United States, and sexism expressed in her own family. She weaves all these instances of rape/"rape" together seamlessly; indeed, except for a few backslashes to indicate pauses within lines, she uses no punctuation at all. She uses repetition to establish and maintain rhythm, together with a long, freewheeling line reminiscent of jazz improvisation on a single chord. The two of these give her the range of both voice and space she needs to cover global territory and to manifest her profound self-assertion and anger.

But Jordan begins and ends with her ". . . personal and idiosyncratic / and indisputably single and singular heart" (89). Using the details of her own life, she begins to understand the interrelatedness of different forms of domination, and from her own experience, she creates the will to resist. For this reason, "Poem" is perhaps the strongest example of Jordan's feminist impulse to develop coalitional voice, to nurture her own "perpetual birth" and thereby serve "a positive and collective function, without pretending to be more than the one Black woman poet I am. . . ." (1981a 126). Here, she shares the project of coalitional voice with Judy Grahn and other feminist poets, the project of naming her own experience of oppression in order to indict the systems that have oppressed her without erasing difference between herself and other women/oppressed persons. Accordingly, she frames her entire discussion in terms of her own firsthand knowledge of sexual violence against women.

Jordan opens "Poem" in first person, establishing the everyday reality of the threat of sexual violence and simultaneously establishing self-reflexively the ways her experience necessarily inform and shape her poetry:

> Even tonight and I need to take a walk and clear
> my head about this poem about why I can't
> go out without changing my clothes my shoes
> my body posture my gender identity my age
> my status as a woman alone in the evening/
>
> (1980, 86)

Starting with this prosaic example, Jordan illustrates the relentless threats women face. Right away, her lack of punctuation and long lines of accumulating detail create a sense of movement, even of urgency, in the poem. With no caesuras in these lines, the reader/listener is propelled into the body of the poem, carried forward by the lack of breath and the repetition of "my." These elements lend this piece to performance, so that "Poem" seems as much a collective reflection on *women's* lives as "Getting Down" seems one on *African-American women's* lives. The difference, however, is that "Poem" is rooted more emphatically in the poet's own experience, so that her angry energy, precision of description, and formal strategies combine to invite and confront the reader more forcefully.

But this interaction with the reader doesn't come to fruition until the final, explosive lines. Jordan builds toward this by weaving details from her own daily experience with reflections on legal definitions of rape in France, South Africa's interference in other African nations, the C.I.A.'s persecution of activists, and her father's sexism and her mother's internalized racism.[4] As I said previously, Jordan pulls the reader through all these details with her lack of punctuation and her spirited improvisation on the long line using repetition. She also uses the word "and" like one note in the consistent chord; it connects her details and provides beat. But Jordan does establish "movements" in this poem, largely by asking questions. At the end of the first movement, she uses "and" to move from her contemplation of danger on the night streets to "who in the hell set things up / like this" (1980, 86). Immediately after, she writes "and in France . . . ," so the reader feels the force of her confrontive question and yet remains in the poem's thread of connections. Jordan discusses France and South Africa in the second movement, ending with "Do You Follow Me" (87). By capitalizing the first four words in these lines, Jordan highlights the direction she is taking and queries the reader/listener to see if she/he is making the connections between oppressions with her. After discussing the C.I.A. and her mother and father in the third movement, she asserts ". . . the problems / turn out to be / me" (88), and begins the fourth and final movement with the next line: "I am the history of rape" (P 88). This final movement then builds toward the crux of the poem's meaning and purpose in its own final lines.

Jordan also uses the word "wrong" not only to characterize her oppressors' opinions of her but to build rhythm and keep the reader/listener grounded in the poem; she uses it some twenty-seven times. The point of her initial observations on being out alone at night, revealed in the seventh line, is that "I can't do what I want / to do with my own body because I am the wrong / sex the wrong age the wrong skin . . ." (86). In the movement on the laws defining rape in France, she asserts that were she raped there, the act would be sanctioned ". . . because I was wrong I was / wrong again to be me being me where I was/wrong / to be who I am" (87). Similarly, in her ruminations on racism in the U.S., she says, "We are the wrong people of / the wrong skin on the wrong continent . . ." (87) Her father sees himself as wrong because African-American and his daughter as wrong because a girl (88).

Jordan uses the word "wrong" again in the final movement of the poem, and here weaves together all the ways she has used it to illustrate fully the connections between all the forms of domination she has spoken of:

> be-
> cause I have been wrong the wrong sex the wrong age
> the wrong skin the wrong nose the wrong hair the
> wrong need the wrong dream the wrong geographic
> the wrong sartorial I
> have been the meaning of rape
>
> (89)

"Wrong" sums up the process by which forces of social domination use "either/or" formulations to identify the different, the other, as "wrong," undesirable, evil. Jordan understands that this very thought process is a

form of rape, so that she herself is an example of all that is "wrong" is
". . . the history of rape" (88), ". . . the meaning or rape" (89). All of
this, of course, is rooted in her acknowledgment of her personal experience; again in this final movement, she says simply, "I have been
raped" (89).

However, she asserts that her poem itself is an act of resistance. It is
a cry of no against the violence of rape in all its manifestations: "but let
this be unmistakable this poem / is not consent I do not consent" (89).
Again, Jordan returns to her own experience of oppression, her own
experience of rape, in order to make her final and most substantive gesture of rebellion. She inverts/subverts the word "wrong" in her powerful self-assertion of her own name: "*I am not wrong: Wrong is not my
name* My name is my own my own my own" (89). Here Jordan exter-
nalizes her anger fully and in the process claims the power of self-naming. Her refusal to accept the dictate that she is "wrong" gives her her
own self-designation, and impels her out of silence in the same way her
speaking does in "Case in Point." As in "Getting Down to Get Over,"
this is a negative naming, a *denial* of old names, necessary to the struggle for equal power relations.

Perhaps the most dramatic effect of "Poem about my rights," however, is the way in which the reader/listener is invited, as Jordan almost
breathlessly layers the connections between oppressions, to feel what
the speaker feels: a sense of profound injustice and righteous anger.
Jordan in fact builds this mood to the very end of the poem; only in the
last line does she turn her anger directly toward the reader, unnamed
except through her or his sudden recognition of how she or he is connected to the systems of violence Jordan has depicted: "and I can't tell
you who the hell set things up like this / but I can tell you that from
now on my resistance / my simple and daily and nightly self-
determination / may very well cost you your life" (89). The anger here
is unflinching and searing but not alienating. The reader/listener is *inside* the poem by the time she/he reaches the final lines, because Jordan
has used a highly personal voice, established the interrelatedness of oppressions based on her own experience, and propelled the reader/lis-
tener with her through her far-flung observations with performance-
based formal strategies. The result is that, in the end, the reader is forced
into self-examination rather than disgust at her experiences of oppression, and Jordan has accomplished her goal of using "love" to overcome
"either/or" patterns of thinking and social activity.

Into the 1980s

The effect of Jordan's integration of African-American and feminist aesthetics, then, is an empowering coalitional voice and an unflinching recognition of the ways that oppressions interlock, as well as of the responsibility both poet and reader/listener have to confront these oppressions. Jordan's version of the truth-telling, community, and resistance necessary to this confrontation has influenced her poetry in the years since the publication of *Passion*. If anything, her vision has widened, as she has synthesized not only her concerns with gender and race but also class and homophobia. A good illustration is the poem "From Sea to Shining Sea" (1985), in which she traces the daily layering of control masked as "natural order" in the United States of the 1980s. In this poem, the "advances" of consumerism act as metaphor for the commodifying stereotyping of marginalized groups: "natural order" means "you keep the pomegranate stacked inside a wobbly / pyramid composed by 103 additional pomegranates / next to a sign saying 89 cents / each" (1985, 11). The "natural order" does not mean a pomegranate "split open to the seeds sucked by the tongue and lips," but a prepackaged, processed item of consumption, the image of the thing circulating politically as the thing itself. This extends to patriotism itself: "Above all the flag is being replaced by the flag" (11).

Jordan uses a montage of news stories here to illustrate the underside of the false optimism of the era; "this was not a good time to be gay," she asserts, and supplies a story about an episode of mass gay-bashing. She follows by illustrating that this "was not a good time" to be Black, old, young, a child, without a job, with a job, a woman, married, or living in various high-risk locations, from big to small cities, in the U.S. (14–15). This poem is divided into sections, and after cataloging the difficulties of living along the margins of American society in the 1980s, she arrives at first person and asserts disruption of this "natural order": "I am opening my mouth / I am just about to touch the pomegranates / piled up precarious." The next section then proposes an optimistic vision of reaching across difference to resist the oppressive order: "This is a good time / This is the best time / This is the only time to come together." In an almost free-wheeling version of her vertical rhythm, Jordan celebrates this action as "Fractious / Kicking / Spilling / Burly" and as "Raucous / Messy / / Free / Exploding like the seeds of a natural disorder" (20).

The pomegranate as symbol of the sensual supplies a center for the coming together of different identities, the possibility of community; yet this is not a simple affiliation but rather is messy and raucous. The displacement of adjectives implies the explosion, and the words themselves speak of both a volcanic activity ("Spilling," "Messy") and a contentious struggle ("Fractious," "Burly," "Raucous"), but the activity overall results in freedom, a "natural disorder" grounded in a common bond and yet holding forth the liberation gained through the respect of difference. This poem illustrates the full development of Jordan's broad, relentlessly inclusive vision and is full of both anger and hope.

With this poetry, Jordan has continued working in the tradition of both performance-oriented, politically visionary feminist poetry and the African-American tradition of the griot, who carries the stories and vernacular of the people, and reaffirms and rejuvenates cultural values by repeating them in ritualistic performance. But she has also returned to the questions of literary tradition, precisely through claiming her own experience and using it to speak of communal concerns. She begins this journey in *Passion,* in which she includes an essay that asserts that Walt Whitman's poetry is a fruitful mixing of Western ideas about poetry and other, even older cultural forms. For example, she says that Whitman's dictum that poetry be broadly accessible and used by the "ordinary" people echoes that of ancient civilizations for whom poems served a daily, if not religious then at least culturally enriching, function. In Jordan's view, this is a radical poetry that weaves together individual and community, public and private, lyrical and everyday language, urgent political necessities and mythical concerns. She says it is "as personal, as public, as irresistible, as quick, as necessary, as unprecedented, as representative, as exalted, as speakably commonplace, and as musical, as an emergency phone call" (1980, x). In Whitman's poetry, Jordan maintains, more ancient, less dualistic aesthetic understandings function to create a poetry that seems new in the democratic setting of the "New World." It is in this spirit that Jordan finally claims the literary tradition as her own, by using the term "New World poet" for herself and her contemporaries—feminist, African-American, and all the diverse others who write the American experience in poetry.

Four

Survival as Form in the Work of Gloria Anzaldúa and Irena Klepfisz

As feminist poets who reside in the borderlands between the dominant white American culture and their cultural, national, and linguistic backgrounds, Gloria Anzaldúa and Irena Klepfisz explore the precariousness of their position—in which gender oppression complicates the relationship of individual women to their racial/ethnic communities as well as to the dominant American culture, while their racial/ethnic status potentially divides them from American women. In this exploration, they also necessarily extend the limits of formal conventions both in American and in specifically feminist poetry. In the case of both Anzaldúa and Klepfisz, their borderlands consciousness causes them to cross poetic form and genre and issue linguistic challenges as well as to reaffirm the need to name a knowing and known self that survives and even thrives in the margins. The fact of this transgression, or *innovation,* however, has largely not been admitted in feminist criticisms, which have focused primarily on the thematic challenges offered by borderland poets.

Gaining some understanding of these poets' formal innovations is important because both have drawn from the basis of feminist poetry and in turn contributed to the feminist poetry movement based on their experience on the racial/ethnic outside. Both have been activists in the women's movement and in feminist publishing since the 1970s, and as poets and essayists have had notable influence within the feminist poetry movement. Both have also been very active in synthesizing the concerns of women with those of their respective racial/ethnic communities, Klepfisz as a leader in the Jewish feminist and Jewish communities, Anzaldúa as an outspoken organizer and editor for Chicana women and Third World women as well as the Chicano/a culture at large. Both have written on behalf of and to these communities (Anzaldúa and Moraga 1983, Anzaldúa 1987, Kaye/Kantrowitz and Klepfisz 1989). Looking at these two poets together is important as well because as coworkers they have extended their influence further, providing an im-

portant example of the interlocking nature of the feminist poetry movement and of just how central poets of marginal racial/ethnic status have
been to it.[1]

The crucial discovery for Anzaldúa and Klepfisz is that their identities
are both alienated from the dominant culture and devalued in their respective racial/ethnic cultures. As Anzaldúa puts it, her effort to deal
with the racial dilemma she faces involves getting "an accounting with
all three cultures" (white, Mexican, Indian); each in its own way has
proven home and not-home, and her solution is "making a new culture—*una cultura mestiza*—with my own lumber, my own bricks and
mortar and my own feminist architecture" (1987, 22). Her innovations
in form, genre, and language turn out to be parts of a reckoning with
the places she has come from—and lived on the edges of—as well as the
raw material for constructing a new home, a new consciousness, as a
woman. Klepfisz came to writing age in the lesbian feminist poetry
community of the early 1970s and initially wrote only along "the strict
divisions between my Jewish and lesbian life" (1990, 169). Through
the next two decades, she began to discover "a woman's link in the
chain of Jewish history" and thus to conceptualize an integrated identity
as a Jewish feminist (170). Simultaneously, her poetic journey came to
involve intertwining the roots of these two communities—realizing the
intersections of these margins themselves—and inventing ways of
speaking about these intersections.

Anzaldúa mixes poetry and prose and interrupts her prose with fragments of texts not written by her, both oral and written; while she
writes primarily lyrical poetry, retaining the emphases on subjective
presence and the primacy of personal experience, she explores fragmentation and destabilization of self and culture in her cross-genre pieces.
Klepfisz switches from more regulated lines in stanzaic form to broken
lines/lineation to prose poems, and also includes fragments of historical
texts to explore the intersections between the "I" and the cultures she
crosses. For both Anzaldúa and Klepfisz, writing about life in the margins involves the mixing and/or juxtaposing of linguistic systems; they
each write both interlingually and bilingually.[2] These women write not
only away from dominant American literary categories, away from a
totalizing paradigm of identity and writing that denies their otherness
and their experience, but toward some synthesis of identity, some sense
of a surviving self in life and in poetry. This occurs in different, almost
mirror-opposite ways in each poet. While Anzaldúa experimentally ex-

plores the mobility of voice—by mixing poetry with prose, history with autobiography, personal texts with fragments of folk culture—she ultimately relies on the subjective "I" embedded in lyrical poetry to stave off the potential fragmentation and destruction of life in the margins, affirm the cultural importance of her own difference, and challenge the reader at least to come to terms with if not develop a "mestiza" consciousness. For Klepfisz, in contrast, the lyric proves restrictive in that it cannot express an integrated sense of self when none exists; as a result, she expresses her split consciousness by separating her poetry about being Jewish from her poetry about her feminism and lesbianism. Only when Klepfisz discovers the "freedom" of prose poetry, poetry that resembles conversation, and the culture-crossing possibilities of bilingual poetry can she reach some sense of an ongoing, integrated self and relate fully to her communities.

Even this brief introduction leads us to another important conclusion: exploring Anzaldúa's and Klepfisz's work is also important because it deepens our understandings of feminist poetry by situating it relative to other literary phenomena. The particular combination of textual strategies that Anzaldúa and Klepfisz call upon may at some readers' first glance appear distinctly postmodernist, but while challenging the tyranny of form and genre as well as linguistic imperialism are noted characteristics of postmodernist literary practice, stating/reinstating subjective presence is not. Anzaldúa's and Klepfisz's central commitment is to feminism; as a result, they need to define a woman-self in the context of their "minority" history and their present borderlands existence, much as June Jordan does when she asserts "I am not wrong / Wrong is not my name" (1980, 89). However, because the cultural multiplicity of the experience of women like Anzaldúa and Klepfisz so exceeds the boundaries of American culture, it also carries them out of their central aesthetic commitment to poetry, and over the borders of form, genre, and language. They begin with their most urgent need—for self-definition—and move outward to resist form, genre, and linguistic conventions and thereby to challenge readers; in this way, their work is a logical extension of the project of developing coalitional voice begun by feminist poets in the early 1970s.

Feminism as Avant-garde

As I have already noted, while Anzaldúa's and Klepfisz's poetry is grounded in the conviction that racially and ethnically marginalized women can establish identity in the heavily autobiographical lyric and lyric-narrative so often used by feminist poets, they simultaneously challenge and extend those very forms from their positions in the margins of American culture and the women's movement itself. As they locate themselves in relation to feminist poetry in this way, both of these women employ strategies that potentially align them with postmodernism and the avant-garde, in the broad sense of these categories as they operate in American literature. These literary distinctions function powerfully in the late twentieth century to name what is going on both at the center itself—in the postmodernist sense, now understood to be a fiction, and always potentially the site of fragmentation and chaos—and on the edge—where the avant-garde perpetually asserts itself, only to be further usurped by the "newer new."

Both poets, thematically as well as formally, participate in postmodernist self-reflexivity and acknowledgment of the fragmentation of the self. Similarly, they both question history and intertextually challenge existing historical documents. Through these strategies, both writers threaten to undermine authorial and textual authority as they subvert the integrity of dominant cultural discourses and historical narratives. As far as poetry itself goes, however, the label "postmodern" is not very helpful in identifying these poets, because in a historical sense it usually simply refers to poets writing after World War II and/or upon the end of the reign of the high modernists Eliot and Pound. In a more narrow, contemporary sense, postmodernism in poetry is largely identified only with the experimental work of the language poets (Perkins 1987, 331–33). In addition, even the more general literary features ascribed to postmodernism themselves only partially characterize the work of these two poets; these features cannot fully attend to the cultural dilemma that arises in the feminist and racial/ethnic margins of American culture.

Anzaldúa's and Klepfisz's approach to history intersects with but ultimately extends beyond postmodernist appropriations and critiques. Both do subvert narratives of history, particularly as they provide counterpoints to "official" historical texts with their own autobiographical fragments, but this use of history is never parodic or even ironic. These women in fact call upon precise recollections of histories of domination and their own personal stories of oppression as marginalized women in American culture as well as in their own racial/ethnic subcultures, and in doing so rely on subjective voice and experience to correct the historical record and (re)establish the historical presence of their marginalized ancestors. Thus, many of their textual strategies are rooted in the post-modernist impulse to question history, but the demands of writing in the margins of American culture modify this impulse. These women wish to subvert history, and yet they believe they must still make some truth claims about the gaps in Western historical narratives in order to assert their own identities.

This need to subvert history and yet to continue to rely on it also keeps these writers from simply valorizing their revised pasts without question. While Rosaura Sánchez has demonstrated how Chicano writers largely do not establish ironic distance from the past, but in fact often take a nostalgic stance, longing for a "lost period, for a former sense of community" (1987, 10), Anzaldúa clearly does not valorize the past but rather wants to understand it for the ways it can both empower and further oppress her. Similarly, Klepfisz writes history through auto-biography in order to facilitate self-understanding and to establish a basis for future self-understandings, for both herself and other Jewish-American women. Both Anzaldúa and Klepfisz call upon history and especially historical female figures not in a nostalgic move that denies present states of pain and alienation, but in a very contemporary auto-biographical move: they seek to remake these traditions and to make use of them in their own ongoing efforts to survive.[3]

Similarly, these women engage in textual strategies that express the disjuncture involved in living in the margins, strategies which partake in a postmodernist version of "double-or multiple-voicing" (Hutcheon 1988, 44), whether painful or celebratory, while simultaneously constructing narratives of the coherent self. The impulse toward subjective voice and some ongoing functional center of identity runs throughout Anzaldúa's and Klepfisz's work. They write experimentally toward the goal of achieving a single voice, a voice that speaks of survival of the self and yet paradoxically may itself be subject to further revision. Anzaldúa divides *Borderlands/La Frontera: The New Mestiza* into two parts, the first characterized by fragmentation—expressed in crossing the borders back and forth across genre, in inter- and bilingual fragments, and in intertextuality. The second part, however, is a collection of predominantly lyrical poetry written mostly in highly personal voice. In addition, a closer look at the first section of her text reveals that the poetic voice that weaves in and out of it preserves her subjective presence, and in fact that she eventually draws her textual divisions and thematic forays back to a center that resides in the life and voice of the author herself. Throughout her several volumes of poetry, Klepfisz does not foreground textual disruptions of voice and text in the same way Anzaldúa does but rather introduces them within lyrical pieces themselves. Her generic and bilingual challenges come later in her career as a poet and speak a desire not only to express the interconnections between two linguistic and cultural systems but to achieve their possible integration in the consciousness of the writer herself.

It is clear that the mixture of strategies that express both dispersal and wholeness in the work of Anzaldúa and Klepfisz directly reflects their location as both feminist and racially/ethnically marginalized. They recognize the conditions of a postmodern world, but they project a move beyond them in their effort to assert a self with a valuable historical narrative that enables them to survive. In this sense, the political theory and poetics that arise from their feminist and racial/ethnic locations might even be called post-postmodernist.

However, a third, mediating term—the avant-garde—can function in a very useful way to describe the apparent connections between feminism and postmodernism that inform Anzaldúa's and Klepfisz's work, as well as to locate their work relative to the avant-garde or experimental as it is understood in literary, and specifically poetic, history. Maria Damon (1993) has revised the label "avant-garde" to encompass the activity of expressing typically postmodernist impulses that might arise from the social margins and affect the subjectively oriented, tightly controlled form of lyrical poetry. I find Damon's definition helpful because it provides a way to speak of the ways feminist poets like Anzaldúa and Klepfisz—who find themselves in the margins not only because they are women but because they are racial/ethnic minorities—must challenge established literary conventions in order simply to write. Damon asserts that the political and aesthetic effect of life on the margins of American culture is precisely the avant-garde. Her use of the term moves beyond its designation of either a clearly defined historical movement (such as surrealism) or a formally defined one (in which form breaks new ground that is eventually "overtilled" by other, less inventive cultural workers).[4] Damon instead promotes an understanding of the avant-garde that both refers back to the word's etymological origins and reflects the experience of marginalized writers in late twentieth-century America. In the original military sense of the word, the vanguard was composed of the "least-esteemed" members of society, who were sent ahead of the main troops and faced the most immediate peril of death or captivity. In a contemporary, poetic sense, the vanguard is comprised of those who live along the front lines, or the social margins, and who become "guerrilla verbalists" in their very struggle to survive. Damon maintains that the marginalized, "ostensibly most expendable members of the American socius have produced its truly vanguard literature" (xi).

These literary warriors stretch the limits of the acceptable simply because they write; whether or not their work is formally experimental, it "breaks social taboos and formalist rules in its attempt to create a new consciousness borne of heretofore inexpressible experience" (xi). Thus, Damon breaks the impasse between formalist and historical interpretations of the avant-garde and provides an understanding of how feminist poets like Anzaldúa and Klepfisz—because of their attention to life in the margins and to the resulting political urgencies—in fact extend the limits of their aesthetic "base," the feminist poetry movement, and even of the postmodern. As they address the ways that a particular set of material conditions shapes their need for poetic utterance, they necessarily challenge formal conventions rooted in dominant social practices, and they move beyond the ruling literary discourse(s). As Anzaldúa and Klepfisz question and rely on history, as they subvert and reassert individual voice, and as they do both out of a distinctly feminist commitment, they tackle both modernist and postmodernist ideas of the relationship between self and history and between self and community.

Borderlands/La Frontera: The New Mestiza

In the poem "Cultures," Gloria Anzaldúa evokes the feelings of a young girl instructed by her mother to bury garbage in the backyard. The girl is responsible for trying to transform the remains of the dominant culture: "into the hole I'd rake up and pitch / rubber-nippled baby bottles / cans of Spam with twisted umbilicals / I'd overturn the cultures / spawning in Coke bottles / murky and motleyed" (1987, 120). The girl's toil is considered "woman's work" by her brothers, and her returns are small, for even though her mother says that trash "replenishes the soil," ". . . nothing would grow in / my small plots except / thistle sage and nettle" (120). Through the lyrical observations of an adolescent girl, Anzaldúa conveys the dilemma facing the *mestiza,* the Mexican-American woman who must deal with the debris of dominant American culture in her backyard. This poem indicates the futility of burying the "trash," and Anzaldúa's book *Borderlands/La Frontera: The New Mestiza* is itself an examination of the elements of American culture that she must deal with in the "backyard" of her identity. While Anzaldúa consistently returns to such lyrical poems, which rely on voice and feeling to convey the theme, and which build her sense of a surviving self, *Borderlands* also exceeds the boundaries of the lyric and lyric-narrative.

It is for this reason that *Borderlands* has in fact come to be considered one of the landmark feminist works of the 1980s, both theoretically and autobiographically; indeed, the genre-crossing she does in this text (crossing the boundaries of poetry, autobiography, history), as well as the bilingualism and interlingualsim she engages in, appear to have no parallel among feminist poets or writers in general. The Spanish title indicates the unique bilingual/interlingual nature of this work, goes a long way in setting forth the borderlands as a central locale and metaphor for this text, and hints at precisely why this book has been so important. The Spanish word *frontera* means both "border" and "frontier," and carries multiple meanings: it conveys the literal territory along the borders between Texas and Mexico (which was once a "frontier" in American colonialism, though already long inhabited by *Mexicanos*) and California and Mexico; the effects of living in this borderland on/within the individual; the "frontier" that the resident of the borderlands must traverse as she charts new ways of traveling and understanding in order to survive the rigors of a borderlands existence and to assert a surviving self; and the new "frontier" of language, culture, and national identity that Anzaldúa challenges the reader to enter.

The *mestiza* is the new human consciousness that resides in this landscape. As Anzaldúa defines her, the *mestiza* is deeply connected to her landscape and embodies the connections and contradictions among race, cultural and political affiliations, and self-understanding as they are shaped by and in turn shape the borderlands. As a landscape or textual territory, Anzaldúa's text itself is a borderland and Anzaldúa the *mestiza* who shapes it and is shaped by it: it is a journey back and forth across the borders of genre and language, so that the result is a new kind of text, in which borders move and sometimes disappear, and writer, written, and reader all take a *mestiza* shape through the recovery of hidden histories, the autobiographical assertion of oppressed selves, the evocation of both of these in the lyrical voice of personal poetry (which in many ways remains the central literary impulse in the text), and the challenge to the reader to understand and even live a borderlands mentality. Anzaldúa fearlessly exposes the pain and fragmentation of life in the borderlands in the theme and formal structures of her text, while simultaneously constructing a new self-consciousness—and by extension, in her plan, a new form of human consciousness—in which the breaks in the old turn out to be seams in the new.

Anzaldúa divides *Borderlands* into two sections, the first a fluid mixture of lyrical poetic fragments, prose autobiography and history, and quotations from popular Mexican-American culture and "authoritative" American historical texts, and the second a collection of fairly conventional, predominantly lyrical poetry that deals with the themes elucidated in the first section. The first section evokes the borderlands in numerous ways; Anzaldúa's autobiographical pieces concern her growing up along the Mexican-American border and coming to terms with that past, and her historical narratives strive to correct American versions of the history of the region but also attempt to revive the repressed feminine presence in Mexican-Indian history. Her poetry, in both sections, explores all of these themes with the subjective voice of lyric. In terms of both content and form, Anzaldúa explores both the literal and figurative borderlands, unflinchingly expressing the pain and anger intrinsic to a borderland existence and yet looking for some combination of genre, form, and language to describe this experience and a surviving self and voice with which to describe it. She proposes what she calls a "third way" of thinking that violates dualities and through "continual creative motion . . . keeps breaking down the unitary aspect of each new paradigm" (80). As she crosses back and forth across the borders of genre, form, and language, she asserts as a speaking woman in the borderlands, so that author and "life-story" are both there and not there, both inside the text and lost somewhere in its constant disruption. In the process, and especially as interlingualism and bilingualism are added to the mix, the reader is invited into this dilemma, and challenged to develop a mestiza consciousness.

A close look at Anzaldúa's first chapter, "The Homeland, Aztlán: *El otro México,*" demonstrates the textual feel of this disjuncture and blending. The title itself clearly situates Anzaldúa as a Chicana, as she calls on the notion of Aztlán (the U.S. Southwest as the "original" Indian homeland of Chicanos/Chicanas) which originated in the Chicano/a movement of the 1960s and defines the borderlands as the starting point, the original "home" (Anaya and Lomeli 1989, 2–5). The epigraph is a quote from a well-known contemporary song, which locates Anzaldúa's comments in the popular culture of the Mexican-American border; this song asserts that this "other Mexico" is one Mexican-Americans have constructed as a new kind of national territory. This is followed by a quote from Jack D. Forbes's *Aztecas del Norte* in which he maintains that this group comprises the "largest single tribe or nation of Anishinabeg (Indians) found in the United States today" and that some of these Indians call themselves Chicanos/Chicanas and understand their "true homeland" to be Aztlán (1987, 1).

Anzaldúa's voice then enters the text in the first original piece of the chapter—her long poem about visiting the literal border between Mexico and California that is marked by a barbed wire fence running out into the Pacific Ocean, a poem that contains the originating themes and locales for the text. Anzaldúa first notices the edge where earth touches ocean as a kind of border, at times a gentle coming together and at others a violent conflict (1). Anzaldúa transforms the sea into the rising of both her racial heritage and an attack on the fence in Border Field Park, situated on the ocean, and she hears the sea crying and feels "the tangy smell of the sea seeping into me" (2). The fence represents American imperialism and the ways it tore Mexicans from their lands and reconstituted the borders, while the poet also interpolates the fence onto her own body as it calls forth the painful experience of border-crossing Mexican women. Her body becomes at once both a colonized territory itself and a symbol of the divided territory of the Mexican people:

> 1950 mile-long open wound
>> dividing a pueblo, a culture
>> running down the length of my body,
>>> staking fence rods in my flesh,
>>> splits me   splits me
>>>> *me raja   me raja*
>
> (2)

As the female presence in the poem, Anzaldúa metaphorizes the spirit of Mexicans, who like the sea "cannot be fenced," for "*el mar* does not stop at borders" (3). The symbols of sea, land, and fence are interpreted within the poem through the body of the speaking woman, who herself then issues the declaration of rightful ownership as she stands in the sea: "This land was Mexican once, / was Indian always / and is. / And will be again" (3). Anzaldúa writes the final stanza of the poem entirely in Spanish, indicating her need to return to her ancestors' language, and extends the metaphors introduced in the poem to further state the larger themes Anzaldúa has in mind for the landscape of her text as a whole. She says that she herself is the bridge lying/lain down between these two worlds and cries, "Yes yes yes, I am a Mexicana on this side" (3). Within this poem, Anzaldúa seems to establish her own identity as both the starting and the ending point for understanding the borderlands.

The textual strategies that follow this initial poem begin to accrue to produce a feeling of disjuncture. After the poem, Anzaldúa immediately moves into a section of term definition. Her functions as poet and essayist begin to rub up against each other in form even as they complement each other in theme. In a single long paragraph, Anzaldúa defines "border" as the term operates in the lives of Chicanas and others who live in the precarious interstices between cultures and who must mediate between their own identities. She says that the U.S.-Mexican border is an open wound where "the Third World grates against the first and bleeds" and where "the lifeblood of two worlds" merges to form another country, a border culture (3). This of course is her literal point of departure, but she goes on to define borders as those lines established to demarcate the safe and the unsafe, "to distinguish us from them." A border, says Anzaldúa, is "a vague and undetermined place created by the emotional residue of an unnatural boundary." "*Los atravesados*" (the cross-breeds) live in the borderlands, and here she includes "the queer, the troublesome, the mongrel, the mulatto, the half-breed," or "those who cross over, pass over, or go through the confines of the 'normal' " (3). In Anzaldúa's particular history, these "transgressors" are Chicanas/Chicanos, Indians, or African Americans who occupy the U.S. Southwest and must submit to the Anglo-Americans in power. With this definition, the lyrical voice of the initial poem extends into the voice of the social critic whose ambitions for a new kind of borderland identity extend into the collective.

But just as Anzaldúa accustoms the reader to her critical prose voice, she moves into an autobiographical fragment, set off by indentation, in which she watches her cousin run from the immigration police because, even though he is a fifth-generation American, he can't speak English. He is caught and deported to Guadalajara and eventually walks all the way back to the Rio Grande Valley. With this episode, Anzaldúa illustrates the borderland status of Mexican-Americans, and she then immediately moves into the historical narrative of how America was originally inhabited by Indians, how the Aztec civilization came to be, and how the descendants of the Aztecs, combining Spanish and Indian heritages, eventually migrated back into what had become North America. This section is further punctured intertextually as Anzaldúa grounds her history in the cultural forms of the people and contrasts it to the historical records that have attempted to erase it. She includes a poem by the anticolonialist Violetta Parra, two stanzas of a Mexican *corrido* lamenting the invasion of the gringos, and a passage from the historian William H. Wharton's ethnocentric interpretation of the period in American history, in which "the wilderness of Texas has been redeemed" (7). Anzaldúa sews these references into the text without any kind of framing, producing feelings of disjuncture and initially the appearance of pastiche. Nevertheless, Anzaldúa structures her prose commentary directly in response to the quoted fragments, recounting events in the border dispute between Mexico and the United States to reiterate Parra and the *corrido* and to dispute Wharton.

The final fragment is a lyrical prose evocation, with the occasionally rhythmic feel of the prose poem but numerous lapses into Anzaldúa's plainly stated "facts" of Mexican immigration history. All of the formal elements in this chapter—the cultural fragments in quotation form, the autobiographical and historical narratives, and the poetic lyrical "I"—finally work thematically to evoke the present status of Mexican immigrants ("illegal aliens" in the marginalizing discourse of the American legal system) who are returning to their "homeland" in a "silent invasion" (10): "Without benefit of bridges, the *'mojados'* (wetbacks) float on inflatable rafts across *el río Grande,* or wade or swim across naked, clutching their clothes over their heads. Holding onto the grass, they pull themselves along the banks with a prayer to *Virgen de Guadalupe* on their lips *Ay virgencita morena, mi madrecita, dame to bendición"* (11). The metaphorical and factual elements that converge in this chapter finally convey a picture of the borderlands resident/traveler who lives at the outermost extremes of the social margins—and Anzaldúa makes clear that she considers the Mexican immigrant woman to be at the very greatest risk (12).

Regardless of how she crosses the borders of genre, form, and language, this nevertheless remains a chapter, a single unified section in Anzaldúa's larger work, and she strives within it for a synthesis of the various linguistic, literary and cultural strategies that textually appear to be so disparate. Anzaldúa does not mark the boundaries between all of these elements, illustrating her rejection of traditional generic divisions through her disregard for even typographical delineations between them. In addition, the subtitles Anzaldúa utilizes in chapter 1 do not necessarily denote a shift in genre; rather, these shifts may occur within subsections. Nevertheless, the subsections themselves indicate some gradual buildup toward a thematic synthesis and, at the chapter's end, Anzaldúa writes her revised history in the body of the Mexican woman, and in her own body as she represented it in the initial long poem: "This is her home / this thin edge of / barbwire" (13).

Anzaldúa continues with the chapter format throughout the first section of her text; each functions like chapter 1—as a compendium of styles, genres, and linguistic modes that still functions as a whole—and in each the themes and textual strategies Anzaldúa introduces in the first chapter resonate and expand. In addition, the poetry collection relies on divisions that mirror the thematic emphases and the autobiographical narratives established in the first section. The collection as a whole is entitled "*Un Agitado Viento*/Ehécatl, The Wind," referring to the wind as mythical Aztecan presence and using it as metaphor for the journey through the borderlands. The six subsections of the poetry collection lead the reader through Anzaldúa's lyrical journey; she moves from the ranches where she grew up through stages of being lost, crossing back and forth across borders, finding herself through the help of the Aztecan goddess Cihuatlyotl, being continually animated by this goddess, and returning home. The sense obtained from the overall project is of building blocks in a mestiza consciousness: each chapter, each smaller section of poems, and the two main sections of the text themselves represent a different stage in the author's construction of this consciousness, and yet each operates on its own. This further enhances what Anzaldúa herself identifies as the "mosaic" feeling of her text (66) and supports the synthesis of individual and collective voice and story—coalitional voice, or the mestiza consciousness as the consciousness of the *raza*—that Anzaldúa strives for throughout her text.

The combination of voices that emerges in chapter 1—the dominant versus the subversive, the public versus the private—are woven together throughout the whole of *Borderlands*. However, even as the initial long poem about the U.S.-Mexican border establishes Anzaldúa's voice as the originating one in the text and her female body as the lived site of the borderlands experience, her lyrical voice continues to intervene in the brokenness and fragmentation reflected in the border-crossing text itself, and it finally gains full authority as the subjective voice of lyric takes over the text. The "tribal rights" that Anzaldúa seems to be advocating in her descriptions of the dilemma of the *mojado* haunt all of her historical narratives, but her own voice insistently rebels. Even in the Mexican-American culture she goes on to describe, asserting oneself to have rights as a woman or a lesbian is translated as "selfishness," and Anzaldúa's voice begins to dominate the text as she increasingly interprets this tribal history in terms of her own political and sexual woman-identification (18). Even in the first section, though she slips from auto-biographical to poetic to historical/critical voice, the historical interpretations are increasingly skewed toward the plight of women, the female deities rejected by her Indian ancestors, and her own personal survival with the help of these women/goddesses. The thematic progression that accompanies Anzaldúa's assertion of personal voice does not contradict but encompasses both the brokenness and the wholeness implied by textual border-crossing, for she mediates between margin and center through both the art of linguistic "healing" and an emphasis on ambiguity and difference as positive aspects of personal and cultural identity.

Mestiza Forms, Mestiza Themes

Chapter 7 of the first section of *Borderlands,* in which Anzaldúa performs her outline of the mestiza consciousness, lies spatially, numerically, and thematically at the heart of the text as a whole. It functions to indicate the ways theme follows form in the first section of the text—for it is only in this final chapter that Anzaldúa spells out the shape and function of the mestiza consciousness and its connections to her formal experimentation—while it simultaneously prepares the way for a "mestiza" reception of the collection of lyrical poetry that follows. Here as in other chapters, Anzaldúa moves fluidly from the definition of terms into history into autobiography and into highly lyrical poetry, but she foregrounds the theoretical elements of her thematic scheme as they are related to the structural elements of her writing. She thus makes clear that, rather than simply produce disjuncture and fragmentation, the jumps from form to form, genre to genre, and English to Spanish and back, indicate not just the state of life in the borderlands but the tolerance for contradiction in the mestiza consciousness. In addition, the ways that Anzaldúa's use of voice weaves together individual and collective concerns doesn't merely question generic requirements (for poetry and autobiography versus history, for instance), but further extends the connections between personal and political that have so radically informed feminist poetry. The synthesis she is striving for, for herself, her text, and her readers, is a kind of prototype for a new human consciousness. Thus, though she consistently crosses genres, the first section of the book has an organic wholeness, for in chapter 7 she eventually weaves together the philosophical strands she began laying out in chapter 1 with her definition of "border."

Anzaldúa in fact explains her role as a writer to be itself defined by the borderlands and says that breaking down divisions in writing is a practice related to the "ethno-poetics and performance of the shaman" in her Indian heritage (66). The shaman, she says, "did not split the artistic from the functional, the sacred from the secular, art from everyday life" (66). If the writer writes in the shamanic tradition, "story (prose and poetry)" has the ability "to transform the storyteller and the listener into something or someone else" (66).[5] Here, the border between individual (writer or reader) and community (invoked by the text, writer and reader together) begins to break down (67). Anzaldúa also maintains that the idea of "virtuosity" (the tyranny of the genius) dominates Western aesthetics (68). This echoes the Native American views voiced by Joy Harjo (1993) and Wendy Rose (1992) and further indicates that Anzaldúa's writerly impulses are indeed rooted in an anti-Western (or pre-Contact) orientation, so that Western categories of genre, form, and linguistic code are automatically displaced. Thus, while Anzaldúa must consciously write *against* Western literary modes since she is a racially marginalized, Spanish-speaking woman who writes literature in English, she is also drawing on ancient ideas about the relationships between art and everyday life. In this process Anzaldúa adds a significant non-Western critique to the view of poetry as functional and culturally productive in feminist poetry. Maria Damon's idea of the avant-garde may also be fruitfully modified by Anzaldúa's notion that writing on the front lines is mestiza, a confluence of Western and non-Western traditions. Rather than purely oppositional in a progressive sense, the mestiza mode of writing combines the old and the new.

In asserting the shamanic tradition, Anzaldúa understands the writer to be a "shape-changer," one who can combine textual shapes in the process of transforming self and reader. Even in the midst of the writing itself, she comments on its constantly shifting structure: "I see a mosaic

pattern (Aztec-like) emerging, a weaving pattern, thin here, thick there
. . . This almost finished product seems an assemblage, a montage, a
beaded work with several leitmotifs and with a central core, now ap-
pearing, now disappearing in a crazy dance" (66). Once again, however, Anzaldúa completes a movement within this text (a chapter) with
a return to herself as originator of the text. She self-consciously performs the role of the shaman within and for the community but always
returns to her own subjective needs within the borderland juxtaposi-
tion/fusion of ancient and contemporary elements that contextualizes
her writing: "I sit here before my computer, Amiguita, my altar on top
of the monitor with the *Virgen de Coatlalopiuh* candle and copal incense
burning . . . Writing is my whole life, it is my obsession" (75).

Female Presences and the New Mestiza

This dialectic between self and community continues as Anzaldúa attempts to deal with the Mexican history of repression of both the female
divine and historical women. A trio of female spiritual "presences"
move back and forth through Anzaldúa's history and autobiography,
and the poetic sequences become broken, even trancelike. The Virgin of
Guadalupe, the good mother, together with the raped and abandoned
mother *la Chingada (Malinche)* and the mother who seeks her lost children (*la Llorona*) move snakelike through the text, leading Anzaldúa to
herself through *la facultad*, the "capacity to see in surface phenomena
the meaning of deeper realities," which the marginalized rely on so
"we'll know when the next person is going to slap us or lock us away"
(38–39). Thus, the history of these lost female deities and Anzaldúa's
work to find them ultimately leads her back to her communities—the
borderland residents, especially women and gays and lesbians, who
must survive in the face of incredible odds, and who ultimately will
inherit the mestiza consciousness. But again, it is only through self-
exploration that she is able to identify the ways she has "split from and
disowned those parts of myself that others rejected" (45). She identifies
the "Shadow-Beast," the "protean being" who resides within, and then
removes from it the projections of evil placed on it by her culture and
consequently herself; this part becomes the serpent (the Aztec symbol
of the feminine) and as representative of both evil and fecundity, both
death and healing, enables the mestiza consciousness. The spirit of the
serpent brings her ultimately back to the pursuit of a coherent self:

"And someone in me takes matters into our own hands, and eventually, takes dominion over serpents—over my own body, my sexual activity, my soul, my mind, my weaknesses and strengths . . . And suddenly I feel everything rushing to a center, a nucleus. All the lost pieces of myself come flying from the deserts and the mountains and the valleys, magnetized toward that center. *Completa*" (51).

Interestingly, the lyrical poetic segments in these passages operate like a trance, with the speaker alienated from her own psyche: "she has this fear that she has no names that she has many names that she doesn't know her names" (43). It is in the prose section in which the "lost pieces" come flying together, and the redemption of the lost woman—split off from society and exiled to the borderlands, split off from herself by self-hate—is accomplished. Thus, the voice of the "I" expands beyond the borders of the lyric in this particular section of the text; prose accommodates the poet's most assertive statement of self, and further disrupts the divisions between genre and among forms within genre. In this same way, the blending of individual and coalitional voice is also accomplished and/or constantly postponed.

In fact, this tension between the collective and the individual is inherent to the work of the shaman or "storyteller," the writer in the margins who seeks at once to recover her "home" culture(s) from the dustbins of imperialistic histories and to resist the imperialisms themselves—to "empower" those like her living in the margins and to "educate" those who have enough cultural power to avoid the margins. As Trinh T. Minh-ha puts it, the storyteller "sets out to revive the forgotten, to survive and supersede it" (1990b, 126); she simultaneously saves and destroys. She attempts, too, to belong to and speak for/with more than one collectivity; Anzaldúa speaks out of her Mexican, Indian, American, lesbian, and feminist identities. It is out of this need to "recover" that Anzaldúa moves from one collectivity to another, mediating between them through her own consciousness as a form of coalition. But this consciousness itself thrives on ambiguity—not necessitating the postmodernist idea of multiplicity of identity but what Anzaldúa calls "mental nepantilism" or the mental ability to understand that identity and culture are full of contradiction and difference rather than to see them only in the simplistic, dualistic terms of Western rationality; Anzaldúa notes that "nepantilism" is derived from an Aztec word meaning "torn between ways" (1987, 78). This consciousness emerges after the borderland resident undergoes "the coming together of two self-consistent but habitually incompatible frames of references" and thus "a cultural collision," and consequently must choose between adopting a counter-stance that preserves the "duel," the dualistic oppositions of oppressor and oppressed, and an alternative consciousness in which she "learns to juggle cultures" and "nothing is thrust out, the good the bad and the ugly, nothing rejected, nothing abandoned" (78–79). Thus, Anzaldúa advocates not a survival in spite of splitting, nor a stalemate between opposing powers, but that the self add a "third element" (79), which essentially is the energy of "continual creative motion that keeps break-ing down the unitary aspect of each new paradigm" (80). Her fluid text moves in this way and demonstrates the way the consciousness works to bring writer and reader, to bring communities, to one another, always mindful of difference and change.

The Surviving Self and Poetic Voice

Anzaldúa does mean, then, to express at once both communities that thrive on ambiguity, change, and difference and a self that survives the constant transformation. While in section 1 of *Borderlands* she formally and thematically prepares the reader for her idea and embodiment of the mestiza consciousness, in section 2, she writes about her experiences as a mestiza in authoritative subjective voice. Thus, within this one text, Anzaldúa illustrates the capability of the mestiza consciousness to hold both the stability and the constant deferral of self-identity.

Anzaldúa does write poetry that complements her themes of section 1, although in more conventional form. The one exception to lyric here is her poem "We Call Them Greasers," which is in its title the reworking of a well-known historical work on *Tjana* history. Anzaldúa contributes to the rewriting of the history of the Mexican-American border by adopting the persona of a gringo landowner who rapes and murders a Mexican woman and then orders her husband lynched. The details in this poem are graphic; the speaker describes closely his rape of the woman and how, after raping her, "in that instant I felt such contempt for her / round face and beady black eyes like an Indian's" (135). The tone of this poem is subversive of the landowner, however; since it is so cold and distant in its description, it provides no identification, and in fact a feeling of contempt for the landowner himself, thus invoking the emotions of the multitudes of Mexican women who were brutalized by such men. The landowner is further distanced from those he oppresses by his misuse of the Spanish language. The only two Spanish words in the poem simply serve to demonstrate the gringo's disdain; he says he "found" the Mexicans "growing corn in their small *ranchos*" and that he showed them a piece of paper, told them they owed taxes, had to pay up "or be gone by *manana*" (134).

But most of Anzaldúa's poetry in section 2 is autobiographical and lyrical. "Poets have strange eating habits" (which she dedicates to Irena Klepfisz), for instance, evokes Anzaldúa's spiritual journey to the Aztec goddesses. She projects herself as a human sacrifice to the "strange eating habits" of the void she must throw herself into in her search: "I feed it my throat my hands / let it glut itself on me / till it's pregnant with me. / Wounding is a deeper healing" (140). She eventually gives birth to the goddess, named Leyla, who inhabits the long lyric-narrative "Interface," and mirrors Anzaldúa's own condition as insider and outsider:

> Last Christmas I took her home to Texas.
>   Mom liked her.
> Is she a lez, my brothers asked.
>   I said, No, just an alien.
> Leyla laughed.
>
> (152)

In "*Nopalitos*," Anzaldúa invokes her insider/outsider status in her home community along the Mexican-American border. As she pulls the *nopalitos*—cactus leaves—and prepares them for making *chile colorado,* she ponders the neighbors, a man watering his flowers, women sitting on their porches laughing and talking. She knows that her journey away from this place sets her apart from these people and always will: "I left and have been gone a long time. / I keep leaving and when I am home / they remember no one but me had ever left" (113). But she projects herself as the caretaker of their culture, one who can nourish what they have provided her with a mestiza consciousness: "I have more languages than they, / am aware of every root of my *pueblo*; / they, my people, are not. / They are the living, sleeping roots" (113).

In the final poem of the collection, Anzaldúa bequeaths her mestiza identity to her niece, and thus closes the text with a lyrical evocation of the necessity of communication and care in the preservation of both her culture and individual women's identities. She begins the poem with instructions: "Don't give in *mi prietita* / tighten your belt, endure" (202). She establishes the cultural condition of the young Mexican-American woman, whose ancestors were raised in the Rio Grande Valley by strong women, who herself was raised by strong women, who will always be threatened by oppressing outside forces. Anzaldúa maintains, however, that no one can ever take her pride of being mestiza. Though her descendants may be dying of hunger, they will be the "members of a new species," a mestiza people able to face power, to "look at the sun through naked eyes" (203). She writes that this people will "rise up, tongue intact / carrying the best of all the cultures." What is now a sleeping serpent, she says, will wake up, and the "old skin" of submissiveness and silence will fall away. Then, she says, "Like serpent lightning we'll move, little woman. / You'll see" (203).

Language and the Nepantil State

In spite of Anzaldúa's dependence on lyrical voice in section 2 of *Borderlands,* one kind of disjuncture that she introduced in section 1 remains in place and thus continues to pose the greatest challenge to readerly sensibilities—including non-Spanish-speaking feminist readers' desires for feelings of collectivity. This disjuncture involves language codes. Anzaldúa consistently switches from Spanish to English and back throughout the text, using both interlingualism and bilingualism throughout the "mosaic" text of section 1 and the poetry collection in section 2. It is in this area of linguistic codes that Anzaldúa most fully expands feminist poets' ideas about the connections between feminist writers and feminist readers; it is the place where native English-speaking feminist critics like myself find themselves most uncomfortable, both because of limited Spanish language ability with regard to the Mexican-American context from which Anzaldúa's language patterns arise, and because the fluidity of the text feels most disrupted by the language switches and the reading difficulties (both in terms of the page and the language itself) posed by them.

The whole question of language-switching involves the role of Anzaldúa as translator. Even as she relates Mexican and Indian history, that is, "translates" it for Americans not of or not familiar with Mexican heritage (and Chicano/as unfamiliar with their backgrounds), so she is faced with the necessity to translate all of her thoughts/writings in Spanish in order to attract the obviously desired American audience. She does translate in many instances, but in more than a few, she simply refuses. The result is a jarring reading experience. When, in one instance, Anzaldúa writes a sentence in Spanish and then translates it in the following one, she also moves right into a poetic fragment written entirely in Spanish and not translated at all (54). In some instances, she translates the fragments from Mexican-American popular culture (29); in others, they simply stand in Spanish, an enigma to the non-Spanish-reading reader (55). In many instances, the Mexican words Anzaldúa uses are integrated into the English text, and their meanings are identifiable by context; this use of Spanish is interlingual, that is, the use of Spanish and English impinge upon each other, are mixed up and most reflective of the ways Mexican-Americans mix the languages; as Anzaldúa asserts, Chicano/as speak "a patois, a forked tongue, a variation of two languages" (55). In other instances, Anzaldúa "splits" the text bilingually, so that a single section is repeated in both Spanish and English; these separations may occur typographically or within a single paragraph, the latter giving them a parallelist feel.

Within this text, this insistence on mixing the languages is perhaps the most resistant and most avant-garde move, and also potentially the most fruitful for feminist poetry, for it is the most telling and most disturbing textual consequence of Anzaldúa's borderland experience. It marks her difference not only from non-Spanish speakers but from those who actively engage in linguistic imperialism, who insist that any American who would write must write in standard English.[6] It also marks her difference from non-Spanish-speaking women, as well as from other Chicanas; she narrates her conversations with the latter, often conducted entirely in English because they are afraid their own variant brand of Chicano English will be somehow "inferior" (56). Thus, the ways that Anzaldúa constantly switches or blends linguistic codes are guerrilla tactics toward self-definition in the face of the Western literary tradition and Western cultural imperialism, and simultaneously develop both the outwardly focused critique offered by feminist poetry's Woman as well as the inwardly focused emphasis on Women, on difference between women as integral to their relationships with one another. Anzaldúa writes: "Until I can take pride in my language, I cannot take pride in myself . . . Until I am free to write bilingually and to switch codes without having always to translate, while I still have to speak English or Spanish when I would rather speak Spanglish, and as long as I have to accommodate the English speakers rather than having them accommodate me, my tongue will be illegitimate" (59). This very statement operates in the same way that Anzaldúa's insistent use of Spanish throughout *Borderlands* does, for precisely because she *does not* use Spanish in this statement, she demonstrates her desire that non-Spanish speakers get the point.

History and the Mother Tongue: The Poetry of Irena Klepfisz

Like Gloria Anzaldúa, Klepfisz's life story is integrally connected to and revealed in her writing. By 1940, nearly half a million Jews were locked inside the Warsaw Ghetto; by the time Klepfisz was born there in 1941, the penalty for attempting to escape was death. Many died within the walls of the ghetto from hunger and disease; many more were deported to face death in the concentration camps. Klepfisz's father, Michal, was killed in April 1943 in an act of heroism in the Ghetto Uprising. Because her mother spoke fluent Polish, and Klepfisz as a baby girl was able to pass, the two were hidden by Polish peasants and eventually emigrated to Sweden after the war, and to the United States when Klepfisz was eight years old. In New York, she went to public schools, where she spoke English, but was otherwise immersed in a Jewish world in which Yiddish was the primary spoken language, the history of Jewish struggle and loss during the war years permeated daily life, and the radical political claims of the Jewish Labor Bund shaped her secular Jewish consciousness.

Also like Gloria Anzaldúa's, Irena Klepfisz's borderlands are both literal and figurative. While Anzaldúa subverts and rewrites history to revalue her territorial home along the actual borders between the United States and Mexico, Klepfisz was pushed from her original home and exists along the margins of American culture; both her racial/ethnic status as a Jew and her extraordinary historical status as a child survivor of the Holocaust keep her crossing from inside to outside and back. While Anzaldúa seeks to recover lost or glossed-over historical figures and narratives, Klepfisz must engage history because its diverse claims together threaten to overwhelm her. History traps her among the pain of losing family and community in the Holocaust, the realization that she barely missed death herself, the memory of brutality and thus the brutality of memory, the hope for the possibility of endurance and survival, and the need to love women and to recognize them in her history. While the geographical origination of her marginalized existence is the

Warsaw Ghetto and the United States is the borderlands to which she
is exiled, the set of historical events that created that original borderland
in the Ghetto continues to dominate and determine her life on another
continent, in another decade. While even in the United States her
Yiddish culture creates in Klepfisz a vital Jewish consciousness, the demands of history itself create in Klepfisz a split between this consciousness and her feminist consciousness and her political and literary
practice in women's communities. Until Klepfisz can question and
somehow come to terms with the power of death and the suppression
of women's voices in her history, she remains unable to embrace survival and to begin integrating her disaligned identities. As a "child survivor," Klepfisz faces the challenge of leaving the threatened, terrified
child behind and claiming the power of being a survivor, while as a
Jewish woman, she must discover how to call forth the presence of
women in her history as a healing and preservative force in the midst of
radical destruction.

   Klepfisz experienced her formation as a writer in the early days of the
feminist poetry movement, which at least partially explains her heavy
reliance on the free verse lyric as she began her career as a poet. But
for Klepfisz, the lyric proved restrictive in that it could not express an
integrated sense of self when none existed; she has said that her early
poetry "reflected the strict divisions between my Jewish and lesbian life"
(1990a, 169). As a result, in the poems of *Periods of Stress* (1975) and
in other poems from that period, she expresses this disjuncture by using
a broken line, jagged lineation, all lowercase letters, and no capitalization; by writing "quoting poems" that establish her enthrallment with
history;[7] and by spatially separating her poetry about being Jewish from
her poetry about her woman-identification. Later in her career, Klepfisz
reaches the conclusion that the demands of her history and her particular situation in the margins exceed those of any single form, genre, or
language. She then calls upon the narrative capability and detail of prose
and prose poetry, the emphasis on difference in poetic "conversation"
with other women, and the culture-crossing possibilities of bilingual
poetry to attain some sense of a surviving, integrated self. While some
of Klepfisz's strategies intersect with Anzaldúa's, they fit together in her
work with a primary difference: hers function to provide variations
within the enterprise of poetry itself while Anzaldúa uses poetry as one
genre among others only to revert finally to the lyric. This difference
coincides with yet another significant one. Anzaldúa's formal innova-

tions are collected in and determine the shape of a single text, while Klepfisz improvises her formal challenges during the course of her poetic career. Their evolution in fact occurs through two volumes of poetry into a collection of these volumes that also adds a newer series of poems.[8]

Self vs. History: Disjuncture in Klepfisz's Lyric

Klepfisz opens her collection of poems *A Few Words in the Mother Tongue* with two early poems (1971) never before published. Ironically, these poems work to establish Klepfisz's struggle with history, and so function like archaeological signs to her poetics. The first, entitled "Searching for My Father's Body," captures the poet's dilemma: she is caught in a history that she did not determine, that she did not write, that nevertheless centrally involves her own father, who died when she was still too young to remember him. The sense of disjuncture lies in the dilemma of dealing with the seeming inevitability of history, especially as it is memorialized and even commercialized through written texts and public discourse,[9] while trying to understand the self in relation to it. While "Searching" functions as a lament for the father, it also works as a kind of contest with him. He is there only in written texts—in fact, he is emblematized as martyr and hero—and not-there in any physical sense, both because she cannot remember him herself and because he lies in an unmarked grave. While Klepfisz searches the Warsaw death indexes for her father, "hoping to see the name / and to catch sight of a familiar grave," she mourns his unnameability, for the location of his grave is not known (1990b, 29). She longs to lay him to rest, but instead he remains alive, and actively resistant to the danger and death, in the fragmentary narratives of the Warsaw Ghetto Uprising that interrupt the text. In two long quotations (set off in italics), Michal Klepfisz's fellow fighters narrate his heroic act of throwing himself onto a German machine gun so his comrades can escape an ambush. As Leonard Diepeveen has described the exact quotation within a poem, it "complicates and decenters the subject" (1993, 18). Klepfisz's voice is indeed destabilized by the hero-narratives, for she is not capable of any full elegiac expression of grief; she is haunted by a lack of closure and in fact invites the disjuncture of yet another quotation, which describes her father asleep among the graves in a cemetery while working for the underground. Thus, Klepfisz's search for a completion to her father's life and to this historical narrative is postponed: "It is here I see him most clearly / as he sleeps leaning against a tombstone / and dreams, never considering / where he himself will one day be buried" (1990b, 34).

The shadow of the father falls over the second poem, too, which begins with an epigraphic quotation stating that "the widow Rose and small daughter Irena survived and now reside in New York" (35). The highly irregular lines of this poem focus on the transformation of Rose from young wife of Michal, who "never believed / that he might die," to mother, Holocaust survivor, widow, and finally dressmaker in New York. The daughter, in contrast, is "a moving monument"; she stands a testament to her father and lights candles for deceased children at Holocaust memorial meetings (37). In the last half of the poem, the imagery grows stark as the widow and "half-orphan" live in a New York apartment "with an ivy-covered fire escape / which at night / clutched like a skeleton / at the child's bedroom wall" (37). The skeleton is the poet's father's; he refuses to give up "his strategic position" and is always present with the mother and child, as both "hero and betrayer," so that they "taste his ashes" when they sit down to meals (38). By virtue of the quotation at the beginning of the poem, Rose and Irena textually "survive" only in relation to the father, and they remain trapped in the history of his heroism and death.

History's control over the poet continues through the poems about Klepfisz's Jewish identity in *Periods of Stress* (1975). This volume is divided into two untitled sections; the first continues to explore the events and effects of the Holocaust, while the second includes poems about Klepfisz's self-exploration in terms of gender and her relationships with other women. In two poems about her father, Klepfisz again finds herself suspended between the legacy of her father and the desire for historical closure. In "pow's," irregular spacing in broken lines gives a feeling of inconclusiveness and only half-understood truths, and disrupts the smooth self-expression expected from the lyric. The broken lines convey a ghostly dream image barely there, as well as the poet's desire to begin to see her father realistically:

>   he was old   and tired
> and so scarred   so very unlike   the image
> i have of him   he pulled his hat   down

over his eyes   ashamed   of his years   his
        shabbiness

(44)

In the final three lines of the poem, the speaker reflects on her own life
and the spaces become longer and longer in the pain of loss and grief
and her corresponding lack of clarity of identity:

                                    i am now   almost
        thirty-
two   should have borne   him a grandson   to carry
        his name   he came home   a bit   early

(44)

The lack of capitalization in this poem also indicates a destabilization of
voice, a very uncertain assertion of subjective presence in an ostensibly
lyrical piece.

"about my father" functions as a selective catalog of details about her
father's life and functions to subvert the "official" historical accounts of
Michal Klepfisz's life. Therefore, this poem indicates the poet's desire
to understand her father as a complex human being rather than as a
looming, legendary presence—he both "refused to hit me" by saying
"his hand / was too large" and "wrote to his aunt that he hoped the
baby would be a boy" (48). But the final important details—that he
jumped from a train bound for Treblinka, was shot at and actually
wounded and yet returned to Warsaw, that "he believed in resistance"
(48)—at least partially undermine the poet's desire to create her own
historical narrative of her father. Nevertheless, signs of the longing for
a coherent and final portrait of her father exist; though no capitalized
letters are used, the lines remain more uniform in length and unbroken.
Each long line is marked by dashes at the end, marking each of them as
a separate, important detail, but also signifying each as a separate item
in a historical accumulation of facts. With this past, Klepfisz challenges
the "official" written historical texts with her own personal history of
her father, breaking the chain of transmission and positing details to fill
in the gaps that keep her so tied to her past.

The rest of the Holocaust poems in *Periods of Stress* deal with women
characters, further revealing Klepfisz's desire to recover something from
her history that she can use to pursue survival. None of these, however,

are personal poems, indicating Klepfisz's continuing inability to express her surviving self in relation to her Jewish past; only one includes any autobiographical detail, and not in connection with the Holocaust figure described in the poem. Two of these are persona poems, in which Jewish women relate their experiences. In "herr captain," a Jewish woman succumbs to the sexual violence of a soldier in order to save her own life, while in "death camp," two Jewish women go to the death camps together. In "death camp," the speaker remembers going to the gas chamber with a rabitsin and crying out to her:

> i screamed   into the wall   as the blood burst from
> my lungs   cracking   her nails in women's flesh   i
>   watched
> her capsize   beneath me   my blood in her mouth   i
>   screamed
>
>   (47)

Klepfisz here not only adopts the persona of a person forced into a concentration camp and finally into the gas chambers, but she speaks as this person after death. In the final four lines of the poem the spaces become more uniform and the lines even rhythmic, so that the horror of death in the gas chamber and of cremation afterward are related in a kind of peace:

> my smoke
> was distinct   i rose quiet   left her
> beneath
>
>   (47)

In "perspectives on the second world war," Klepfisz relates in third person the narrative of a woman trying to hide her child; only in the final stanzas of this poem (the last in this section of the volume), does the poet herself become the speaker. Here, she begins to hint at some knowledge of her own experience, but she is still afraid to express it. She knows it would not be considered thoughtfully, but rather easily, as just another part of this emblematic history of the Holocaust, and nothing special because it involves women:

> listening to conversations   over brandy
> i am always amazed at their certainty

> about the past   how it could have been
> different   could have been   turned around
>
> (50)

She wishes to tell them her own experience, but feels intimidated, daunted by the carelessness with which they discuss such details. Again, the speaker feels trapped between the inevitable tragedy that weighs upon her through her father and the desire to speak her experience to others and potentially to be empowered into survival through it:

> it would be too impolite
> of me to say   my mother hid me
> for two years among ignorant peasants   who
> would have turned us in   almost at once
>
> (50)

Klepfisz continues to use the broken line, uneven spacing, and jagged lineation throughout these poems, as she does the lack of capitalization, further indicating the disjuncture she experiences between her Jewish self and her self as a woman. Nevertheless, they do represent a desire to express her woman-identification, and in this serve as a hint of the synthesis she attempts in her later poetry.

The most telling reference to her own life in fact comes at the beginning of this section of poems rather than at the end, in an untitled poem that functions almost like an epigraph; only ten short lines, this poem seems almost a guilty admission of survival, as if the speaker really did not deserve to escape the fate of the millions who perished in the Holocaust; the poet relates that during the Holocaust, German soldiers were known "to pick up infants / by their feet / swing them through the air / and smash their heads against plaster walls" (43). Again, this is historical detail, but this time she follows it with an autobiographical statement: "somehow / i managed / to escape that fate" (43). Because it is titleless, this poem operates as a kind of shadow to the poems it introduces. The poet's own history is still subsumed under the death count, the horror, of those who actually perished, whether her father the absent hero or Jewish women, those unsung heroes whose stories are largely absent from the historical record.

In the searingly personal poems of the second section of *Periods of Stress,* Klepfisz continues to use strategies of rupture within the lyric, indicating at once a desire to connect with self and to communicate with individual others and the incompletion of these acts. In "dinosaurs and larger issues," for instance, Klepfisz writes a dissection of the progress of a relationship in seven sections. While the poem outlines the process of developing intimacy, the breaks in line emphasize the ways this is not a continuous, enjoyable experience, as well as the ways that the two parties in the relationship themselves struggle to maintain identities separate from each other. Klepfisz here does not forge a statement of self-identity within the relationship; the joining of these two people overwhelms the poem, so that it finally is a statement about the power of women loving each other, rather than about women alone. Nevertheless, the two women together do somehow begin to recover a certain history. They share "the moans of an ancient language" that "echo through the cave" (61). Their intimacy mirrors the relationships of women through time, so that the poet delves deep into evolutionary history to express their union, and they become "tame and huge so much larger than we dared imagine" (62).

In "edges," however, a woman character does try to locate her own boundaries. The sections thus read something like a journal, and yet the broken lines retain the sense of disjuncture. But this poem, like "perspectives," is written in third person. The "I" is not present in this poem; the poet and subject do not converge. As Adrienne Rich has noted, the strategy of "deliberate distancing" through use of third person may be utilized by women who long for an identity but do not feel capable of expressing it directly or wholly (1979, 40). As in many instances, Klepfisz here uses natural imagery to illustrate lyrical feelings, a move that emphasizes her desire to know intimately some part of herself that she can only identify with a geographical location in landscape. She substitutes natural presences for the missing core of self: "the only reason she was not able to make it on her own / though she'd been on her own and alone most of her life / was that she'd never before been forced to distinguish / herself from trees or sand and sea . . ." (1990b, 76). The hyphenation at the end of the fourth line here indicates a desire for a line of a standard length, but what kind of line is not apparent: does she desire a poetic line or the justified line of prose writing? Thus, the twelve sections of this poem have the feeling of prose diary entries. They chronicle a series of days in which a woman fends off her fear and rage by contemplating nature as a mirror and studies the growth cycle of seeds. The bedroom also functions as a thread through these sections:

the shoreline scares the speaker, and the bedroom and the plants are her refuges. She cooks and freezes food and studies books about plants "try- ing to remember / old words she once knew: viscera   sta- sis   inchoate" (80). Finally, however, "it culminated in a rage she could not contain" (81). In the last section of the poem, the bedroom door is blown open by a draft, and she no longer attempts to separate herself from the ocean and becomes a kind of madwoman performing a ritual design and transferring her horticultural desires to self-preserva- tionist ones: ". . . she walked for a mile collect- / ing all the fish skulls she could find and arranged them in / concentric circles   placing a rock in the middle.   finally / she carried some large stones to the foot of a bluff   hoping / to prevent erosion" (81).

The poems that sandwich this section, "conditions" and "self-dia- logues," illustrate the conflicted nature of the poet's search for some sense of self. In both, her speaking self speaks to the nonspeaking self, while in "conditions" the unspeaking self is potentially unruly and must be punished, and in "self-dialogues," a constructive conversation be- tween the two selves actually begins. In "conditions," the speaker speci- fies the good behavior the nonspeaking self must display in order to be acknowledged at all:

> . . . and if: you want to go   and
> want to come   with me   back and forth
> smoothly   easily   you can   if: you do every
> thing exactly   precisely   as i want.
>
> (54)

In "self-dialogues," however, the nonspeaking self is spoken to with compassion and even taken care of in the end. The speaker dreams she is a tree and the nonspeaking self climbs in to rest: "wherever your human skin / touched my rough bark   i / sprouted branches   till / lush with leaves   i grew" (94).

Klepfisz synthesizes the emphases of these two self-exploratory lyr- ics—one toward dispersal, one toward wholeness—in the theme of the long poem "Two Sisters: A Monologue." Like the two early poems "Searching for My Father's Body" and "The Widow and the Daughter," this poem is published only in *A Few Words*, even though it dates from 1978. It functions as a kind of bridge between the earlier and later work, and was actually written between *Periods of Stress* and *Keeper of*

Accounts. This long poem in seven sections offers the tension between two forces—history and survival—in Klepfisz's experience and resolves them in favor of the survivor. Within the text *A Few Words,* it functions similarly to chapter 7 in Anzaldúa's *Borderlands;* it identifies a mode of consciousness that can integrate both the pain of life in the margins and somehow supersede it in a bid for the survival of an ongoing self.

In the ways it deals with history, "Two Sisters" is not so unusual. Here, Klepfisz provides the official historical account of the lives of the two sisters and then creates their feelings within the poem. In this way, she doubles back to her use of historical detail in the two early poems, although the historical account does not disrupt but introduces the poetic text here. It is significant that the historical account appears first; it demonstrates the poet's acknowledgment of that history but not her overt reliance on it. She states the account but then moves into poetic detail arising from her own interpretation of the facts, an interpretation that in turn also relates to her own journey.

In the historical account, she relays that Helen and Eva were born in Hamburg, Germany, in 1936. The girls were separated from their parents for a few months during the war; they were sent on a children's train to Holland, but their aunt and uncle never arrived to pick them up, so they spent the rest of their time away from their parents in a Catholic orphanage. In 1939, the Hesse family emigrated to the United States. The two sisters grew up, married; Eva became an artist, divorced, and was diagnosed as having a brain tumor. She died at age thirty-three, in 1970. Klepfisz then shares that the poem is a monologue by Helen Hesse, sole surviving member of the Hesse family. Helen is the speaker of the poem and the survivor; thus the tension between past and present is resolved in favor of the woman who wishes to endure. The two sisters serve as doubles, one a hard-edged survivor, the other consistently overcome by the past and finally unable to go on. These sisters—one of whom survives "just by my own will" and one who dies because "young death is suicide no matter what" (104)—represent the options available for a woman tied to history as Klepfisz is.

Besides ostensibly paying tribute to the Hesse sisters, this poem also functions as a kind of eulogy for Klepfisz's close friend and contemporary Elza Frydrych Shatzkin, a child survivor of the Holocaust and gifted writer who committed suicide when she was twenty-five (1989, 165–67; 1990a, 167–68). In the final line of the poem, Helen mourns the final demise of her double: "Eva, sister—what dreams we both had"

(104). But this sentence of nostalgia is itself preceded by the first clear bid for survival in Klepfisz's poetry; Helen chooses survival through her children, of whom she says ". . . I want them to know / how easily these battles are   lost" (104).

The Self in History: Keeper of Accounts

This reckoning with history comes to full fruition in Klepfisz's next volume, *Keeper of Accounts*. In the first section of this work, she still relies on persona; "From the Monkey House and Other Cages" explores female oppression through the experiences of entrapment and despair of two females monkeys born and raised in a zoo. In stark diction, Klepfisz metaphorizes women's desire and their inability to help each other under brutal conditions. Again, broken lines indicate the pain involved in such a social location; at the end of "Monkey II," one female mourns the death of another and longs for another place: "dizzy / with messages i would lie / down dream of different / enclosures" (128). "Different Enclosures" is the title of the second section, a series of autobiographical poems about the relationships among women office workers, and a direct parallel to the situation of the monkeys. In "Work Sonnets, with notes and a Monologue about a Dialogue," Klepfisz expresses her own experience in a variation on the sonnet; she adds one line at the end and uses no rhyme scheme. In "Notes," she relates in prose diary form her conversations with another office worker, who resists her ideas that they should demand more for themselves in their job, and her speculations about the worker's life and why she remains in such a low-level job. In "A Monologue about a Dialogue," the poet adopts the persona of the other worker herself to explore the assertions of the poet that she wants to do something more, she wants " 'to do special important work' " (149). This use of prose indicates Klepfisz's increasing discomfort with the restrictions of poetry; she moves between the extension of the traditional form of the sonnet into purely prose segments to express women's experience fully. Similarly, the voice in the lyrical love poems in the section "Urban Flowers" is more assured, better able to express women's feelings of connection and separation using more standardized line lengths, fewer broken lines and more uniform spacing, and capitalizations and punctuation.

In "Inhospitable Soil," the fourth and final section of *Keeper of Accounts*, Klepfisz fully challenges "official" historical texts with the assertion of her own experience and the historical personages of other women, and she does both of these with a bold subjective presence. It is also in this section that Klepfisz presents her most innovative formal challenges: the erosion of the boundaries between poetry and prose and the use of Yiddish bilingually with English. The poem *"Bashert"* lies at the core of this section. In its highly ritualized first two sections, Klepfisz writes her own memorialistic history of the Holocaust. In the four sections that follow, she unflinchingly relates, in alternately straightforward and lyrical prose, her own and her mother's harrowing experience of the Holocaust.

Unlike the poem's prose sections, the first two sections are not numbered, indicating that they are more transcendent, less autobiographical; Klepfisz clearly intends these sections to fulfill a public function as memorial texts. Their chantlike repetition has a ritualized feel and brings to mind the Kaddish. As James McCorkle has noted, these sections are *"as if* they are sacred, and as such, through the transformative process of incorporating the clearly ritual trope of anaphora, they *become"* sacred texts (1992, 180). The first section offers the memory of those who died in the Holocaust without reverting to simple nostalgia; that is, rather than become heroic emblems of a certain era, the people in Klepfisz's ritualistic remembrance function as human beings in all their complexity. They become sacred ancestors without losing the faces of their real lives, and in the process history does not gain so much power that it robs human beings of individual desires and frustrations or of their singular struggles in the face of massive destruction. This is evident in the first seven lines:

> These words are dedicated to those who died
> because they had no love and felt alone in the world
> because they were afraid to be alone and tried to stick it out
> because they could not ask
> because they were shunned
> because they were sick and their bodies could not resist the
> disease
>
> (1990b, 183)

These lines call to mind the somber dedication to the act of remembering that characterized the Jewish *akademyes* (memorial meetings) that Klepfisz regularly attended as a child in Brooklyn. Klepfisz has written that she found *di akademyes* "frightening and upsetting" while they simultaneously "instilled in me an enormous sense of pride in Jews, most of whom, under the worst circumstances, showed humaneness and heroism" (1990a, 146). These gatherings, she recalls, gave her a sense of "peoplehood"—the unity of Jews who were not to blame for the suffering they experienced (146).

However, even as this text too becomes a tool for such powerful rememberings, it is accompanied by a parallel memorializing text for those who *survived*. With this move, Klepfisz ritualizes her belief that the lives of those who died must be connected to those who can go on living, and that those who go on living should be able to endure the pain and suffering contained in memory and to survive. Both those who died and those who lived on were subject to history as it is *bashert*—inevitable, (pre)destined. Even as those who died are not given complete power through valorization, the survivors too are understood as complex humans subject to history:

> These words are dedicated to those who survived
> because they refused to give up and defied statistics
> because they had faith and trusted in God
> because they expected the worst and were always prepared
>   because they were angry
>
> (1990b, 185)

In these highly stylized, ritualized pieces, Klepfisz avoids the broken line; though she has used it in almost all of her poetry to this point, she does not use it here both because it would defeat the anaphoric pattern and the rhythm of the chant and because through these she wishes to convey the way that deceased and survivor are conjoined. They form a seamless group relating to the same history, rather than a valorized past and a completely fragmented future. While the feeling of control comes and goes in her earlier work, Klepfisz seems in full command in *Bashert*. She purposefully creates a sense of history as not only important but highly personal and vital to survival. Klepfisz begins to write history herself, through the lives of individual Jews, Jewish women, and her individual experience of the Holocaust. In other words, as she develops a full sense of the personal, the political no longer overwhelms her; instead, she is able to make the connections between them and to assert both a sustainable self and a relationship to her respective communities.

The four numbered prose sections of *Bashert* that follow are intensely revealing; they trace Klepfisz and her mother's harrowing, life-threatening experiences in Poland and their escape and then Klepfisz's journey, as an adult, toward some understanding of her status as a Holocaust survivor. This move into prose indicates a willingness on Klepfisz's part to convey as precisely as she can her experience as a woman in relation to Jewish history and to do this together with the ritualistic remembrances of all those who were affected by the Holocaust. Though the broken line and uneven lineation will no longer work to express Klepfisz's marginalization and her desire for a surviving self, neither can she, it seems, trust an even, rhythmic line for narrating her own story. She wants to relate it as precisely as possible, and so she turns to prose. The prose itself slips in and out of the lyrical, moving from prose poem to simple prose and back to the prose poem. At the end of the first section, "Poland: My mother is walking down a road," for instance, the details of starvation, passing, and unceasing fear have accrued to build some narrative suspense. The last two paragraphs bring a hopeful denouement, as her mother meets, quite by accident, one of her father's former teachers: "They do not cry, but weep as they chronicle the dead and count the living. Then they rush to me. To the woman I am a familiar sight. She calculates that I will not live out the week, but comments only on my striking resemblance to my father. She says she has contacts. She leaves. One night a package of food is delivered anonymously. We eat. We begin to bridge the gap towards life. We survive" (189).

The second and third sections are especially significant in that they bridge the gap between Klepfisz's childhood in Poland and her adult life in the United States; they are set in Chicago and Brooklyn respectively, and chart the development of Klepfisz's own consciousness of herself as a marginalized citizen of the United States, as a racial/ethnic, lesbian outsider and a perpetual citizen of the historical borderlands. Finally, she is able to address at once both her Jewish past and her lesbian feminist present. This is nevertheless a painful juncture. In the second section, as she walks home at midnight, she understands that "the city is alien" and that she feels isolated, "baffled at how to make a place for myself in this larger, gentile world which I have entered" (190). The landscape of the inner city threatens demise—"Everything is waiting for the emptiness to close in on itself" (190). Amidst this despair, Klepfisz remembers her friend Elza, recounts her struggle as an orphan after the war, her adoption, her promising career as a writer/

scholar, and her suicide at twenty-five. She remembers that her mother instructed their friends to keep the news of Elza's death from her; Rose was fearful that her daughter also lived on the edge. Through Elza, Klepfisz remembers two very important episodes that become central to her conception of history. In the first, a shopkeeper says to the young Elza, " 'Very accurate. Just like a Jew. Perhaps you are a little Jewess?' " (192). In the second, Elza tells Klepfisz that "Jews . . . made a terrible mistake," that is, they stopped acting like human beings (192). At this point, Klepfisz ponders the meaning of history: "Are there moments in history which cannot be escaped or transcended, but which act like time warps permanently trapping all those who are touched by them?" (192). She says then that she begins to "develop perspective," as she understands that "no one simply passes through. History keeps unfolding and demanding a response" (193). History strikes in a multitude of ways: "I see now the present dangers, the dangers of the void, of the American hollowness in which I walk calmly day and night as I continue my life. I begin to see the incessant grinding down of lines for stamps, for jobs, for a bed to sleep in, of a death stretched imperceptibly over a lifetime" (193). Finally she begins to understand that history does not necessarily discriminate, that her own history has been repeated many times. In the life of Chicago's poor, she begins to "understand the ingenuity of it. The invisibility. The Holocaust without smoke" (193).

In section 3, Klepfisz articulates the ways her split selves begin to cohere. She wants to know herself as Jewish woman, as a Jewish feminist. She finds that she is "almost equidistant from two continents" (194)—one dominated by the history her father represents, the other by her immersion in the desires of the young students she teaches, all themselves on the margins of American culture by virtue of their racial/ ethnic status. In the center of this section, Klepfisz retreats into memory to illustrate her inability to know a coherent self under the effects of history; she recalls lighting a candle at a memorial meeting, and feeling herself "dissolving" (195). But in the present, she longs to become a natural element connecting the two continents, recalling her identification with landscape in "edges": "I am almost equidistant from two continents. I look back towards one, then forward towards the other. There is a need in me to become transparent like water, to become the salt water which is their only connection" (196). When a student asks, " 'What are you?' " Klepfisz answers that she is a Jew, and begins to pull her split selves into a whole: "In my muscles, my flesh, my bone, I balance the heritages, the histories of two continents" (197).

In the final section of "*Bashert,*" Klepfisz completes the historical project she began in the first two chantlike sections; she proposes herself "a keeper of accounts," reexamining Jewish history for the stories of women's lives. This approach to history represents one completion in her struggle to bring together past and present, self and community, woman and Jew. Of course, "keeper of accounts" has multiple implications; not only does she "account" for women's lives in Jewish history, but she wants to tally their individual experiences and their general power as part of her reckoning with the past. These meanings transform the stereotype of the Jew as miser (" 'Perhaps you are a little Jewess?' ") by giving it a positive function for the Jewish feminist. Representing the ways Klepfisz understands that she must break form, genre, and language in order to speak a surviving self, this section is both the thematic fruition of her poetic themes and the broadest formal challenge. She combines prose and poetry, unbroken and broken poetic lines. She uses capitalization and punctuation in some fragments and not in others, and she interlingually uses Yiddish and English.

When encountered with the stereotype of the miserly Jewess, she says, "Yes. It's true. All true. I am scrupulously accurate. I keep track of all distinctions. Between past and present. Pain and pleasure. Living and surviving . . . Between life and death. Yes. I am scrupulously accurate. I have become a keeper of accounts" (198). She calls on the lives of "shabby scholars" and "inhuman usurers and dusty pawnbrokers" who were subject to "the magistrates that drew the boundaries of their lives and declared them diseased"; like "my despised ancestors," she says, she has become a keeper of accounts. But the most important move occurs next, when Klepfisz calls forth the women who had less power than Jewish men, including "the matriarchs, the wives and daughters, the sisters and aunts, the nieces, the keepers of button shops, milliners, seamstresses, peddlers of foul fish" (199). Significantly, it is at this point that Klepfisz returns to poetry, rhythmically "accounting" for the lives of women

> who understood the accounts but saw them differently
> who knew the power of human laws, knew they always
>   counted

> no matter what the revolution or the party or the state
> who knew the power of the words *Zyd, Jif, Jüde*
>
> (199)

Klepfisz asserts these women as the primary creators and users of Yiddish culture; they "argued in the common tongue" (199). With this account of Jewish women's experiences, Klepfisz fully enters history, rather than being overwhelmed by it. Upon claiming herself as a Jewish feminist, and committing herself to the lives of her Jewish women ancestors, she is not afraid of the "legacy" of Jewish history, of the Holocaust. The self she asserts is now able to move back and forth between past and present, from historical texts that picture for her "the hair being shaved" or "the endless fields of hair" to survival. She holds a sense of self in spite of her marginalization. She loses any sense of time, and "like acceptance like the refusal to deny," answers for herself the question "Perhaps you are a little Jewess?":

> Yes. It is true.   I am a keeper of accounts.
> *Bashert*
>
> (200)

The poet is able to leave behind the fragmentation of being caught between her heritage and the dominant culture by claiming herself as a Jewish woman intimately connected to the history of her people.

Interlingualism and Celebrating History

In the new poems grouped under the title "A Few Words in the Mother Tongue," Klepfisz develops her concept of interlingual poetry; this reclamation of her Yiddish culture is the logical extension of her coming to terms with her history as a Jewish woman. "*Di rayze aheym*/The journey home" reenacts the joining of two continents that provides the energy for "*Bashert*." This poem is written in third person, but also uses first-person plural, giving the sense that Klepfisz is writing for herself but also for other Jewish women—herself, her mother, other survivors— and is providing an anatomy of the process of constructing a bridge between the American present and the Jewish (Yiddish) past. In section 1, the woman looks out the window where "all is present" and "the shadows of the past / fall elsewhere" (216). All she sees is "wilderness" in which ". . . our tongues have become / dry . . ." (216). Significantly, no Yiddish appears in this section; Klepfisz is representing the experience of Jewish-American women alienated from their "mother," Yiddish culture, and the "mother tongue," Yiddish. It is "forgotten speech" in the present (216).

In the poem's second section, the woman searches for her history and realizes "It is there / *di gantse geshikhte* / *fun folk* / the entire history / of the people" (217). In the third and fourth sections, she flies back to the European continent and rests on a wall, only to sight a wasteland on one side and a cemetery on the other. In sections five and six, she asks questions of the past and becomes ashamed that she has forgotten so much that "even the ghosts / do not understand me" (221). The seventh and eighth sections deal with her fears that the "strangers" of both her past and present will not understand her language, and she begins to force out sound:

> unformed sound:
> a
> *der klang*
> > the sound
> o
> *dos vort*
> > the word
>
> > > > > (223)

With this speaking of the "mother tongue," the woman accomplishes, in the final section, "the journey home." She realizes that this place, though full of strangers, is her home. The revision of history is only complete with the recovery of the native language; with the memories and the spoken tongue, living as a marginalized one "among strangers" in the "wilderness" of America becomes bearable, and "*Ire zikhroynes* / her memories / will become monuments" (224). This final line is very significant, for the Jewish woman creates monuments with her Yiddish language, rather than solely acting as a monument in her own life; she takes charge of utterances of history, rather than being controlled by them.

In "*Etlekhe verter oyf mame-loshn*/A few words in the mother tongue," Klepfisz goes on to further revise stereotypes of and differences among Jewish women by playing on Yiddish words and their meanings. She defines each Yiddish word and then reinterprets the definition: "*di kurve* the whore / a woman who acknowledges her passions / / *di yidene* the Jewess the Jewish woman / ignorant overbearing / let's face it: every woman is one" (225). Klepfisz connects her own sexuality to the use of Yiddish by women, defining the term lesbian in that language: "*di lezbianke* the one with / a roommate though we never used / the word" (225).

Of Klepfisz's linguistically innovative poems, this one comes closest to being bilingual. The third section is written entirely in Yiddish. The words used in this Yiddish passage have all already been defined by the context of the first section, however, so that the impulse seems to be to invite the reader to use the language with the interpretive tools provided by the poet. Any words not identified in English within the poem are translated in a glossary in the back of the text. In this use of bilingual poetry, Klepfisz differs from Anzaldúa; she wishes to preserve what she considers to be a culture in danger of extinction, while Anzaldúa asserts a language spoken by more and more people in America. Klepfisz is not uncomfortable with the role of translator but rather offers her bilingual poetry certainly as a challenge to the centrality of English but centrally in expression of her own integrated sense of herself as both Jew and American, both participant in Yiddish culture and language and American citizen. Through this use of Yiddish, she also continues the project of reclaiming the importance of Jewish women to the daily evolution of culture; she simultaneously praises *di lezbianke* and the one who goes to market "where she buys / *di kartofl un khalah* / (yes, potatoes and challah)" (225–26).

Conversation and the Self: "East Jerusalem, 1987"

Klepfisz ends *A Few Words in the Mother Tongue* with a new poem, "East Jerusalem, 1987: *Bet shalom* (House of Peace)," which is also prefaced with historical detail. This time, however, the historical narrative is of Klepfisz's own particular form of resistance as an adult, resistance that involves activism on behalf of both Jewish and Palestinian women. In 1987, Klepfisz met in East Jerusalem with a group of Jewish women writers (both American and Israeli) and Palestinian women "to express feelings and responses" to the Israeli occupation of the West Bank and Gaza (237). The ongoing historical implications of this poem are marked by Klepfisz's comment that she could not write about the meeting until after the *intifada* began, and she dedicates it to one of the Palestinian women, whom Klepfisz says she is afraid to name because of the danger such public recognition could bring. In this poem, Klepfisz intersperses pieces of the conversation at the meeting—she narrates a historical event—and in doing so, interposes her own poetic musing amidst the words of others. In contrast to the poem "Search for My Father's Body," Klepfisz here is not overwhelmed by history but seeks to help write it. She explores her own identity as a Jewish woman and as a woman concerned about the fate of other women, about the differences between women and how they may be worked out. Significantly, the voices of various women are woven throughout this poem. The spacing between stanzas is tripled, giving the impression of various voices mingling in discussion. Occasional stanzas even rely on a "we," alternately the collective voice of the Israeli women, the Palestinian women, and the Jewish-American women. And sometimes the voices of the various communities blend together, as one woman tells the writers to share her story, and the writers respond: "You mean: Our voices carry. / Yours alone does not" (239). The final two stanzas of this poem convey the deep understanding of history, and thus of the importance of valuing difference, that Klepfisz has reached through her poetic innovations and thematic explorations. She leaves the conversation, and later imagines the Palestinian women with "battered suitcases" and "stuffed pillowcases." She imagines "children running to catch up" and realizes the power that one group can have over another, the same power that caused her own childhood migration during the Holocaust (239). In the last stanza, Jerusalem—the geographical center of her Jewish history—becomes the symbol of both her own necessary attention to her own history and her ability to see in it the history of others. She understands that attention to history and attention to differences among Jews, among women, carries the responsibility of remembering: ". . . if I / forget thee oh Jerusalem / Oh Hebron may I forget / my own past my pain / the depth of my sorrow" (240).

Conclusion: Rewriting History, Writing the Self

Both Anzaldúa and Klepfisz conduct challenging experiments with individual voice and poetic form, genre, and language. Both seek to rewrite histories that have marginalized them in order to cope with the effects of their own location as women on the racial/ethnic borders of contemporary America. Both seek to write a surviving self in the process. However, the differences between them are also instructive for a feminist poetics. While Anzaldúa challenges the genre of poetry itself by engaging it within a multivoiced, multigeneric text, Klepfisz revises and refines poetic forms themselves and the ways voice can be constructed within these forms. While Anzaldúa needs to rewrite a history that was imposed upon her by the dominant culture, Klepfisz has to reckon with the absence of women within Jewish history and the very power of history itself to situate her not only on the margins of the dominant culture but between life and death. While Anzaldúa theorizes and then attempts to enact textually a "mestiza" consciousness, Klepfisz conveys the integration of her fragmented identities through quiet formal shifts occurring over several works of poetry.

These differences can be very fruitful for further exploring the diverse perspectives of feminist poets writing from the racial/ethnic margins of American culture. While feminist poets in the margins necessarily write an avant-garde poetry—by virtue of their social location, they challenge the limits of current literary practice(s)—and while they employ similar strategies, these strategies shape each poet's work differently and produce a rich body of poetic direction that further expands the importance and influence of the feminist poetry movement.

Five

History, Myth, and Empowerment in Joy Harjo's Poetry

> That's what I mean to tell you. On the other side of the place
>   you live stands
> a dark woman. She has been trying to talk to you for years.
> You have called the same name in the middle of a nightmare,
> from the center of miracles. She is beautiful.
> This is your hatred back. She loves you.
>
> (1990a, 59)

In the poem "Transformations," the Creek poet Joy Harjo releases the hold that racism and sexism have had on her by "giving back" these hatreds to their source, which her use of second person suggests may even be her reader.[1] This single passage illustrates Harjo's location as a Native American and feminist poet of the 1970s and 1980s, when both these groups did significant work in establishing strong poetic traditions related to the political and historical contexts of their respective communities. Much like Gloria Anzaldúa, Harjo needs to identify an ongoing, surviving self in the face of devastating cultural and political oppressions, while at the same time she cherishes her roots in a tribal culture that does not separate art from life and she wishes to develop a collective and functional poetic connection to readers in general as well as to her Native and her women's communities.

My objective in this reading of her poetry is to understand exactly how Harjo blends Native American and feminist politics and aesthetics, weaving together Native Americans' and women's mythical and real-time stories, and developing a subjective and coalitional presence that resists oppression. Harjo's task is not easy because of the difficulties involved in crossing back and forth between two very different cultures, and especially in light of the extent of the cultural destruction Native Americans have experienced at the hands of Anglo-American society (out of which feminist discourse arises). I will explore how Harjo uses her concept of "empowerment" to combine the community-oriented aesthetics and mythological grounding of Native tribal traditions with the focus on difference and celebration of women's lives that feminist poetry's coalitional voice allows. I will then examine, in two volumes of Harjo's poetry, how this combination "empowers" the poet herself not only to survive her marginalized status as both Native American and woman but to persuade her respective communities to act against destructive social forces. In *She Had Some Horses* (1983), Harjo writes third-person narrative poems, highly lyrical expressions of personal revelations, and the heavily ritualized, performance-oriented "She Had Some Horses," which work together to achieve a personal, communal, and hopeful use of myth, story, and history in the attempt to survive. In *In Mad Love and War* (1990), Harjo moves toward coalitional voice—and thus fully toward collective empowerment—by writing deeply personal prose lyric-narratives and long-line lyric-narratives that can both bear the burden of a detailed history of destruction and achieve individual and community survival through myth and story.

Connecting Tribal Life and Feminism

Like Anzaldúa and Irena Klepfisz, Harjo faces some difficulty in synthesizing her multiple cultural traditions and political locations. As Harjo herself has stated, the relationships between Native American life and feminism have historically been very complex and varied. While Dexter Fisher has asserted that for many Native American women poets, "feminism is synonymous with heritage, and a search for one yields a concern with the other" (1980, 13), Harjo herself asserts that the roots of feminism in Western ideas of individual rights and freedoms and its tendency to emphasize a vision that deals with only one half of the community makes it in many ways an alien concept in tribal settings (1990b, 60).[2] While Harjo uses the word "feminist" for herself in the American context off the reservation, she says, "The word 'feminism' doesn't carry over to the tribal world" (60).[3] By utilizing a different word that encompasses the aims of both Native and feminist communities, Harjo arrives at an understanding of feminism compatible with Native life, even though all the cultural trappings of the women's movement are not readily understood or accepted in Native cultures. While the cultural bases of the political philosophy of the women's movement make feminism a foreign term in Native tribal life, she asserts that "a concept mirroring similar meanings" *would* work. She says, "Let's see, what would it then be called—empowerment" (60).

This notion of empowerment, as Harjo develops it, involves a constant dialectic between individual and community in the conviction that, out of this relationship, a rich cultural life and positive political change can occur; this notion certainly resonates with the feminist conception that art and life, art and politics, and the personal and the political are not separable. Thus, Harjo does fit the profile of the Native American woman poet that Dexter Fisher supplies—she understands her work as a Native American and as a feminist to be coterminous— through the understanding of empowerment as essential to the survival of both Native American and women's cultures (Fisher 1980, 13). Harjo is engaged through her poetry in the project of recovering and/ or building a sense of women's ability to persevere and survive as well as of women's community; she conducts a parallel exercise on behalf of her Native culture; and finally she understands both these moves as intimately connected to and supporting one another.

Harjo faces a related dilemma, however; she writes poetry, a Western literary form, a fact that complicates her allegiance to Native understandings of the cultural and collective relevance of art. As Silvester J. Brito has noted, Indian songs, chants, and prayers are oral narratives located in an ancient tradition and oriented to communal life, and all of these have been erroneously identified (by Westerners) as poetry, which is the textualized expression of individual consciousness. He goes on to point out that young Native American writers, as a result of the profound changes that colonialism has wrought in their cultures, have nevertheless turned to poetry (1984, 27–28). Like feminist poets, these Native Americans have developed their own poetic tradition (Brito calls it "protest poetry") that works inside and yet against the Anglo-American literary tradition. This poetry is important first of all because, together with other Native American writers as well as feminist poets like Anzaldúa and Klepfisz, Harjo must overcome personal, internal barriers to speech, which are sometimes conditioned by her respective communities themselves. But in poetry she can also emphasize community; out of her commitment to both Native and feminist aesthetics, she can shape poetry to incorporate the understandings of the functional and communal nature of story and art that are part of her Native heritage, simultaneously connect to feminist understandings of coalitional voice and collective survival, and also communicate in a form that circulates in the dominant American culture.

Harjo has stated clearly that she understands the responsibility that the cultural function of art in Native American life places on the artist, and the integral relationship between community and individual implied in this responsibility: "I feel strongly that I have a responsibility to all the sources that I am: to all past and future ancestors, to my home country, to all places that I touch down on and that are myself, to all voices, all women, all of my tribe, all people, all earth, and beyond that to all beginnings and endings. In a strange kind of sense it frees me to believe in myself, to be able to speak, to have voice, because I have to; it is my survival" (quoted in Bruchac 1983, 92). This responsibility is thus the basis not only for cultural but for personal survival, and it is at the heart of the difference between the aesthetic orientations of dominant American culture and Native American tribal cultures. Harjo has described the value of the artist in Western societies and pointed to the "ideal community" in tribal life as an example of a more culturally significant art. In contrast to American culture, in which "many artists have separated themselves from the community" and "art has been separated from the community" and turned into "big business," "in tribal communities, the value of the visionaries—the musicians and writers—was in what they did (and still do) for the community, and their contributions were seen as crucial to the community's health." In an ideal society, Harjo says, artists would be respected and valued for their work and "would be paid to do that work by the rest of the society because of what they give back" (1993, 93).

The Hopi feminist poet Wendy Rose has written extensively on this matter, and echoes Harjo's assertions. Rose's comments focus especially on the artist her/himself and the artist's role in the community. She says that while the artist in American culture is conceived to be the epitome of the demand for personal freedom, and must produce works of art in solitude and apart from the flow of everyday life, the artist is an integral member of daily community life in Native traditions. Rose maintains that in Western aesthetics, artists form a "special elite" who are "nonutilitarian, self-expressive, solitary, ego-identified, self-validating, innovative," while in Native traditions, "art must be community-oriented . . . , it must be useful, it must be beautiful and functional at the same time (the ideas are inseparable, for functioning is part of beauty, and vice versa), it is good if more than one person has a hand in its production," and many times a "party (or feast, or ceremony) is part of the art form" (1992, 411–12). In Native life the artist is not separated from society; she or he is understood to contribute a vital skill necessary to the ongoing life of the community.

Feminist poetry as it was developed beginning in the late 1960s shares many of these characteristics, although they were developed from *within* the Western tradition and in resistance to it, while Native understandings of story and art are ancient and self-sustaining. Nevertheless, feminist poets' notions of the functional and collective dimensions of art do coincide with Native beliefs, and therefore Harjo has a cultural bridge over which she can pursue her goal of empowerment. Describing the specific ways she crosses this bridge, however, first requires a deeper exploration of her relationship to both the Native and feminist literary traditions, as well as of her understandings of Native American metaphysics.

History, Colonialism, Language: Native American Women Writing

Harjo joins other Native Americans to participate in a relatively new Native written tradition in order to assert alternative interpretations of history and the ongoing importance of myth for Native Americans and in fact to maintain that these considerations of memory and history can be important for non-Native Americans as well. The imposition of written language on the oral tradition of Native Americans has been part of the effort by Anglo-Americans to supplant indigenous cultures with colonialist structures since the mid 1800s, and the effects have been devastating. Harjo is one descendant of a group of writers who began "to tell their side of the story" and to rely on sources from the oral tradition to build a written tradition so that "the word continued to be equated with ways of knowing and of passing knowledge on" (Fisher 1980, 7).[4] Thus, Harjo asserts in the poem "Autobiography" that the version of the history and effects of colonialism imposed on Native Americans by the United States cannot destroy the memory and cultural meanings her people hold dear: "We were a stolen people in a stolen land. Oklahoma meant defeat. But the sacred lands have their own plans, seep through fingers of the alcohol spirit. Nothing can be forgotten, only left behind" (1990a, 14).

The survival of any cultural tradition depends in part on language, and Native American writers have realized how important it is that the very structure of their tribal languages involves a particular worldview. Harjo has said that English "is a male language, not tribal, not spiritual enough" (1981, 9). She has used English as her primary language, and even as she expresses herself in this language, she recognizes the differences between her own tribal linguistic heritage and the Indo-European linguistic system: "I have learned to love the language, or rather what the language can express. But I have felt bound by the strictness imposed by its male-centeredness, its emphasis on nouns. So, it's also challenging, as a poet, to use it to express tribal, spiritual language, being. But maybe all poets basically are after that, and sometimes it isn't enough and that's when those boundaries become frustrating" (quoted in Bruchac 1983, 62–63). In contrast, says Harjo, the center of tribal languages "often has nothing to do with things, objects, but contains a more spiritual sense of the world" (63).

Nevertheless, Harjo also says that an element missing from English that one finds in tribal "land-based" languages is "a spirit of place" (63). She has a sense of the way human interaction goes beyond spoken language and the way that language emanates from the land. In "Eagle Poem," prayer "to sky, to earth, to sun, to moon" opens language into its essential physicality:

> And know there is more
> That you can't see, can't hear,
> Can't know except in moments
> Steadily growing, and in languages
> That aren't always sound but other
> Circles of motion
>
> (1990a, 65)

The conclusion of her poem "Bleed-Through" addresses the fundamental power of sound itself: "There are no words, only sounds / that lead us into the darkest nights / where stars burn into ice / where the dead rise again / to walk in shoes of fire" (1990a, 36). For Harjo, as well as for many other Native American writers, landscape emits sound, which becomes human utterance and eventually systems of language. This view partakes of Native metaphysics, in which the land—material surfaces—"bespeaks" the spiritual; human beings, as one group equal and not above earth and its creatures, nevertheless express the spiritual in the unique forms of language.[5]

As a Native American who uses English but recognizes the importance of her own tribal language, Harjo also writes about the experience of living between languages, using one because of its cultural prevalence and yet identifying with the other. This is the theme of "For Alva Benson, And For Those Who Have Learned to Speak." In this poem, Harjo explores the "land-based" language from a Native perspective as she writes that the Navajo language is deeply connected to the earth in the act of birth:

> And the ground spoke when she was born. Her mother heard
>   it. In Navajo she answered
> as she squatted down against the earth
> to give birth . . .
>
>   (1983, 18)

The child learns both "voices," but though she speaks in both Navajo and English, she sees people in urban areas unable to ". . . hear the ground as it spun around / beneath them." She adopts the spiritual position of the ground through fostering her understanding of the spiritual roots of the Navajo language: ". . . She learned to speak for the ground, / the voice coming through her like roots that have long hungered for water." When her own daughter is born, she too is gifted with the ability to be ". . . in either place / or all places . . ." (1983, 18–19). Similarly, Harjo speaks to the spirit of Anna Mae Pictou Aquash, an American Indian Movement (AIM) activist who was secretly buried by Federal officials and only later given a proper Sioux burial, "the second time in Lakota, a language that could free you" ("For Anna Mae Pictou Aquash," 1990a, 8). Even in death, Aquash may not be properly united with her people unless her community asserts the importance of her tribal tongue.

These Native views of language came under attack when Western models of education were forced on Native Americans by the U.S. government in its effort to supplant indigenous culture entirely. As Paula Gunn Allen has noted, Indians found little use for written traditions for they had relied on oral traditions for centuries before Europeans began arriving on the continent. In addition, as Allen says, since "instruction in literacy" was one tool of colonialization and was enforced through separating children from their families and forbidding them to speak their native language, "their reluctance to take up pen and write is hardly surprising" (1989, 15). While in the nineteenth century Indian men shared narratives with missionaries, folklorists, and ethnographers, and while some of them became journalists and cultural critics, not until the twentieth century did Indian women really begin recording their own stories. Paula Gunn Allen maintains that women generally were reluctant to share their stories with men; Rayna Green has likewise demonstrated that many of these earlier writers were dedicated to the survival of their cultural traditions in the face of Euro-American educational and cultural practices but were inhibited by the white, often male, interlocutors who "assisted" them in transferring their words to the page (1984, 4; Allen 1989, 15–17).

Women like Emily Pauline Johnson (1861–1913, Mohawk), Ella Deloria (1888–1971, Sioux), Zitkala a (1876–1938, Sioux), Humishuma (1888–1936, Okanogan), and Mourning Dove (1888–1936, Okanogan), however, moved from recording tribal practices and stories to writing their own works (Green 1984, 3; Fisher 1985). These women, who have received critical attention and have been increasingly republished since 1980, form a powerful heritage for contemporary women Native writers; they established a transitional body of work, moving from the oral traditions of the tribes into Western forms and opening up communication with the dominant culture. Their increasing focus on Western notions of literature—on creative expression through fiction and poetry—expanded and refined the idea of the artist as the transmitter of culture in Native environments. The effect of this early tradition is crucial, for while contemporary Native women writers rarely convey Native ceremonial stories and chants themselves in their entirety, as Green asserts, the "psychic and symbolic landscape of Indian country—complete with animals, spirits, parts of the natural landscape—combines with specifically tribal or pan-Indian social references—foods, dances, ceremonies, joking" to provide the Native setting for much of their work (1984, 5). The contemporary literary scene is increasingly peopled by talented and visionary Native American women who rely on this heritage.[6]

As Green goes on to say, even as many Indian writers address their connections to their Indian heritages, they must also refer to the context of contemporary life. The Native world is not background—it is central—but Native American literature is not just a compendium of all of the old stories. Rather it is a new mixture, a blend of ancient and new, a combination of traditional and contemporary ideas and practices. In this kind of literature, the "half-breed" has played a special role. As the racially mixed, as the one with ties to both Native and non-Native culture(s), the half-breed especially signifies the ways the traditional Native and the modern non-Native worlds have clashed and commingled. Herself of mixed Indian and European ancestry like Harjo, the writer Louise Erdrich says this "dual citizenship" is fruitful for literary expression, and yet the Indian voice is stronger and more insistent because it is "culturally different" (1987, 77). The half-breed, being both inside and outside, is more aware of the value of tradition and more committed to expressing her/his multiple backgrounds.

Feminist Women of Color Writing

In addition to her obvious connections to other Native American women writers, Harjo has also established a very direct line between herself and feminist poets of color, thereby extending her literary heritage across the borders of her Indian and non-Indian, her Indian and feminist affiliations. Harjo herself has had the experience of being identified and excluded as a woman of color in white women's organizations, and the exclusion she has felt in these settings mirrors that of many other women. Harjo says that "many women's groups have a majority of white women and I honestly can feel uncomfortable, or even voiceless sometimes" (1990b, 61). This illustrates how the intersection of feminism and Native American cultures is further complicated by varying degrees of sexism and racism. Many women in Native American societies have had more social power in gender structures that have often been egalitarian, while other Native American women have faced sexism as Native American communities have adopted Western practices (Cook-Lynn 1987, 71; Halsey and Jaimes 1992).[1] Likewise, in the feminist movement, racism has alternately held sway and been condemned.

Harjo's work stands in especially close relation to that of Audre Lorde. In the acknowledgments for *In Mad Love and War,* Harjo thanks Lorde for "her warrior self, her fierce and tender poetry" (see also 1989, 7; 1984). Herself marginalized to some degree in all of her communities, Lorde understood the tensions involved in the relationship between the individual and the community and the challenging work that can be produced if this tension is addressed. In Lorde's view, a "disciplined attention" to inner feelings means they can "become sanctuaries and spawning grounds for the most radical and daring of ideas" (1984, 32). In turn, this leads to a fearlessness about speaking and calling the community to be accountable for individual as well as collective silences: "We can learn to work and speak when we are afraid in the same way we have learned to work and speak when we are tired. For we have been socialized to respect fear more than our own needs for language and definition, and while we wait in silence for that final luxury of fearlessness, the weight of that silence will choke us" (44). Similarly, Harjo remains adamant about the power of writing to provide a sense of self to women who have felt silenced: "I don't believe I would be alive today if it hadn't been for writing. There were times when I was conscious of holding onto a pen and letting the words flow, painful and from the gut, to keep from letting go of it all." Harjo remembers that this was when she was young and full of internalized racism and sexism, and writing helped her to overcome her silence. She writes: "if we, as Indian people, Indian women, keep silent, then we will disappear, at least in this level of reality. As Audre Lorde says, also, 'Your silence will not protect you' " (1990b, 58).[7]

Lorde is indeed a powerful, groundbreaking example of a poet who mined her own cultural and racial history in order to rescue from the past the untold or buried stories of heroic women's lives, to create for herself a stronger identity because of the examples of these women, and to establish a substantial cultural tradition for readers who are similarly seeking to establish connections with feminist and racial heritages. With her volumes *The Black Unicorn* (1978) and *Our Dead Behind Us* (1986), Lorde made a highly significant contribution to the search for history on the part of women of color. In her poem "A Litany for Survival," she honors the ones who live in the gaps, who are caught in the in-between, caught between knowing fullness and being trapped in emptiness. The speaker identifies herself with this group by using the refrain "those of us who" and by exploring the effect of fear—"learning to be afraid with our mother's milk"—on the daily pressures and pleasures people face. Hunger produces the fear that "we may never eat again," but full stomachs produce a fear of indigestion. Likewise, the presence of love produces the fear that "love will vanish" and its absence the fear that "love will never return." The final fear Lorde lists is that "when we speak we are afraid / our words will not be heard / nor welcomed / but when we are silent / we are still afraid." The final line of the poem affirms the need to go on speaking and the importance of memory to recognizing the significance of the speaking act: "So it is better to speak / remembering / we were never meant to survive" (1978, 31–32).

In Harjo's "Anchorage," dedicated to Lorde, Harjo traces this process of survival through the history of her own Indian peoples. The reminders of emptiness in Lorde's poem occur in physical and emotional sensations; in Harjo, natural images—glaciers, a "storm of boiling earth," "spirits we can't see"—remind of the emptiness and fullness that have been available to her people. And the figure of a woman— "someone's Athabascan grandmother"—is the link to this past, the reminder that survival is connected to history and remembering. The poet says the task is to ". . . claim her / as our own history, and know that our dreams / don't end here . . ." (1983, 14). The poem ends with the story told by her friend Henry, who was shot at eight times and not hit, and was extremely surprised to find himself alive. The need to tell these stories and connect them back through the grandmother to the natural and cultural histories bound up in Indian life is indicated in the final lines, which echo and pay tribute to Lorde's poem: "Because who would believe / the fantastic and terrible story of all of our survival / those who were never meant / to survive?" (15). These lines function as an ironic comment on the impossibility and the actuality of Indian survival, as well as on the likelihood that non-Indians will not believe such stories of heroic daily life.

Harjo has similarly established her connections to June Jordan. She uses an excerpt from Jordan's poetry about survival to preface the first section of *In Mad Love and War*, entitled "The Wars": "We are not survivors of a civil war / We survive our love / because we go on / loving" (Jordan 1980, 90–91). In "Hieroglyphic," the poet addresses Jordan directly and speaks of her own heart as a "phoenix of swallowed myths" in which angry angels stalk the street and "tether skeleton horses" and then "tell you there is no heaven or hell; it's all the same" (1990a, 53). To deny memory and overlook the power of myth is equivalent, Harjo writes, to being driven underwater by a crocodile, "the spin of / broken sky replaced my meager human memory." These associations with the mythic dimensions of Egyptian history/culture (and the devastation of these myths) lead ultimately, however, to the poet's memories of the destruction of her own people and their myths. This destruction, she realizes, cannot be acceptable; it is not "all the same." Instead the poet offers "my rebel spirit up to living" and attempts to describe in language what is really too heavy to be written: "It goes something like this: When the mythic spiral of time / turned its beaded head and understood what was going on, it snapped" (53). This realization of the ongoing power of myth and her responsibility to share it she wishes to tell to a fellow poet who is engaged in the same project: "All / these years I had been sleeping in the mind of the snake, June. I have to tell / this to someone" (54).

In another poem written with Audre Lorde in mind, Harjo further establishes the importance of "the book of myths" in a time when "there is no more imagination" and "myths / have taken to the streets." She sees the trickster figure Rabbit shaking "his dangerous bag of tricks" into the world as she and Lorde go in search of "sweet and bitter gods" who can "whisper madness" in their ears. The central mythical figure in their constructions of poetic vision is a "fiery goddess," a "sweet trick of flame" who tells the stories "that unglue the talking spirit from the pages." The result for Harjo and Lorde is a love for expressing the heritages that are theirs through the power of the mythical figure of a woman. And Harjo states the importance of this woman for the mythical dimensions of her own contemporary existence as a Native American woman who lives in a dominant culture she sees as virtually devoid of any meaningful myths, and particularly lacking in empowering myths for women: "There is a Helen in every language; in American her name is Marilyn / but in my subversive country, / she is dark earth and round and full of names" ("The Book of Myths," 55–56).

This reading of the mythical figure of a woman in Native American culture reflects the deep connections between woman, animal, and earth—the interconnectedness of all life—and also acknowledges the historical dimension of betrayal that Indian women have experienced. Unlike the figures of Helen and Marilyn Monroe, however, these figures of women belong to a land-based tribal culture and illustrate the importance of the connection of the individual to the whole as well as the significant mythical role that women play in cultural survival. Thus, through her poems for other feminists of color, Harjo establishes the deep connections between Native American myth and the ongoing struggles of real-time women.

Mythical Time and the Insistence of Memory

In the poem "Skeleton of Winter," Harjo establishes lyrically her relationship to ancient beings and the earth through memory and a metaphysical understanding of the interconnectedness of all living things and all points in time. As Harjo has said, the tribal understanding is that the "world is not disconnected or separate but whole" so that "all persons are still their own entity but not separate from everything else" (1987, 92). She conveys this relationship in the final stanza of "Skeleton of Winter":

> I am memory alive
> > not just a name
> but an intricate part
> of this web of motion
>
> > > > (1983, 31)

The speaker is not just a name, not just identified by her use of human language, but she is part of the physical world and is known in its language of sound and motion. This sound and motion is mythically charged as well; Harjo evokes rabbits who get run over by cars at night but emerge alive. She understands that "there are still ancient / symbols / alive" as she dances "with the prehistoric horse / years and births later / near a cave wall / late winter" (30). Here animals serve as representations for mythical realities past and present and thus enable the poet herself to understand how she is bound up in the "web" of time, the mythical, the physical, and both personal and collective meaning.

Throughout Harjo's poetry, the past, the present, and the future are bound up together in a cycle of time. She sees memory as "not just associated with past history, past events, past stories, but nonlinear, as in future and ongoing history, events, and stories" (1990b, 67; see also Allen 1989, 59). From Harjo's Native American viewpoint, history involves remembering, and yet time is not linear, so that the "facts" do not necessarily correspond to one point in time but to a continuing condition. In the prose poem "Santa Fe," Harjo writes: "The wind blows lilacs out of the east. And it isn't lilac season . . . Oh, and it's a few years earlier and more. That's how you tell real time. It is here, it is there" (1990a, 42). In the single long paragraph that makes up this poem, images and events flow into and out of each other in a single moment: a woman the size of a fox who "dangles on the arm of cocaine" and devours her lover flows into St. Francis bronzed on the lawn into the poet herself, "seventeen and shy and wild," into a man on a

Harley-Davidson with lilacs growing out of the spokes of its wheels. The Indian belief that time is cyclical and space is spherical determines the fluidity of this collage lyric-narrative, and is referred to directly in the poem's text. Harjo writes that the woman/fox's act of murder is true and then isn't true anymore. When the poet becomes herself at seventeen, "there is no woman . . . , for that story hasn't yet been invented." The man's face the poet "will never remember, and never did." In this poetic vision, time cannot be viewed as a series of points on a scale but involves a cycle of points that are all equally important; space, likewise, is only "as solid as the bronze statue of St. Francis, the fox breaking through the lilacs, my invention of this story, the wind blowing" (42).

In "Original Memory," Harjo blends elements of Creek mythology with images from contemporary jazz (itself a musical form indigenous to the United States and yet invented by African-Americans) to comment on the radical differences between Native American and Western conceptions of time in particular. This poem is also written in prose form and begins in the familiar formula of the first line in many Native creation myths: "When Rabbit doubted the miracle of creation at the beginning of the world" (1983, 47). Rabbit is a trickster figure in Creek mythology who introduces uncertainty, tragedy, and humor into the patterned balance of life. The poet understands that Rabbit enables her to mediate between the non-Native and Native worlds she inhabits. Rabbit was present for the act of Creation, and "doubt sprang from his heart and humans were created." But the poet later imagines Doubt as a white man who "worships invention and calls it love." In "Western time," while playing saxophone duets with a friend, the poet is drawn into the Muscogee world where Doubt is "beautiful lovers who left in the same way a day turns on the heels of sunset to go on to some other world of its creation." Through a series of musical notes, she imagines time in the Muscogee world as a fusion of past and present, so that each day becomes "a repetition, a variation on a theme of others," and "love" is the only exercise that makes moving from one world to the other bearable:

> Love is always love but we're convinced there isn't enough
>   there either, so we
> pull ourselves out of our ceremonial spiral of prayer,
>   understood relationship,

into this other world because whatever world we are entering or leaving we are still looking for love.

(1990a, 47)

Nevertheless, only in the Muscogee world can the violations of love (beginning with "original memory" "as old as Rabbit's heart cracking open") be healed; here, "one would have a circle of relatives (everyone is ultimately a relative) recalling similar events, to establish connection, and to convey the event lovingly into a past." In honor of this community, the speaker and her friend recreate in their urban environment the ceremony of joining past and present, of preserving memory and love, in their late night music session: "We sip wine, do a hit of courage, each of us imagining another spin of the wheel, and take up our horns again" (48).

Deer—traditionally of great importance as sustenance for the southeastern tribes, including the Creek (Muscogee)—appear in poems more heavily lyrical as well as in those more oriented to narrative. While deer seem to function as figures of women in Harjo's poetry, they also operate as mythical signs of her Creek heritage. In the lyrical "Song for the Deer and Myself to Return On," the speaker, who lives in "a house near downtown Denver," uses a Creek hunting song for calling deer into her house. When they arrive, she works with them to invent a song to take them all back "home": "Now the deer and I are trying to figure out a song / to get them back, to get all of us back, / because if it works I'm going with them" (30). Home seems to represent not only the physical space in eastern Oklahoma where the Creek tribe is based but also the Creek way of life itself. In "Deer Ghost," a doe comes to find the poet in her urban setting where "nameless" "night ghosts," who have forgotten their heritages, wander. This deer "is no imaginary tale" but the mythical representation of continuity and memory:

. . . This is

> what names
> me in the ways of my people, who have called me back.
> The deer knows what it is doing wandering the streets of this
> city; it has never forgotten the songs.

(29)

Similarly, in the prose poem "Autobiography" the dreams of Creeks in their Oklahoma homelands do not consist of "malls and hotels" but come from "the hearts of deer," who carry memories and understand the significance of "the death count from Alabama, the destruction of grandchildren, famine of stories" (14).

In other places, the urban landscape itself mixes with animal imagery to remind the poet of her Creek origins. In "Autobiography," for instance, she meets a homeless man from Jemez, New Mexico, who reminds her of her father; through her, he remembers "his daughter, the chili, the songs," while she talks to him as if he were her father "with that respect, that hunger" (15). These two men merge to symbolize her Creek past—both its despair and its promise—so that she experiences another cycle of personal and tribal renewal by moving toward the east through memory and ceremony: "Yesterday there was rain traveling east to home. A hummingbird spoke. She was a shining piece of invisible memory, inside the raw cortex of songs. I knew then this was the Muscogee season of forgiveness, time of new corn, the spiraling dance" (15). The hummingbird works as a transition between the desolation of contemporary Indian life and the memory of and celebration of the promise of the Creek harvest season.

In fact, these two sets of images—urban imagery and seasonal harvest imagery from the Creek tradition—illustrate the tension between and convergence of Harjo's displacement as an Indian who does not live on the reservation and her deep connections to Creek ceremony and belief. Perhaps more than any other natural image could, the "time of new corn" evokes the ceremonial center of Creek identity. For many southeastern tribes, the Busk or Green Corn Ceremony was, long before contact with Anglo cultures, and still is the most important feast celebration in the seasonal calendar (Green 1984, 310; Martin 1991, 34–42). Joel Martin notes that for the Creek in particular, the Busk has traditionally functioned not only to celebrate the new corn and pay tribute to the mythological woman who gave it to them, but "to renew . . . collective life and public spaces," "to rekindle a sense of the sacrality of life," and especially since the arrival of Europeans, "to strengthen Muskogee cultural traditions during a period of intensive cultural contact" (1991, 34). Marked by fire rituals, feasting, and dancing (which is of particular importance in Creek life year-round), the Busk then is the defining collective moment in Creek life. As corn has special significance in many other Native traditions as well, Harjo's use of corn imagery calls forth an identification not only with her own Creek heritage but also with the general Native concentration on actual harvests and harvest imagery as sites of the ritual enactment of myth through the power of ceremonial space, memory, and tradition.

The image of corn takes on added significance, however, in the contemporary context of Indian life in which traditionalism and the cultural disintegration caused under colonialism coexist and collide. In Harjo's prose poem "Grace," which works as a kind of preface to *In Mad Love and War,* the speaker recalls when winter cold "froze imaginary buffalo" and "the haunting voices of the starved and mutilated broke fences." Amidst this desolation, the speaker and a friend turn to the hope of the harvest, hope for cultural preservation and renewal, as they conduct "the epic search for grace" in a truck stop on a winter morning and find "a promise of balance" through which they again understand "the talk of animals," and spring is "lean and hungry with the hope of children and corn." Promise and harvest together comprise the calendar of Native life, and the desolation of "winter" or "the memory of a dispossessed people" is only transformed by "grace" in the springtime of promise and planting (1990a, 1). These images of Indian life and myth work together to create a sense of empowerment for contemporary Native American individuals and communities.

All of these examples demonstrate how Native American ideas of time and space affect Harjo's approach to history. The word she most frequently uses for history is "story." This word more clearly communicates the importance of the oral tradition in tribal life and the meaningfulness of mythical figures, events, and lessons. In her acknowledgments in *In Mad Love and War,* Harjo thanks the writer Leslie Marmon Silko (Laguna Pueblo) for helping her to "understand the importance of story, and my place in it." Silko has said, "You don't have anything if you don't have the stories" (1977, 2). This meaning of "story" has often been misread by non-Indians, for the effects of Western historical understandings on Native American life and history have been not only to skew the "facts" of European American treatment of Native Americans from the 1500s to the present day,[8] but to obscure, or create silences about, the centrality of memory and myth in Native American readings of "history." In delineating the meaning of history in tribal cultures, Trinh T. Minh-ha has assessed the effects of the Western conception of history on these cultures: "Story-writing becomes history-writing, and history quickly sets itself apart, consigning story to the realm of tale, legend, myth, fiction, literature. Then, since fictional and factual have come to a point where they mutually exclude each other, fiction, not infrequently, means lies, and fact, truth" (1989, 120). In contrast, in Native American traditions, myth in story is a primary vehicle for the transmission of communal identity and sacred truths, and has traditionally been crucial to cultural survival. As Paula Gunn Allen has stated, "The tribes seek through song, ceremony, legend, sacred stories (myths), and tales to embody, articulate, and share reality, to bring the isolated self into harmony and balance with this reality . . . The artistry of the tribes is married to the essence of language itself, for through language one can share one's singular being with that of the community and know within oneself the communal knowledge of the tribe" (1986, 45). Thus "story" is based not on the unity of time, space, and action and the primacy of the individual life, but on collectivity and shared belief in the ongoing relevance of mythological beings and meanings.

Harjo's Evolution of Voice

As she works toward empowerment in these two volumes, Harjo weaves together images—from the natural world, from the worlds of Indian myth and ceremony, and from women's bodily and dreamed existences—to confirm the Native belief that one thing may in fact become another, and that the physical is but one manifestation of the real, as well as the feminist belief in the personal as political. However, Harjo's body of work demonstrates not only the development of her notion of empowerment but also the evolution of her voice, from personal lyric to heavily ritualized lyric to the prose lyric-narrative. Like many other feminist poets, Harjo in her earliest work concentrates on developing a subjective presence, while in her later work, she moves toward a more complex understanding of the relationship between individual and community precisely through linking her own self-exploration to collective concerns with history and survival.

Harjo's earlier poetry is especially lyrical, concentrating on reaching self-understanding through personal expression. However, some of these poems, such as "Early Morning Woman" and "The Blanket around Her," seem to be stretching toward communal recognition of a mythical "woman" or toward historical "woman" ("oh woman / remember who you are / woman / it is the whole earth"), but they nevertheless rely on very general imagery in free verse forms. They thus read more like lyrical, symbolic dreams than contextualized, collective evocations. Other early poems, such as "I Am a Dangerous Woman" and

"Conversations between Here and Home" use similar form and imagery but are infused with an anger about the conditions in which women live that foreshadows Harjo's later, very specific explorations of her location as a marginalized woman: "angry women are building / houses of stones / they are grinding the mortar / between straw-thin teeth / and broken families."[9]

Only in her later poems does Harjo move toward integrating her self-discovery with more communal concerns through coalitional voice. The poems in *She Had Some Horses*—including third-person narratives, highly personal lyrical revelations, and the ritualized, communal long poem "She Had Some Horses"—establish Harjo's desire to deal with her own experience and simultaneously to interact with, to empower, her communities with meditations on history, story, and myth. In these poems, she moves toward, and even to some extent establishes, coalitional voice. However, it is only in the highly personal detail that emerges in Harjo's lyric-narratives and prose lyric-narratives in *In Mad Love and War* that she is able to deal adequately with her personal experience of both survival and cultural celebration and thereby to address collective concerns in the tradition of coalitional voice established by feminist poets. That prose poems dominate in Harjo's evolution into coalitional voice in *In Mad Love and War* is really not at all surprising, for with this form she moves away from the more individualized forms of modern poetry and toward the traditional forms of oral storytelling in Native traditions.

Because in all these formal manifestations Harjo explores empowerment and transformation chiefly through women figures—whether mythical, metaphorical, or historical—and these figures form the thematic and imagistic matrix in both *She Had Some Horses* and *In Mad Love and War,* I focus on these as they function as locations of integration of Native and feminist elements within Harjo's poetry. Therefore, in the following discussion, I will explore Harjo's evolution of style and voice in relation to the ways she uses women to reckon with history, celebrate and use myth, and build stories that lead to survival.

Earth/Animal/Woman: The Woman Figure in the "Horse" Poems

Harjo's relationship to myth and memory reflects their centrality to the tribal community and the ways they hold the community together even in periods of threatened disintegration.[10] She consistently draws on earth and animal imagery, as well as images and stories of women, to create mythical meanings and to emphasize the importance of memory, and she draws many of these from ancient tribal systems, especially the Creek. However, because the locations in her poems are often nontraditional, urban settings and because the complexities of contemporary life demand loosening ties to "home," Harjo also uses this imagery to reestablish or reinforce her connections to tribal traditions. Her more lyrical work of course heightens a sense of separation, while her third-person narratives and the ritualized "She Had Some Horses" demonstrate an especial desire to establish the collective "story" that contextualizes the individual in both the Creek/Indian world and women's communities and empowers her and these communities to act.

In *She Had Some Horses,* Harjo establishes her commitment to women's stories in her most detailed meditation on the status of women, the third-person narrative entitled "The Woman Hanging from the Thirteenth Floor Window." In this poem, a woman's life and spirit teeter on the edge of self-destruction. Harjo has said that the woman in this poem came to her as a kind of composite of many different urban Indian women she had read about but that she has had many readers say they know the specific woman she was writing about (1989, 11). This underlines the way this character is both lived, in terms of the actual conditions many American women must face on a day-to-day basis, and mythological, in terms of her larger significance to women, her ability to represent processes going on in many women's spirits. The woman hanging from the thirteenth floor window has been married twice, is both daughter and mother, is ". . . all the women of the apartment / building who stand watching her, watching themselves" (22).

The tenement building she hangs from sits on Lake Michigan, across from the "tall glass houses" in which the rich live; in the tenement buildings all around hers, she sees other "women hanging from many-floored windows / counting their lives in the palms of their hands / and in the palms of their children's hands." She hears many voices, giving her different options: voices from her past that pull her back to her life (and yet only "to have another child to hold onto in the night, to be able / to fall back into dreams"), voices yelling for her to jump, and the cries of those mothers on the street below who wish to help her. As the woman's mind "chatters like neon and northside bars," she remembers her parent and her children, and she ". . . knows she is hanging by her own fingers, her / own skin, her own thread of indecision." At the conclusion of the stanza the woman surveys all the elements of her life so that here, a short final line sums up what her central need is: "She would speak." Instead, she can only survey her life and make a decision to hang on or to let go, either of which Harjo implies is a viable choice for the woman hanging from the thirteenth floor window:

> She thinks she remembers listening to her own life
> break loose, as she falls from the 13th floor
> window on the east side of Chicago, or as she
> climbs back up to claim herself again.
>
> (22)

Very significantly, speaking is not available to this woman precisely because she is from "the Indian side of town" (22). Thus, even in the urban setting, Harjo is concerned about the convergence of Native and gendered identities. In "The Woman Hanging," the woman faces an uncertain future; Harjo's use of third person and her refusal of narrative closure hints both that she has not discovered a way into empowerment by connecting personal and collective stories and that she wishes to. In other poems in *She Had Some Horses,* she strives for this empowerment by merging the figure of the horse with women figures. In the lyrical "Night Out" (which presages the poem "Deer Dancer" in *In Mad Love and War*), the poet evokes Native Americans sitting in despair in a bar, but yet as the night wears on comes to understand them as "powerful horses" and no longer ". . . the wrinkled sacks of thin, mewing / spirit, / that lay about the bar early in the day / waiting for minds and bellies." These horses are the power of memory of ancestors trying to break through the seemingly endless possibilities for despair in Native American contexts: "You are the circle of lost ones / our relatives" (21). The past seeps into present time, so these Indians may reenter the mythic worlds that sustained their ancestors. Similarly, a rainbow made up of the "colors of horses" informs the poem "Vision"; emerging in the rainbow are the "horses that were within us all of this time / but we didn't see them because / we wait for the easiest vision / to save us" (41).

The "She Had Some Horses" poems form the core of this volume, however. The point of the poems in this series is to overcome the polarities inherent in Western thought and life and to provide a more integrated view of existence, influenced by Native American philosophy and spirituality, but also centrally influenced by feminist theory; indeed, as Paula Gunn Allen has noted, Harjo "believes that the view she describes of the inside being the outside has come to her from American feminists" (1986, 166). As bearers of the mythic who move from past to future, from self to other, the horses in these poems contradict either/ or dualities; they are feminine figures that abound in creativity and energy for turning the inside out, the outside in. The form and arrangement of these five poems pulls them together as a communal ceremonial: the first and last poems have a ritualistic, chantlike quality, while the three in between are lyrical evocations of the pain and possibility the horses bring to women's lives, and one of these is a lyrical evocation of the poet herself as a horse, which grounds the entire cycle in the poet's own self-realization.

In the title poem, "She Had Some Horses," the mythical woman figure "owns" horses of so many different and conflicting types that the contradictions begin to melt together. The woman in this poem is identified in no other way than as "She." "She" structures the poems, but is not personalized so that the individual woman, women, and community merge into a collective, even mythical, female presence. As the horses symbolize the inner life of the "She" who "owns" them, they point up the futility of rigid polarities and illustrate the way each individual, each community, the world, holds all these "contradictions" within, without being destroyed and in fact potentially being made more "whole" by this condition. The poem is divided into stanzas of various lengths, each line beginning anaphorically with "She had horses . . ." The stanzas are separated by the refrain, "She had some horses," which reiterates that these horses all "belong" to "She" and serves to create a sustained feeling of the "contradictions" beginning to collapse into each other. The contrast between tribal ceremonial imagery and images of the despair of urban Indian life again provide a contrast in these poems, and "She" runs her horses through these images to understand how they may be transformed into one another: "She had horses who like Creek Stomp Dance songs. / She had horses who said they weren't afraid. / She had horses who lied" (63). In another stanza, the horses become material representations of the mythical. They are both the names of material objects themselves and the realities that those material objects merely represent:

> She had horses who called themselves, "horse."
> She had horses who called themselves, "spirit," and kept
> their voices secret and to themselves.
> She had horses who had no names.
> She had horses who had books of names.
>
> She had some horses.
>
> (64)

At the end, Harjo whittles the stanza form down to a single couplet that reveals the central contrast and a final, isolated line in which the poet asserts what the rhythm and repetition of the body of the poem has been building to, that these horses, though so different and seemingly contradictory, are of the same whole:

> She had some horses she loved.
> She had some horses she hated.
>
> These were the same horses.
>
> (64)

In the second poem in this series, "Two Horses," the figure of the horse enables the speaker to understand herself as she relates to the mythical world, and establishes the connections between the more performance-oriented sections of the poem and the poet's lyrical exploration. The figure of the horse breaks down the Western imposition of division between mundane and sacred, between present and past:

> My heart is taken by you
>   and these mornings since I am a horse
>   running towards
> a cracked sky where there are countless dawns
>   breaking
>   simultaneously.
>
> (65)

At the outset of "Two Horses," the speaker muses that she had thought her love of and carefully cultivated connection to the natural ("the sun breaking through Sangre de Cristo Mountains" and "wild musky scents on my body") would "unfold me to myself." Her other, mythical self, however, is the revelation of "many colonies of stars / and other circling planet motion" and she is unexpected, a gift. In this poem, the subjective "she" discovers the horses of the mythical, who bring personal wholeness and a vision for collective life (65).

The poems "Drowning Horses" and "Ice Horses," in contrast, deal with the pain of oppression and victimization, the trauma of living as an unwanted "other" in the nontribal world. In "Drowning Horses," the speaker cannot encourage a friend not to commit suicide because she herself understands the extent of the despair experienced at ". . . the cliff edge of the talking / wire, . . ." The speaker's final "yes" to her friend can be read as the affirmation of reasons to commit suicide or a "yes" to all she has experienced and the affirmation of another life informed by the realization that the "either/or" is not the only solution, which once again is symbolized by the horse: "Her escape is my own. / I tell her, yes. Yes. We ride / out for breath over the distance. / Night air approaches, the galloping / other-life. / / No sound. No sound" (66).

"Ice Horses" recognizes and celebrates women who can endure and escape the horses of victimization and seek out the horses of freedom, and recalls Lorde's celebration in "A Litany of Survival." The horses of pain and oppression are frozen in ice, who "chased deer out of your womb," while the horses of freedom and wholeness move toward the fire and hold the woman like an infant herself:

> They are the horses who have held you
> so close that you have become
> a part of them,
> > > an ice horse
> galloping
> > into fire.

> > > > > > (67)

The transformation of ice into fire again indicates resistance to the notion of polarities. The horses move from cold into hot, melting away the ice of oppression with the fire of caring and new vision.

In "Explosion," the final poem in the "Horses" series, Harjo invents a contemporary, alternative creation story for Creeks and uses these horses as the central figures. Once again using anaphora and listing, Harjo echoes the ritualized form of section 1 of "She Had Some

Horses," thus framing the middle three, more lyrical sections and establishing the entire poem as a performance-oriented piece. The physical event that forms the basis for her mythical speculations in this last section is the explosion of the "highway near Okemah, Oklahoma." Maintaining that every physical being or object or event has a spiritual correlation ("There are reasons for everything"), Harjo provides possible scenarios for this new creation event. Maybe, she says, there is a new people, another tribe, coming forth; this tribe too might be hated and "live in Moskogee on the side of the tracks / that Indians live on. (And they will be the / ones to save us.)" In other words, this "new" tribe might be a mythical rebirth of possibility for the Creek tribe as it already exists. At the center of the emergence of this "new" tribe are "lizards coming out of rivers of lava / from the core of this planet," coming "to dance for the corn, / to set fields of tongues slapping at the dark / earth, a kind of a dance"; in this way, they repeat the creation cycle of the Creeks, arriving from the center of the earth to enact the seasonal cycle. But maybe, the poet suggests, "the explosion was horses" who emerge to wait for "evening night / mares to come after them" (68). These horses might, the poet speculates, ride over the night into the dreams of fields in Oklahoma, into "wet white sheets at midnight" where humans sleep, into frogs, into a "Creek woman who dances shaking the seeds in her bones," into Mexico and Japan, and into Miami "to sweep away the knived faces of hatred." These horses carry the possibility of self-knowledge and community renewal; they may bring with them new people and new corn for more than just the Creek tribes themselves. But the recognition of these horses rests on the belief that there are "reasons for everything" and a physical event like a highway explosion might indeed lead to an eruption in the "night mares" of average humans and the natural world. Consequently, some will not even see these horses, while others will see them and understand how they hold within themselves the possibilities for eruption, for participating in the new creation: "But some will see the horses with their hearts of sleeping volcanoes / and will be rocked awake / past their bodies / to see who they have become" (69).

This series of poems gets at the heart of Harjo's poetic message. Native beliefs can bring renewal to contemporary Indian life, particularly through the horse/woman figure. In turn, this equation of horse and woman conveys the potential that Native beliefs hold for empowering women to combat oppression, and ironically reestablishes a connection between women and the earth that has been eroded through feminist attacks on essentialism. Harjo sees the possibility that Native American and feminist perspectives and imagery can empower each other through using myth, revising history, and attacking the hierarchical oppositions imposed by Western thought and culture; each can provide the other with cultural energy that has been depleted in ongoing struggles with dominant American culture.

Deer Dancers and Warriors: Mythical and Historical Women in *In Mad Love and War*

Extending out of this volume into *In Mad Love and War,* Harjo uses animal figures, mythical women figures, and the lives of actual women to develop the synthesis of her Native American and feminist worlds and to maintain a surviving identity in the dominant culture. She does this effectively because she establishes coalitional voice by exploring and coming to terms with autobiographical and historical detail in the effort to create a communal sense of resistance, celebration, and survival.

The speaker in the prose lyric-narrative "Grace" imagines that grace might be "a woman with time on her hands" (1990a, 1). A mysterious woman whose family is "related to deer" dances naked in the "bar of misfits" in "Deer Dancer," revising the myth of Deer Woman common among the southeastern tribes before removal (5). A "slender, dark woman" signals the possibility of intimacy with both other humans and the earth in "The Bloodletting" (22). Inside a saxophone is "a secret woman / who says she knows the power of the womb" in "Bleed Through" (36). In general, Harjo evokes the empowering and sustaining power of the mythical realm through the figure of a woman.

In the prose lyric-narrative "Deer Dancer," the figure of a woman dancer corresponds to the figure of the deer, who reminds a bar full of despondent Indians of their past and their responsibility to it. On "the coldest night of the year," a woman who is "the end of beauty" appears in the bar to all the "hardcore" gathered there, the "Indian ruins." Though the woman herself is not recognized, the group knows instinctively that her tribe is "related to deer." This woman carries, represents, becomes the mythical, a reminder of the way the world is in tribal perspective, a reminder of all that is past and future in the way of the Indian, and a taste of another kind of time. She is a revelation: "Some people see vision in a burned tortilla, some in the face of a woman" (5).

She is the one who reinfuses their imaginations with the importance of ceremony, but she does it across all the elements of their mixed-up worlds, across the borders between their lives in Indian reality and white American reality:

> And then she took off her clothes. She shook loose memory,
>   waltzed with the
> empty lover we'd all become.
>
> She was the myth slipped down through dreamtime. The
>   promise of feast we
> all knew was coming. The deer who crossed through knots of
>   a curse to find
> us. She was no slouch, and neither were we, watching.
>
> (6)

In a "bar of broken survivors, the club of shotgun, knife wound, of poison by culture," the people who are themselves now "Indian ruins" are overwhelmed by the advent of this mythical message. For a group of people for whom despair results in forgetting, the woman/deer dancer reminds of their ability to step over into mythical time, where the past, the present, and the future are one and the promise of memory is the "feast to come," the cultural abundance invoked by ceremony. Harjo thus revises the myth of Deer Woman as known to the southeastern tribes. According to Paula Gunn Allen, Deer Woman appeared alternately as a human woman and as a doe and acted as a kind of trickster figure "to bewitch men and women and eventually cause their deaths or descent into prostitution" (1989, 236). In Harjo's revision of this myth, Deer Woman brings sustenance and survival rather than cultural disintegration. She carries the possibility of redemption rather than the inevitability of destruction to contemporary Native Americans who are looking for ways to survive; the "Indian ruins" in Harjo's myth are in search of empowering stories by which to escape evil, and Deer Woman acts as the promise of fullness rather than the signal of demise. In this figure, Harjo also upsets the duality of male versus female and good versus evil in Western culture, paradoxically using a natural female image as the bearer of goodness and life.

Significantly, "Deer Dancer" is a story told by the poet, who is very careful both to establish the near impossibility of expressing the mythical in language and to assert the power of story as it circulates among the community. When struggling to describe the appearance of the dancer, the poet says, "How do I say it? In this language there are no words for how the real world collapses" (5). Then, at poem's end, the poet confesses, "The music ended. And so does the story. I wasn't there" (6). Thus, the poet both becomes the bearer of myth and story and places herself squarely in a community of others who participate in the storytelling, culture-making process. The confidence of the lyrical voice in *She Had Some Horses* is here replaced by a more clear-sighted view of the relationship of poet and community, which emerges as the poet relates her own experience/perspective in relationship to that of the community as a whole.

The mythical understandings formed in these poems resonate Harjo's poems about the lives of actual women. These poems reveal her concern with story and with memorializing the lives of women who have given their strength, and too often their lives, for the sake of their people. Harjo has said both that she envisions herself as a teller of not only myth but of stories of ordinary women, and that these women are "warriors" because they "more than survive" (1987, 91; 1989, 11). Many of these women characters are based on actual historical personages, and some are composites or types that represent the struggles of many women. Most are Native American women, but others are African-American, and some are identified as women only.

The interfusion of the mythical and real worlds fully informs a poem about the life and death of a young Native American woman in the long-line lyric-narrative "For Anna Mae Pictou Aquash." In early 1976, the body of an unidentified woman was found on the Pine Ridge Reservation in South Dakota. The official autopsy attributed death to exposure, and the body was unceremoniously buried after the woman's hands were severed by the FBI and sent to Washington for fingerprinting. A second autopsy was demanded by the friends and relatives of Anna Mae Pictou Aquash, a young AIM member who had been discovered missing. This second autopsy showed that the young woman was indeed Aquash and that she had been killed by a bullet fired at close range. No one was ever convicted in the case.

In Harjo's version, Aquash is "the one whose spirit is present in the dappled stars" (7). She inhabits interlocking physical and mythical worlds, demonstrated in the cycles of nature and of waking and dream time. The poet addresses Aquash out of her own experience and in a kind of tribute. She begins by watching her "own dark head / appear each morning after entering / the next world / to come back to this one, amazed," establishing her own relationship to the mythical realm. She compares her own reentry into the physical world to the crocuses emerging from the ground after lying dormant for a season. Yet she again also contextualizes herself as only one storyteller in the Native American network of intertribal communication, organizing, and celebration: "I hear about it in Oklahoma, or New Mexico, / how the wind howled and pulled everything down / in a righteous anger" (8).

Harjo also carefully historicizes Aquash's death in the long procession of American crimes against Native Americans. She writes that "the way in the natural world" is to understand the place "the ghost dancers named / after the heart / breaking destruction" (7), referring to the ability of myth to free Native Americans and women from the long oppression of Native Americans which is perhaps best exemplified by the United States' massacre of almost three hundred Ghost Dancers— men, women, and children—at Wounded Knee in 1890. The task then is to enter the sacred world, not simply to inhabit it, for it intersects completely with the natural world, as the Ghost Dancers believed. In contemporary Indian life, the sacred is named "after," that is chronologically after, the destruction of imperialism, and also "after" in terms of naming, places of such destruction becoming particularly sacred in the history of this people and informing the life and death of the figure of Aquash, a real woman who occupies mythical realms.

In the line "Anna Mae, everything and nothing changes," the poet asserts that life is made of change, that the wheel of life goes on, and yet the repetition sometimes seems brutal when it involves destruction, especially on such a grand scale as inflicted on Native Americans by Anglo Americans. Aquash initiates movement into the world of the "ghost dancers," the mythical world now infused with the anger of the Indians who have suffered, and part of setting the world in harmony again is exploring that anger and following the Ghost Dancers. Harjo writes that she and other Indians have just "begun to touch / the dazzling whirlwind of our anger," have just begun to see the "amazed world the ghost dancers / entered / crazily, beautiful" (8). Anna Mae Aquash ushers them into this realm, these realizations.

In the prose lyric-narrative "Javelina," Harjo implicitly celebrates herself as a warrior. The struggle the javelina face to survive in the desert environment frames the speaker's reflections on the difficulties of survival away from her Creek home and her transformation from desperate young woman living in exile to the woman who is deeply connected to her home, particularly through her writing. The javelina serve as a constant reminder of Harjo's own journey away from her Creek homeland and into the "desert" of her search for a strong sense of individuality: "I was born of a blood who wrestled the whites for freedom, and I have since lived dangerously in a diminished system. I, too, still forage as the sun goes down: for lava sustenance. The javelina know what I mean" (31). The javelina, in their own daily bid for survival, bear for Harjo the exact symbol of her own struggle to survive, to live on the desolation of "lava sustenance," even in light of the historic rebellious strength that has been passed on to her and that she celebrates in a "mythic world." The past breaks through and Harjo becomes a young woman again, asking in first person if she is looking for a job, if the car has broken down again. She then speaks directly to her younger self, bestowing a promising future: "*The mythic world will enter with the subtlety of a snake the color of earth changing skin . . . Your son will graduate from high school. You have a daughter not yet born, and you who thought you could say nothing, write poetry*" (31). She then establishes her ongoing struggle through the years, saying that for years she prays for rain, for the young woman's (the poet's) "beaten spirit to lift up and rain and rain" (31). In the mix of personal meditation and collective hope that Harjo achieves in this prose poem, she calls on the empowering cycle of time and myth to devise an ending for herself as a young woman, for other women who share similar struggles, and by extension for the woman hanging from the thirteenth floor window.

Whether the woman hanging from the thirteenth floor window decides to survive or die, she lives on as a warrior in Harjo's sensitive, compassionate portrayal of her plight.[11] Harjo seeks to empower this woman character through her language and imagery, utilizing her synthesis of Native American and feminist perspectives on myth and history. However, the poet remains rather distant from this woman and her fate, while in Harjo's first-person attempts to reckon with history in the lyric-narrative evocations of mythical and historical women figures in *In Mad Love and War,* she is able fully to develop the relation between self and communities that is self-empowering and empowering to the members of these communities.

Women in the Real Revolution

The poem "Transformations" is perhaps the central example of how Harjo understands the ways empowerment results in transformation and how she achieves a relationship with her communities by exploring her own voice and experience. "Transformations" is both poem and letter, both personal statement of self-assertion and ongoing communal event that invites response from members of the community (the readers). This poem is a letter from the "dark woman" who simultaneously relies on Indian myth and memory and confronts the ways that the Indian, and particularly the Indian woman, have been constructed in the American consciousness. As the racial and cultural "dark woman" in a predominantly white, non-Native culture, the writer of this letter asserts that she is at once both inside and outside. She sees herself as both nightmare and miracle, warrior and visionary. While she uses her honed skills to recognize and understand her "enemy" ("This poem is a letter to tell you that I have smelled the hatred you have tried to find me with; you would like to destroy me"), she also relies on a Native understanding of the interconnections between myth and reality to proclaim the ways that, even as "you can turn a poem into something else," hatred can be transformed. The mythical potential for a poem to turn into a "bear treading the far northern tundra" or a "a piece of seaweed stumbling in the sea" also resides in the "right words, the right meanings" in the heart that can turn hatred into love (59). The poet identifies herself as the unusual bearer of this ability for change, and as she offers the possibility of change to the one who hates her, she also affirms herself and returns—or refuses to be controlled by—the hatred directed at her. The speaker states that she means this poem as a letter; though it is mostly written in prose poem form, it is clearly addressed to another person and is a direct plea for that reader to listen, to understand, and to change. Significantly, then, Harjo breaks the prose form of this poem and introduces line breaks in the final five lines of the poem, drawing tension and heightened power into her final statements of direct indictment and self-assertion.

As a powerful statement of self, a treatise on the value of myth and poetry and a kind of "love letter" to the reader, "Transformation" contains and exemplifies the multiple layers of meaning and intent in Joy Harjo's poetry. It is quite obviously a lyrical evocation of the speaker's self-love and her desire for community. But its deeper meanings are derived from a combination of Native American understandings of the relationship between art, myth, and history and feminist critiques of the hierarchical assumptions that underlie Western thought and culture. This synthesis characterizes Harjo's work in a vital, contemporary sense, for she embraces it out of her dilemma and her potential as a "half breed"; in her life and work, she is both Indian and non-Indian, and in a parallel sense, both feminist and nonfeminist. Indian traditions converge and/or collide with the demands of modern urban life and Indian and non-Indian ideas and images eventually conjoin and redefine one another.

"Transformations" acts in *In Mad Love and War* as a kind of manifesto of Harjo's poetics of empowerment. In the earlier "I Give You Back," Harjo starts the project of transforming self and other through utterances of her life as a woman and of her Native American history. In lyrical voice, she "releases" her fear, the fear engendered in her ancestors by their white conquerors and passed down to her: "I release you, my beautiful and terrible / fear. I release you. You were my beloved / and hated twin, but now, I don't know you / as myself . . ." (1983, 73). In a highly incantatory section of this poem, Harjo utilizes anaphora to ritualize her action of freeing herself of fear: "I am not afraid to be hungry. / I am not afraid to be full. / I am not afraid to be hated. / I am not afraid to be loved" (73). But, in releasing her fear, Harjo finds in her empowerment that she has compassion even for this emotion itself: "But come here, fear / I am alive and you are so afraid / of dying" (74). Even in this earlier work, Harjo makes clear that the object of this synthesis, this empowerment, is a communal life in which difference is valued, in which difference is actually an enlivening principle of everyday life. She speaks from her location as the racial/cultural outsider to propose that the solution to conflicts over difference lies in mutual empowerment rather than in alienation, hostility, and oppression.

This early poem seems to indicate that yet another enlivening principle lies behind the idea of empowerment in Harjo's poetry: the poet's notion of real love, of both self-love and a corresponding love of the community, and of the ways this love creates the desire for both personal and communal survival. But, as Harjo indicates in a poem about her own attempts to understand the struggle of indigenous peoples up and down the Americas, this very notion of love is rooted in the perseverance of Native American culture and myth in spite of a history of devastation, and in her own experiences as a woman. While visiting Nicaragua, she turns away a potential lover and instead considers her history:

> I do what I want, and take my revolution to bed with
> me, alone. And awake in a story told by my ancestors
> when they spoke a version of the very beginning,
> of how so long ago we climbed the backbone of these
> tortuous Americas . . .
>
> This is not a foreign country, but the land of our dreams.
>
> (25)

As Harjo seeks to empower both self and community, "the real revolution is love" (24). Here, Harjo echoes Jordan's belief in the power of "love" to create both communal celebration and respect for difference, rooted in a recognition of "the personal as political."

The synthesis of her experience and her aesthetic and political vision that Harjo achieves in her notions of empowerment and love enables her to rely in her work on both feminist and Native American thought and experience, and it is precisely through this synthesis that Harjo in many ways fits the profile of the contemporary feminist poet: she identifies with various feminist themes and yet questions and modifies them as she explores her own distinct cultural heritage, and vice versa. The relationship between her feminist and Native American heritages is in some ways most profoundly evocative precisely because they are so different; Harjo's work provides a very fertile ground for revising feminist poetics through combining the aesthetic concerns of both the Native and the non-Native feminist writer. As a central voice in the women's poetry movement of the 1980s, Harjo is a prime example of how the relationships among feminism, racial identity, and cultural traditions can prove fruitful rather than debilitating.

Six

Motherhood, Eroticism, and Community in the Poetry of Minnie Bruce Pratt

>   Then the river
> bends,
> the standing water at the lip, hover, hover,
> the moment before orgasm, before the head emerges,
> then over suddenly, and sound rushing
> back from my ears.
>
>   (1990, 23)

In this passage from Minnie Bruce Pratt's poem "Down the Little Cahaba," images of a river's force, sexual pleasure and the sensuality of childbirth merge as the poet and her two young sons float in inner tubes on a hot August day. Throughout the volume *Crime Against Nature,* Pratt's poetic enterprise involves relentlessly exploring and recharting not only the physical and symbolic terrain of her own body but the ideological constructs of gender, sexuality, and the "natural" in her homeland, the South. Pratt creates a new cartography to resist the cultural and legal dictum that the "unnatural" expression of lesbian desire cannot coincide with the "natural" expression of maternal love. In a gesture of irony, she uses nature imagery—in fact, conflates her sexual desire, the erotics of maternality, and elements of natural environments—to upset the essentialist binaries that structure heterosexual relations, the duties of the mother, and the criminalization of lesbianism in Western culture. Creeks, rivers, and snakes in particular act as symbols in Pratt's attempts to erode the dichotomies between "natural" and "unnatural," culture and nature, male and female, heterosexual and homosexual. These natural images become signs of constant destabilization, signs of the possibility of moving back and forth "between more than one self, more than one end to the story" ("Crime Against Nature," 1990, 115).

Pratt's need to evade fixity initially grew out of her complete displacement as a mother. After discovering her lesbianism, Pratt's ex-husband threatened her, using North Carolina's sodomy statutes, with complete loss of rights to her sons if she did not follow his wishes for primary custody. He would not even allow the children to visit her new home, so she and they found "there was no place to be simultaneous, or between" ("No Place," 18). In this poetry, on weekend visits, the three of them travel back and forth, over the borders of creeks and rivers, between the remnants of their former, stable life and an uncertain future. They soon discover, however, that while the place defined for them by law and society feels like a void, they can experience this wilderness differently; after exploring the extravagant spawn of life in a small creek, they begin to understand "the in-between places" ("The Place Lost and Gone, The Place Found," 38).

Pratt asserts her desire and her maternal experience on the edge of and in bodies of water as the in-between from which she can question not only the equation of maternality with moral virtue (enforced in her experience through the cultural institution of motherhood in the South) and the concomitant legally and culturally enforced conventions of heterosexism, but also any defiant and yet finally paralyzing valorization of lesbian sexuality or women's communities/culture. She and her sons swim alongside/like snakes in these waters, discovering fluid notions of sexual identity and experience and of the mother-child relationship. In the sensual flow of the creek (which "comes down in snaky rapids, / huge muscles, ripples over rib bones"), the poet and her sons face the mystery of deciding who they will be in a world that has had no place for them. Underwater, they grapple toward, "wrinkled, undeciphered, a message left for us, mysterious words seen / through the huge eye of the creek" ("Dreaming a Few Minutes in a Different Element," 92–93).

This in-between never presents an ultimate solution; Pratt does not portray it pastorally, as timeless, painless, or always green, but rather as historically bound, rarely peaceful, even occasionally ugly. It is not merely a place of escape but a previously uncharted territory in which she can carry out her ongoing inner dialogue along more than one axis of identity (chiefly her sexuality, but also race, class and region) as well as her dialogue with family members, other lesbians, other women (including feminists), and the cultural systems that have enforced and/or condemned her identity(ies). In this environment, Pratt both inscribes the "wilderness," undoing heterosexual domestication in order to proclaim her lesbian body, and exceeds it, so that ultimately "lesbian" eludes categories of good and evil and "mother" may be heterosexual or lesbian. Rather than rigidify essentialist notions of the "natural" (heterosexual) mother and the "unnatural" (or even the "natural") lesbian, Pratt's choices of nature imagery open up into the liquid, ever-evolving and highly various forms of eroticism involved in both lesbian sex and the birth process.

Women, the Unnatural, and the Lyric-Narrative

Pratt states within this volume that she could not write this poetry earlier, before her sons reached adulthood, when they were still young enough for "either law or father to seize" them from her completely ("Crime Against Nature," 120). The roots of this later volume do appear, though, in Pratt's *We Say We Love Each Other* (1985). Many of her earlier pieces are love poems, exploring myriad expressions of lesbian desire using fruits, vegetables, and garden soil as metaphors. These poems celebrate a lesbian domestic space without delving into the intense pain of loss or critiquing accepted definitions of home and family. Still, Pratt hints at deeper understandings of the variousness of lesbian sex and its relation to other sensualities, including motherhood:

> We have called love *transformation*. I have thought
> of the pain as growing pains, my womb clenched,
> laboring, after my water broke, drenching me.
> ("Earth and Water," 1985, 56)

In these poems, Pratt also spells out her feminist vision. When she and other women meet and talk, the past shifts and breaks, and the idea of a new map emerges: "We locate forbidden places, the kind marked *dangerous / swamp, unknown territory* on the old charts . . . Our bodies become lodestones to the future. *We imagine / a place not marked yet on any map*" ("Reading Maps: One," 9). This poem is informed by Pratt's experience in women's liberation groups in North Carolina and as one of the editors of the journal *Feminary,* which was published by a Durham-based collective during the 1970s and 1980s and geared especially to southern lesbians and their experiences of woman-identification and racism.[1] Pratt and these other women understand the need to remap social constructions of women's sexual desires and political self-understandings, starting with their own bodies.

In *Crime Against Nature,* Pratt remains hopeful that the in-between spaces she explores are indeed the same ones sought by other feminists. In the poem "No Place," the poet dreams that she and her sons have crossed a creek into "the place where everything is changed, the place / after the revolution, the revelation, the judgment." In this dream place where "groups of women pass by," the three of them are still at a loss in the "unfamiliar huge openness" (1990, 18). While she and her sons feel "awkward," the new place is vast and a revolution has occurred.

Nevertheless, while the tone of this dream sequence is hopeful, Pratt is clear here that new configurations of mother-child relationships have not yet been thoroughly conceptualized or put into practice by feminists or lesbians. Indeed, in charting the details of her loss of her sons in *Crime Against Nature,* Pratt discovers that she cannot rely on any easy notion of women's or lesbian community, nor can she easily move into coalitional voice. Her task, she discovers, is to relate the painful particulars of her experience and in the process confront and transform the underlying assumptions about motherhood and sexuality that structure her relationship not just with the culture at large but with other women and lesbians as well. In fact, her efforts to tell her story are themselves born partly out of the lack of understanding she experiences from other women, including feminists. This is illustrated in "My Life You are Talking About," in which the poet reacts against the "ugliness, the stupid repetition / when I mention my children, or these poems . . ."; she describes how angry she becomes when a woman "tries to make my life into a copy of / an idea in her head, flat, paper thin" (67). With the question "How can I make any of this into a poem?" Pratt brings the voices, the questions, of other women into the poetic text to illustrate the complicated differences and misunderstandings at work among women. The result is a poem of broken narrative and prosaic fragments of conversations. The first woman to speak is ". . . supposed to be a feminist and / understand something," but her questions make Pratt want "to slap her with anger" (68). When the woman says she didn't know Pratt had children, the poet tells her she lost custody of them and that loss is the subject of her writing:

> She says: *You're kidding.*
> I say: *No, I'm not kidding. I lost my children because I'm*
>   *a lesbian.*
> She says: *But how could that happen to someone with a Ph.D.?*

(67)

Pratt brings three other voices into the dialogue of this poem, one that of a young lesbian mother who does not conceive of older lesbians as mothers and asks the poet if she has ever thought of having children herself. The beneficiary of gay and lesbian activism, this woman has a child of her own but cannot imagine children for any lesbians of older generations. In addition, a student in a class Pratt is teaching asserts that it is *"not good for children to be in that kind of home"* (70). Pratt's response, in staccato sentences in a single quatrain, indicates the level of her anger: "I am stripped, naked, whipped. / Splintered by anger, wordless. / I want to break her, slash her. / My edged eyes avoid her face" (71). Even a longtime acquaintance discounts the possibility of Pratt's dealing with such a subject; when Pratt tells her about the poems she is working on concerning her sons, the woman replies: "Oh, how sweet. How sweet" (71).

These voices cause pain precisely because Pratt is very conscious of what poetry is supposed to do. She is aware of the intimate relationship between the feminist author and her reader/listeners that is especially valued by feminist writers and their communities. Pratt comments on the ways "the carry-over of metaphor / and the cunning indirection of the poet (me)" is supposed to lure "the listener (her) deeper and deeper / with bright images, through thorns, a thicket, / into a hidden openness (the place beyond the self . . ." (68). Pratt asks angrily, however, why she should offer her poems as maps when she gets disbelief while standing physically in the same room with a woman who identifies herself as a feminist: "Why give her a poem to use to follow me / as I gather up the torn bits, a path made / of my own body . . ." (68).

As a result of these realizations, Pratt insists on difference, within and between women, and avoids essentializing "woman" or "lesbian" as either biological or political identities. She also uses a long line in lyric-narratives full of prosaic detail, in order to question the interpretive and informative dimensions of poetry (even as understood by feminists, as "My Life" indicates): she wants to make sure that the full implications of her journey into the in-between of natural settings become clear to feminists and lesbians as well as to men and women invested in maintaining the heterosexual contract, but she also just wants to make sure that the full story gets told. Diane Freedman says the lyric-narrative results in a "patchwork" of genres (1992, 117). In Pratt's poetry, however, the lyric-narrative at once exceeds formal categories and inhabits its own. It permits Pratt to move fluidly from interiors of the self to natural environments to the politics of her relationships with other individuals and with cultural/legal institutions. It both produces a powerful sense of coherence that allows Pratt stylistically to tell a story, thus breaking the literary/political silence about the experience of lesbians and lesbian mothers like herself, and leaves Pratt room within the poetry to explore the boundaries and needs of her self, including her experience of both fragmentation and coherence. In this case, the poet needs to document the precise details of her experience and simultaneously to imagine sexual and maternal identities that do not rely on dualistic/essentialist notions of gender. She uses the lyric-narrative to accommodate her desire both to represent as clearly as possible the experiential consequences and political implications of her resistances and to explore the blending of personal identities she formulates in the in-between.

Thus, in *Crime Against Nature,* narrative elements function internally to the poems in this volume, which in turn operate together as an autobiographical document, while at the same time Pratt uses the in-between both "authentically" to narrate her lesbian experience and lyrically to invite destabilization. The central story, of Pratt's separation from her sons because of her lesbian sexuality, the aftermath of this traumatic loss, and her and their attempts to build an alternative life, works as the dominant structuring event in each of these poems and yet extends throughout into lyrical meditations that both support and undermine narrative endings, social definitions, and personal and political identity/ies.

The overall narrative is in many ways cyclical and grounded in Pratt's lyrical insistence on avoiding any final story or any single self, but likewise lyric follows narrative, for the arrangement of poems within the volume suggests that emotional discoveries emerge from the narrative development itself. *Crime* begins with the highly lyrical "Poem for my Sons," which speaks specifically of Pratt's sons' births and sets up the journey from anesthetized new mother to self-defined woman poet. The long middle poem, "Shame," addresses her experience of grief, shame, and loss and provides a series of narrative accounts of her and her sons' journey together into a happier present. And the final poem, "Crime Against Nature," relates Pratt's anger about the ways lesbian sexuality has been defined/criminalized and proves to be her clearest statement of the ways storytelling and metaphor can destabilize these laws. The narrative encompasses Pratt's journey from wife and mother to lesbian mother, from disempowered artist's wife to powerfully creative artist. It also finally focuses on the stories of other women who have experienced the "wilderness." This focus grows out of Pratt's personal realizations about the subversive potential of the lesbian body, lesbian desire, and the erotics of maternality, and the need to rebel against the criminalization of the lesbian/the lesbian mother. This move toward a celebratory sense of community is always tentative, however, as it is rooted in Pratt's ongoing recognition of the power of difference and oppression to divide women in destructive ways.

Throughout the lyric-narratives that comprise *Crime Against Nature,* Pratt's desire to document as well as to ponder her experience always also affects the texture of her language and lineation. She alternates between cadenced language to express the self she claims/proclaims and broken, elliptical phrases to express the pain and fragmentation caused by the identities assigned to her and the shifting ground of her own self-definition. Similarly, she relies on long, prosaic lines to document narrative detail but resorts to uneven shifts and abrupt drop-offs to express turbulent currents of grief, shame, and anger, and to rhythmic, more regulated lines to express hope and the celebration of the self and intimate relationships. These structural characteristics facilitate and reflect Pratt's exploration of sexual and maternal experience both as these were formulated for her and as she formulates them for herself through her poetry. And they arise out of her social location as a lesbian in late twentieth-century America; indeed, Elizabeth Meese suggests that a lesbian must reinvent language in order to survive.[2] This echoes Maria Damon's definition of the avant-garde and places Pratt in the company of her feminist contemporaries Anzaldúa and Klepfisz, who offer innovative and resistant writing out of their racial/ethnic identities as well as their lesbian subject positions.

Lesbian Body/Lesbian Poet

The opening "Poem for my Sons" demonstrates precisely that the notion of what poetry is and does must change when the lesbian begins to write. This poem both registers Pratt's libidinous body—a body that has given birth twice—and roots the act of writing itself in her challenge to the conventions of sexual expression, marriage, and motherhood. She inscribes her sensual relations to her children and her proclamation *to them* of herself as "lascivious" and "voluptuous, a lover, a smeller of blood / milk . . ." (13). She also understands that she must actively resist a tradition that has rejected the vociferous woman, and particularly the woman writer (not to mention the lesbian), as a transgressor incapable of adequately fulfilling her assigned, domestic role. Against this tradition, Pratt insists on the convergence of her lived bodily desires and experiences, her commitment to her sons, and her writing. The identities lesbian, mother, and poet merge.

In this vein, Pratt establishes a sharp contrast between her own relationship to her sons and that of the classical poets she spent years studying. Recalling the days after the birth of each of her sons—when she was sore, exhausted, and even unconscious—she rereads Coleridge's and Yeats's poetic meditations on parenthood. Yeats's "prayer that his daughter lack opinions, / his son be high and mighty, think and act" both belies the father's "loud eloquence" against the "mother's exhausted sleep" and reflects the gendered arrangement that confined Pratt herself to motherhood while her husband wrote ("Your father was then / the poet I'd ceased to be when I got married" [13]). Right away, Pratt distances herself from the traditional treatment of parenthood—written by the creatively empowered father—and embarks on a new poetic journey, away from culturally prevalent ideas about both poetry and the role of the woman and mother; she rejects the notion of the poet as male and the wife/mother/muse as female.

Pratt signals the move from the domesticated interiors that have historically "housed" this gendered arrangement to a free, uncharted territory when she tells her sons she has been traveling toward "an unknown place where you could be with me, like a woman on foot, in a long stepping out." She walks away from the house of the "father poets" and from the institution of motherhood that requires her own sexual and poetic urges be suppressed; in the end, she is able to invoke for her sons a different landscape, a place where traditional gender patterns are destabilized:

> I can only pray:
>
> That you'll never ask for the weather, earth,
> angels, women, or other lives to obey you . . .
>
> (14)

Within this single poem, then, Pratt predicates the move from anesthetized postpartum numbness to exuberant creativity out of which she can freely define herself. She rejects the visions of her literary predecessors and sets out on her own poetic journey.

The second poem in the volume, "Justice, Come Down," relates the heavy narrative weight of Pratt's long years of telling her story over and over again (verbally, in numerous settings), and develops an extended lyrical meditation on the power of her slow-burning but fierce anger. Significantly, it also introduces what becomes the central erotic image in this volume: water. Water is ice in the beginning of this poem, representing Pratt's previous entrapment in silence, a silence about her history as a lesbian that now begins to break up under the heat of the angry sun that shines when she writes: "Tongues of ice break free, fall, shatter, / splinter, speak" (17). The hard work of the writing itself, the intense and often angry telling of her experience, thaws her grief and isolation, and waters begin to flow freely; Pratt's "stony circle where I am frozen, / the empty space . . ." (17) begins to loosen here and melt into the creeks and rivers of subsequent poems. While "Poem for my Sons" introduces Pratt's grief over the loss of her sons and her personal transformation into a full and defining lesbian desire, the anger and pleas for justice in "Justice, Come Down" mark this poetry as the site of daring storytelling and a very public lesbian rebellion. Her lesbian body becomes a cultural and poetic site of resistance as she unflinchingly challenges social constructions of the lesbian as unnatural by countering others' appropriation of her body with her own erotic reconstruction of it.

(Hetero)Sexism in Southern History

While creeks and rivers in the South become significant and innovative symbols for Pratt, they are initially important as they represent the currents of southern history. Pratt is particularly concerned with the meanings of woman, wife, and mother in the South, meanings that first deeply affected the region in the antebellum era. Pratt experiences herself and her heritage as distinctly southern and displays throughout her poetry and prose profound concerns with issues of gender, sexuality, and race in this region in particular. She herself has written that, in the patriarchal agricultural society of the Old (and by extension, she argues, in the "New") South, women were equated with the land (1991, 43). The land, tilled and productive, *controlled,* ran as the "pure" lifeblood through southern society—blessed by the purported purity of white women, mastered by white male landowners, and maintained through the labor of African slaves. Ideologues of the South believed that, like the land and the slaves, the southern woman was at base potentially uncivilized, "wild," if not controlled and led toward what landowners and ministers called her higher instincts. The southern woman was thought to obtain her highest natural state only through being "owned" by her husband, by serving as his obedient wife, and by focusing all her energies on maintaining his power, the order of his household, and the passing of this order to their children. As Pratt understands it, the patriarchy forced these women to exchange their bodies for their positions in society, while positing the very existence and continuation of civilization on the moral fulfillment that women presumably obtained through accepting and holding these positions.

The historian Anne Firor Scott demonstrates that the myth of the southern "lady" became important to slaveholders precisely because maintaining the rigid relations of a patriarchal household was essential to maintaining the system of slavery itself. Scott goes on to point out that, though southern patriarchs sustained this discourse on the southern woman, and the wives of wealthy landowners across the region attempted to live up to this "ideal," the everyday realities of these women's lives belied the myth in numerous ways (1970, 16).[3] (Of course, the wives of yeoman and poor farmers literally had no time even to attempt such a life, and African women were considered utterly incapable of the sexual/moral propriety essential to "civilization.") But, as Pratt maintains, the ideal of the southern "lady" and her hallowed relationship to the land has persisted in the South. Living under the power of the vestiges of the myth, Pratt says, "I . . . learned that I could be either a lesbian or a mother of my children, either in the wilderness or on holy ground, but not both" (1991, 43). This configuration of the land as either sacred or wild and corrupt coincides with the conception of women as "natural" if they submit themselves to the rule of (male) civilization and unnatural if they do not; this is the backdrop against which Pratt reckons with traditional images of "wild" women and challenges these through her own body and images from the very landscapes of the South itself.

While Pratt is able to use water imagery freely and fluidly from the outset, she must reclaim the image of the snake from Christian mythology, in which all women are especially prone to carnal transgression because of Eve's attention to the serpent, the most earthbound and therefore the most evil creature, in the Garden of Eden. Powerful men of the Old South characterized diverse transgressors—disobedient women, African-Americans, Indians—as demons, a practice necessary to preserving rigid dualities and carried by the Ku Klux Klan into the twentieth century. Pratt discovers these monstrous images in fact still linger; she finds herself cast as the serpent, which is correspondingly mirrored in the unearthly, science fiction "other," alien and threatening:

> I blame this on too much church, or TV sci-fi, me cast
> as a mutant sexual rampage, Godzilla Satan, basilisk
> eyes, scorching phosphorescent skin, a hiss of words
> deadly if breathed in.
>
> (1990, 114)

From this general representation, in the poem "Crime Against Nature," Pratt goes on to begin questioning directly the attitudes of her ex-husband and mother, both shaped by southern culture's attitudes toward women, both adamantly enforcing the criminalization of her sexuality. Pratt does not begin a new stanza, indicating the connections between the views of her mother and ex-husband and the broader ones she has just outlined, but her questions ("How could they be so / certain I was bad and they were not?") begin at midline, producing an abrupt, charged tone of anger. They acted, says the poet, as if she had begun to "to spin / my skin completely off . . .":

> until, under, loomed a thing, scaly sin, needle teeth
> like poison knives, a monster in their lives who'd run
> with the children in her mouth, like a snake steals
> eggs.
>
> (114–15)

Pratt's mother is complicit in the ideology of the southern "mother-woman."[4] She and Pratt's ex-husband "abhorred" her lesbianism as unnatural; they hate her "inhuman shimmer" like that of a snake, her "crime of moving back and forth / between more than one self, more than one end to the story" (115).

Pratt understands that these people are culturally privileged to name *her*—"the one who tells the tale gets to name the monster . . ." (115)—and that the real threat she poses to the cultural order lies in her insistence that she does not have to live by patterns of sexual behavior and mothering practices forced on her foremothers: "And what are the implications for the political / system of boy children who watched me like a magic / trick, like I had a key to the lock-room mystery? / (Will they lose all respect for national boundaries, / their father, science, or private property?" (119). Pratt recognizes the political intentions behind the ideology of the "natural" woman. Its proponents know that, by refusing heterosexual arrangements and the traditional role of the mother, she may cross into "capable power" (119) with the potential to throw their hierarchical social and legal systems into disarray and even offer other configurations of sexuality and gender that do not sustain patriarchal relations and the oppositions between man and woman, heterosexual and homosexual, lesbian and mother.

Pratt's poetry is deeply informed by her need to break out of these representations. She knows she has to escape from the confining domestic space dictated by heterosexual relations. Therefore, armed with her knowledge of the history of white women in the South, Pratt simultaneously reckons with the equation of the lesbian with diabolical forces and refuses to grieve the loss of privilege she faces by tearing herself/being thrust out of the tradition-bound relation between the southern man and his wife. Pratt's poems about her separation from her husband do not succumb to any kind of domestic panic; that is, even though she deals with feelings of shame that she left her sons behind (ever mindful that she was *forced* to), she does not mourn her privileged position. She also consistently refuses, however, to respond by retrenching and simply valorizing the devalued (lesbian, exiled mother, feminist) end of these oppositions. She does not posit herself purely as victim or victor; while she dares to explore poetically her oppression as a lesbian, Pratt also strives to escape the oppressed/oppressor pattern.

The poem "No Place" provides an example. In the first anecdotal episode in this poem, Pratt's husband demands that she choose her family or life as a lesbian: "Man or woman, her or him, / me or the children. There was no place to be / simultaneous, or between" (18). Pratt does not respond equivocally but rather wishes for some place outside the duality between mother and lesbianism that her husband offers her. She refuses his equation by refusing to choose, and though she ultimately must live apart from her sons, she actively begins to use undomesticated natural environments to configure her and her sons' sense of grief and loss and to move from "no place" to a new place—the new gender arrangement that will allow her to be both lesbian and mother, living her desire and surviving with her sons.

Correspondingly, the interior space of the house in which her ex-husband and sons live is only inhabited in these poems prior to the separation, and these are not sentimental portraits but instead are marked by extreme pain and anger. The very title of "The Place Lost and Gone, The Place Found" indicates movement from a faded place to a discovery; in this poem, Pratt writes of her first visit to her sons after her forced departure. They guide her over to sit in their favorite tree in the yard, and it replaces for the three of them what is now no longer hers but only "their house":

> . . . Their house
> slides away across the lawn to the edge.   Now
> we are in the middle.   Now they show me the inside.

> (37)

Similarly, in "The Laughing Place," Pratt laughs over some memories with one of her sons, flashing back to her and her lover creeping around outside her ex-husband's house in order to try and catch him keeping a woman there overnight; this effort to "steal" is a further extension of Pratt's escape from that domestic arrangement. In discovering the vulnerability of her ex-husband, she admits that she had "thought the house / was brick" but designates those nights of slipping around as the time of "making my escape" (100).

Imagination in the Wilderness

In Pratt's larger narrative, she and her sons move out from the site of the broken domestic arrangement, onto the rivers and creeks and amidst the thick foliage and brush of the southern terrain. They metaphorically begin their search for a new way to be, a new place to survive, as they cross "river after river in the dark, / the Reedy, the Oconee, the Cahaba, all unseen" while going to visit for a weekend at her mother's house because her ex-husband considers Pratt's new house a potentially harmful environment (19). They journey through a no-family's land, constantly crossing the boundaries between the old and the unknown. Pratt says their need to find some in-between place initially leads them into a "huge void / as if that was where we were going, no place at all" (19);

however, in subsequent poems, full of natural settings in which she and her sons reconfigure their relationship in light of the lesbian mother's choices rather than by their culture's dictates, Pratt and her sons begin to define this space for themselves.

At the heart of this revolution is Pratt's eroticism. Her relationship to her sons, her political understandings and undertakings—all of these are determined by her lesbian desire. Throughout this volume, the water imagery—while predicating new patterns for mother-child relationships—is first and foremost sexual, indicating the centrality of Pratt's erotic longings and deeds. She writes that coming out was "a kind of doubling back to myself," the difference between a "stale fountain" and "the creek, pure unknown upwelling, sex." Though she lost custody of her sons, as a lesbian she felt welcomed, "like me running down to be the first to meet, / enter, and be taken by the creek in the early morning" ("Dreaming a Few Minutes" 91).

Pratt's sons appear in these poetic evocations of natural space as reminders of the gender conventions she wishes to escape but primarily as tropes for the new sensualities she is constructing and experiencing. In "Down the Little Cahaba," Pratt's erotic evocation of landscape, sex, and childbirth forges her grief into a searing recognition of her bodily connection to her sons:

> The youngest caught in the
>   rapids:
> half-grown, he hasn't lived with me in years,
> yet his head submerged at a scrape of rock pushes
>
> pain through me, a streak inside my thighs,
> vagina to knee.

                                                              (23)

Pratt recognizes the connections between bodily expressions both within the individual and across relationships. Cultural definitions of the "proper" mother and acceptable sexual behavior for women, both lesbian and heterosexual, have severed these sensual desires from one another.

She believes, in contrast, that her own sexual awakening as a lesbian shouldn't be, indeed cannot be, separated from her sensual ties to her sons, and establishes this natural connection in order to work against the cultural dictum that a lesbian cannot be a mother. Passages from the highly lyrical "Declared Not Fit" illustrate Pratt's insistence that the body's functions and sensations exceed their cultural regulation. She knows she is figured as the other, "Filthy, unfit, not to touch: / those from my womb, red birthslime, come by my cry of agony and pleasure." She is defined as filthy because "sweaty, salty, frantic and calling out sublimely / another woman's name, hands unclenched, I brought down / a cry of joy, then my mouth, mind, hands became / not fit to touch." Then, in a single phrase that begins abruptly at midline, Pratt asserts the astonishing truth about the bodily contact and fluids exchanged in these relationships: "The work is the same" (21). In "My Life You are Talking About," her lover is skittish but the poet insists on making love while her children sleep in another room: ". . . While I whisper, hot, heat / in my breath, how I lost them for touch, / dangerous touch, and we would not believe / the mean knifing voice that says we lose / every love if we touch" (70).

Pratt also confronts and attempts to understand her sons as gendered and sexual beings, like and unlike their mother. In "At Fifteen, the Oldest Son Comes to Visit," she sees "the indelible mark, sketched / on his belly, tattoo of manhood, swirled line / of hair, soft animal pelt, archaic design, / navel to hidden groin." This sign of physical (sexual) development reminds the poet of the ". . . thick line of fur, / navel to cunt" caused during pregnancy by his presence in her womb, and is struck by this "remark on my strict ideas about men and women" (101). In the body of her son, she at once recognizes her own physical traits and sees that he is his own person. As the two of them walk along the edge of the river—"At a distance seen as man and woman, not son / and mother"—she wonders about the fluidity of their separate and fused identities, how "in the next years we might diverge from those selves, those ideas." She wonders, "at this flux of violent water bound downstream," where the river current will take them (107).

Acknowledging these complexities of gender and sexual expression, Pratt does not project an environment in which she and her children could exist without the effects of existing social conditions, however oppressive, or the ways her own choices have been affected by these conditions. In "Dreaming a Few Minutes in a Different Element," she and her sons swim in a creek in which they are "afloat . . . in water steady as our blood, but cold, and older." This also becomes, in her grief and shame, an "anti-creek," a "mean, barren place" where ". . . there is /

water, but it is always the same airless water / pumped around, shallow spray, falling, smelling / of chlorine, dead. It is a place of no feeling" (88–89). While it is the somewhere between a life together in the old, unquestioned setting of heterosexual relations and family and the new, uncertain setting of lesbian sexuality and reconfigured parent-child relationships, the creek does not symbolize an uncomplicated relationship with her sons, but one in which she can relate to them freely out of her own continuing attempts to invent a surviving self. It is a place where together they can *imagine* a better future, a changed world. They stand at the creek's edge, "where everything mingles, simultaneous, undivided" (87). Then, they are underwater, which becomes a simile for the places they will yet go on their adventure into new forms of relationship:

> Submerge,
> and use the green underwater like a lens,
> open the eyes, looking for what is there,
> dreaming a few minutes in a different element.
>
> (93)

While feelings of guilt and shame lurk under the lyrical surfaces of many of the poems in *Crime Against Nature*, these are for her loss of daily contact with her sons, and she makes clear that they are justified only internally to her relationship to her sons and never in terms of the cultural context that has forced their separation. In section 1 of the poem "Shame," she writes in jagged, elliptical phrases that indicate the brokenness caused by her pain: "I ask for justice but do not release / myself. Do I think I was wrong? Yes. / Of course. Was wrong. Am wrong. Can / justify everything but their pain" (45). Pratt means here that she did everything she could without relinquishing her choice to live as a lesbian, and the rest of the responsibility lies in the hands of the institutions that mandated her separation from her children: "I did the best I could. It was not / enough. It was about terror and power. / I did everything I could. Not enough" (24). She understands the connections between her own survival outside the heterosexual contract and the survival of herself and her sons as a family. She is not the "virtuous" mother. She is not the threatening lesbian. Rather, she is a woman looking for another way, and the natural environments she and her sons travel through in these poems symbolize her freedom from the confines of gender polarities as they are traditionally enacted in domestic arrangements. She is grateful her sons have ". . . survived, no suicides, / despite their talk of walks in front of cars, / smashing through plate glass. Despite guilt . . ." ("Shame" 47). When she finally returns again to domestic space, it is the home she and her lover share, and it is the place where her sons visit her after they have all "survived": "Their curious eyes are on life that widens in a place / little known, our pleasure without shame. We talk / and the walls seem to shift and expand around us. / The breaking of some frozen frame . . ." (48). Shame has been replaced by both pleasure and responsibility, and the room grows with their intimations of new models for sexuality, gender, the mother-child relationship, and family.

The Transgressor Talks Back

In Pratt's poetic answers to the society that condemns her, the snake serves as a special sign of transformation in nature as well as a sign of how any sign can take on multiple meanings. With her sons on the riverbanks, Pratt points out a ". . . snake, with a silver fish crossways in its mouth, / just another one of the beautiful terrors of nature, / how one thing can turn into another without warning" (119). The "serpent" points to the ability to cross and recross patterns of self-identification and difference as a beautiful, beneficial, generative process. It is also a terror, threatening in its power to overturn and even destroy old ways of thinking. Pratt's dialogues/arguments with the society that has condemned her are fueled by her insistent proclamation of her lesbian body and during her and her children's attempts to build a new understanding of their lives together. Various voices speak with skepticism or outright hatred about Pratt's being a lesbian or a lesbian mother, and the poet "talks back" to these accusers. As she relates how her former husband and her mother in particular attempted to criminalize her lesbian sexuality according to laws of the "natural," she comprehends the extent of the power they had over her and the force they used without hesitation; these accusers had the cultural power to speak, while she had none. The "conversation" never occurs because the poet is rejected, exiled.

When her mother speaks the poet is literally without response; when Pratt calls to ask if she and her sons can come to stay at her mother's house, she faces complete rejection: "I ask her to take me and not him, and she / refuses.   She says: *He's been like a son to me*" ("Dreaming a Few Minutes," 89). Similarly, in "The Child Taken from the Mother," Pratt extends the metaphor of a male institution, the poker game, for the power her husband has at his disposal in the domestic space of the heterosexual contract and the ways he has victimized her. She understands that the men involved in the game know what's in her hand and that in fact she is trapped both empty-handed and outside the house, while inside, the men undertake their game without her: ". . . Strange men, / familiar, laugh and curse in the kitchen, whisky, / bending over cards . . ." (24). Though she speaks in this setting and continues throughout the years to speak her anger and grief, the men on the inside do not have to listen to her, thrusting her to the outside. She is left alone, excluded, both in terms of her personal relationships with biological family and in the broader social sense.

Pratt adamantly maintains that she is not the guilty party throughout this volume, however, and uses serpent imagery to talk back to the "familiar" men who have mandated her exile. In section 1 of the long poem "Crime Against Nature," for instance, she relates her harassment at the hands of a group of men outside a convenience store, all in triplet, a stanza form she uses in these poems to build dramatic tension. The men taunt her—"*What's wrong with you, girl? . . . You some kind of dyke?*"—for not responding to their overtures. In her angry self-avowal, the poet becomes a serpent, pleased to become the demon they imagine and use her venomous power to resist them: "Sweating, damned if I'd give them the last say, / hissing into the mouth of the nearest face, *Yesss*, . . ." (111–12). While her taunters want to frighten her back down "into whatever place I'd slid from," the poet speaks with courage, which in turn increases her energy for fighting back. She goes on to dream of "an inverted ending," in which she refigures the snake imagery as an empowering dream vehicle for her rage:

> . . . I was shaken out
>
> on the street where my voice reared up her snout,
> unlikely as a blacksnake racing from a drain, fire-
> spitting, whistling like a siren, one word, *yes*

She imagines herself as the fertile snake which can change one thing into another; she has "a mouth like a conjuring trick, a black hole / that swallows their story and turns it inside out" (112–13). This imagined resistance is not overtly violent but actively reworks the men's story so that the denigrating label they have assigned her becomes a designation of strength and the power to name her own identity.

The poker players and the parking lot taunters gain their power from legally sanctioned condemnations of homosexuality, and Pratt also weaves serpentine representations of lesbian eroticism in resistance to codified hatred. In section 3 of "Crime Against Nature," the poet illustrates how the lesbian as monster is in fact systematized in legal statutes: "The hatred baffles me: individual, doctrinal, codified" (116). In a series of unrhymed couplets, the poet begins to fathom that her sexual behavior would have received, in the year she left her husband, "not less than five nor more than sixty years" for "a depraved and perverted sexual instinct." However, in figurative language suddenly carried in rhymed couplets, the monster becomes a prophetic serpent that emerges from deep waters carrying the revolutionary potential of lesbian desire. In this erotic configuration, the finger is like a tongue, and the tongue like a snake that travels inside the lover's body, "winding through salty walls, the labyrinth, curlicue, / the underground spring, rocks that sing, and the cave / with an oracle yelling at the bottom, certainly depraved" (116).

Lesbian Mothers and the Power of Story

Unlike this angry set of poems, the poem "All the Women Caught in Flaring Light" deals tenderly with the attitudes and experiences of other lesbians (other than lovers). This is a poem about the possibility of lesbian community, about public life in a subculture, and yet it centers in the diverse personal stories of these lesbians as mothers. It relies on Pratt's understanding of autobiography, in that she tells her story for the sake of other women like her even as she constantly asserts the differences between women. Pratt here works to deconstruct the idea that women *are* mothers, or are meant to be mothers, no matter what, unless, of course, they are lesbian. She once again counters the idea that lesbianism is unnatural, and therefore is incompatible with motherhood (thought to be the most natural activity of all for women), even as she opposes the idea that woman's highest calling is to bear children, for this itself solidifies the heterosexual bond and gives rise to fear of the lesbian.

In section 1 of the poem, Pratt builds a contrast between a room of women doing anything, perhaps playing cards or having a meeting, and a room of women playing pool and obviously enjoying themselves. The women in the first room are engaged in "ordinary" "womanly" activities and are "naturally" considered mothers ("If we / leaned in at the door and I said, *Those women are mothers,* you wouldn't be surprised, except / at me for pointing out the obvious fact"), while the women in the second room are not thought to be mothers, and are in fact engaged in activity that is socially constructed as male ("If I said in your ear, through metallic guitars, *These women are mothers,* you wouldn't believe me, / would you?") (29).

Pratt self-consciously addresses her own experience as a lesbian mother but also traces the connections between her own life-story and those of other lesbians around her. Her desire to be among them means that she cannot write a purely personal poem but rather must deal with their stories as well as part of their public life together in the lesbian community. She does this in section 2; she does not include the stories of others merely as they reflect on her own but rather discloses precisely the self-related narratives of each woman. She speaks of women by their first names and by their pain: Edie, who raised her children for seven years but has had not even a visit since then; Martha, whose infant was taken from her; and Connie, a free spirit who carefully hides her own tale of a father keeping children from her. Nevertheless, Pratt is clear that these bits of narrative do not provide the whole story. She does not try to recreate the untold portions of these mother's lives but says that each bit of story is as cryptic as the mark that sets them apart as members of this subculture, "the ink / tattoo, the sign that admits us to this room iridescent / in certain kinds of light, then vanishing, invisible" (32). Section 3 is Pratt's commentary on the power of her poem; she understands that it cannot bring all the women and their children together. But it can share their stories, and in so doing, send the pain reverberating with Pratt's own not only through the lyrical rhythms and painful narratives of a poem but through the political goals of an oppressed community. She understands her own narrative to be integrally connected to the stories of other women like herself, all of them challenges to the criminalization of the lesbian and confining definitions of the mother. Pratt encompasses them and the marginalized culture she shares with them in her imagination of the in-between, from which they can imagine the time and place when the lesbian as mother will be accepted.

"the hidden road": Racism and Lesbianism

As she explores her social exile and simultaneously tries to define her connections to communities of women, Pratt realizes that she must also confront the kinds of oppression she herself has perpetuated, namely the racism and classism she inherited from her family. Pratt has always refused to assert that she is completely and finally different and separate from her white father, which, in the words of Biddy Martin and Chandra Mohanty, "would (and in much feminist literature does) exempt the daughter from her implication in the structures of privilege/oppression, structures that operate in ways much more complex than the male/female split itself" (1986, 191).

Pratt first began exploring the connections among race, gender, and class in two of the long poems in *We Say We Love Each Other*. In "Reading Maps: Two," she traces her history as a southern white woman back through her mother, grandmothers, and aunts; again, she works toward understanding through the mother figure, in essence back through her "mothers." Trying to obtain a map of their suffering and survival, she seeks to understand the beauty and pain of their lives as white southern women, but her chief thematic goal is to come to some understanding of how they have dealt with the racism pervading their lives. The form of this poem reflects Pratt's endeavor; different length stanzas with varying line lengths meander down the page, a visual indication of the fits and starts, disappointments and discoveries, of the poet's journey. Pratt longs for her mother and the other women in her family to speak to her, to explain to her how they have survived. About her mother, she writes:

> I want her to tell me
> she doubted them, the men, the women, who taught her to
> live with things the way they were. I want to know
> if sometimes she veered from the road she was told to take:
>   (1985, 36)

Likewise, she wants "to drive into the past now and ask the women / in my family what they thought about what they saw / from the porch . . ."

where they quilted and knitted with "hands that could speak / stitch by stitch . . ." (37). She wants to know what they thought about the roads leading to and from their houses and the now hidden roads crisscrossing their property; these roads are physical symbols of the histories of the Indians who used to occupy the land and the African-Americans who have occupied it since the era of slavery. She remembers that as a child sitting with these women in their communal space on the "porch where men never sat," she herself did not see "the hidden road" marked by "the feet of Choctaw people walking from the Tombigbee / to the mound of the great mother, walking to the west / with the little cry *yaiya ishkitini*." Neither did she see the road "made by the feet of Ibo people stolen / from the land where they hoed their sweet yams, beans, / walking to chop cotton in strange fields at dawn . . ." (38–39).

Here Pratt is attempting to identify a more accurate cartography, one that her ancestresses may or may not have been conscious of. Pratt longs to believe these women had "hidden ways / that they used to change how things were"; she longs to "tell them I want / to alter the pattern we were born into, to ask them / to help me . . . ," but they are all now buried at the end of an "unwinding grey thread" of a road, unable to divulge their secrets (39). The poem concludes with her journey to her mother's house on the same road and her sorrowful realizations that her mother will not tell her what she wants to know. Pratt wishes to discover how her mother felt as she sat on the porch with the other women, "if from there death and sorrow ever looked / like the white men at the courthouse, or herself, / or if she saw how she resembled the woman opposite" (40). Her mother, however, retreats into utter and final silence upon hearing that her daughter is a lesbian: the fact of her daughter's otherness further rigidifies her reticence about speaking about the ways she has been both oppressed and oppressor. Even though Pratt remembers baths with her mother, "the water wide as a creek around us," and even though she has wished they could be "separate, like islands in the bend of the river, apart / from the land we live in, different from how we have been, / and together," she is completely cut off from any knowledge of her racist past through her mother (40). In the end, then, she can only converse with these women—her mother and the other women in her family, as well as the Choctaw and African women—in her poetic imagination. She must undertake the long journey into her racist past alone, out of her experience of being separated from her privilege as a heterosexual, white mother in the southern tradition.

In *Crime Against Nature*, Pratt's poems about being both lesbian and mother surround a group of poems that deal directly with Pratt's relationships to her white family and to African-American women in the South. In "The Mother Before Memory," she writes of both her birth mother and the African-American woman who took care of her from infancy through early childhood. Her first memory is of this nanny figure. She has "no story, no picture of the first memory," but knows the African-American woman held her as they sat alone in a dark room. In her nanny's presence, Pratt remembers, she felt completely safe, but at the time she realizes that an enormous gulf of race and class difference divided them: ". . . I never called her / my mother" (56).

It is difficult to write this kind of memory lyrically without sliding into sentimentality; the writer is often tempted to portray the nurturing nanny without acknowledging the brutal forces of racism that separate woman and child. But Pratt is aware that this is something she is "not supposed to remember"; feeling such a strong attachment to this woman should be hidden, for in racist ideology it erases the rightful place of the white mother. While this memory occupies a single stanza in section 3 of the poem, section 4 is a longer narrative piece on a visit Pratt and her sons paid to her former nanny when the woman had grown very old. Here, Pratt hears of the suffering of this woman in the "sibilant words" of her "delta language." This woman's personal narrative and racial history is marred by the loss of children by force; thus Pratt seeks to understand how they are the same (". . . us two / in the long story of women and children / severed" [57]). But she also understands that she must acknowledge her own feelings of loss only within the larger context of racist violence that has pervaded her native region. In the poem "I Am Ready to Tell All I Know," she writes of a nineteen-year-old man named Michael Donald, who was lynched in Mobile, and seeks to relate her loss as a lesbian mother to the loss Donald's mother must feel: "When my children bleed, my own blood rushes / as if out of me. What if he were one of mine? / But which bloodied one, mine?" (75–76). Again, triplet stanzas provide a tone of urgency under the weight of such violence, as Pratt ponders the effects of racism on motherhood and the difficulty of easily assigning responsibility for oppression.

In the end, just as she does with the lesbian mothers in the smoky bar, she avoids too simple a relationship between herself and these African-American women, for she realizes how cozy notions of women's community have discounted or elided her own difference as a lesbian mother, and she is very much aware of her ability to do this to African-American or any other women. All that remains is her own story, the facts of her interaction with these women, and her open-ended contemplation of the meaning of her relationships with them. Thus, Pratt writes in coalitional voice only insofar as she considers women's relationships and seems interested in presenting the problems inherent in these relationships to her lesbian and feminist listener/readers. Out of the in-between of identity that difference and oppression have forced/invited her to travel into, she avoids any essentialist definitions of "woman" or "women" and returns to the fundamental task of telling in detail her own story, in the hope that other women will respond with theirs.

The Scandalous Ancient Way

From the in-between environments where she queries oppressive definitions of both lesbian and mother, Pratt charts new poetic terrain, insisting that the intimate details of her own struggle do not turn poetry into prose but rather open up within it new possibilities for political and cultural understandings and even self-definition. While she relies on an informal tone to narrate the stark facts of her pain, she creates meaning lyrically by using symbolic imagery and always destabilizes the relationship between self and other, between the individual and culture, and even within the self, by alternately self-disclosing and avoiding the idea of any discrete identity. She evades essentialism precisely by beginning with the body and then moving into free and "wild" space, for the present cultural moment requires that she adamantly claim her own lesbian desire in order to challenge and reconstruct traditional patterns of gender and sexuality. Ever mindful of the forces arrayed against her, she fights back with language, symbol and form, and she gains the ground of telling her story (finally), owning her own sexuality, relating freely to her sons, and relating honestly with other women. Snakelike, she is at once both terror and beauty, a sign of destruction and generation; as she writes in the final lines of "Crime Against Nature," she offers her poetry as exuberant self-celebration and fearless attack: ". . . I advance in the scandalous ancient way of women: / our assault on enemies, walking forward, skirts lifted, / to show the silent mouth, the terrible power, our secret" (120).

Conclusion ────────────────────────────

The poet Audre Lorde's death on November 17, 1992, marked the end of a long, fruitful career for an African-American feminist poet of enormous poetic and political vision. As a leader of the feminist poetry movement, Lorde consistently demonstrated the ways that a feminist poet (or, as she described herself, "a Black Lesbian, Feminist, Warrior Poet, fighting the good fight in spite of it all" [quoted in Lockett 1993, 58]) could inspire a whole generation of women to speak their own lives and dream new dreams in poetry. In her unflinchingly straightforward treatments of the subjects of sexism and racism, however, she proved to be as much a catalyst for change within women's communities themselves as a faithful opponent of the forces of oppression in dominant American culture; she epitomized the need for women to work together out of diversity rather than by inventing and imposing one definition of "Woman." She consistently challenged other women to understand that their work could be defeated by "the inability to recognize the notion of difference as a dynamic human force which is enriching rather than threatening to the defined self" (1984, 44).

As the ties between Lorde and many of the poets I have examined indicate, Lorde's concept of difference was very important in a movement constantly seeking to understand its own multiplicity. Lorde indeed proved to be a warrior, fighting for women's unique and diverse visions, visions that might go to waste if women poets in general, and feminist poets in particular, did not begin to realize the ways they needed to talk to each other as well as to the guardians of the American tradition that had largely excluded women's particular ideas about and needs for poetry. Lorde imagined, lived, and wrote the hard struggle that awaits women who dare explore the sameness and difference that connects them: "we cannot alter history / by ignoring it / nor the contradictions / who we are." But she also understood the potential for women to gain the prize of self-understanding, community, and politi-

cal possibility through exploring their connections: "if we lose / some-
day women's blood will congeal / upon a dead planet / if we win / there
is no telling" ("Outlines," 1986, 9, 13).

The verdict is still out, of course, on whether or not Lorde will be
"disappeared" in establishment poetry as her forerunner Muriel Rukeyser was. But the reception of Lorde's work within the feminist
poetry movement and the enormous outpouring of tribute, among
feminist poets and activists alike, occasioned by the end of her life leaves
no doubt that she will be remembered by future generations of feminist
poets (see Lockett 1993; Christian 1993). While her life and work
proved to be a touchstone for feminists poets in the two decades following the cultural and political emergence of the women's movement, in
many ways her death—and a full recognition of the importance of the
first generation of the feminist poetry movement's leadership—may
have actually marked the beginning of an important new stage in feminist poets' self-consciousness of the scope and depth of their work.

Signs of this self-consciousness were becoming more apparent in the
late 1980s, with the publication of inclusive and self-consciously feminist anthologies like Marge Piercy's *Early Ripening: American Women's
Poetry Now* (1987), which noted the strong connections between the
feminist poetry movement and the social/political women's movement
and offered perhaps the most inclusive selection of poets to date. These
signs continued to appear in the early 1990s, marked especially by Florence Howe's revision of the classic anthology, *No More Masks* (1993),
originally published in 1971, in which she adds poets whose careers are
notably marked by their activity in the feminist poetry movement and
pays special attention to women of color, lesbians, and others who were
omitted in the first edition. Howe's updated anthology demonstrates
that this new self-consciousness is very obviously mindful of the ways
that difference has been used and celebrated among diverse women
poets who simultaneously subscribe to common readings of "Woman,"
in the name of women's community, and write their own unique experiences as they explore the diversity of "women" and the shifting ground
of gender. In her 1993 collection of essays, Adrienne Rich clearly speaks
of feminist poetry as a movement that took hold with great strength in
the early 1970s and is ongoing and vital. These texts show an increased
acknowledgment of the historical relevance and the immense scope of
the feminist poetry movement.

Nevertheless, the bulk of the extensive feminist critical work of fully understanding the work of the feminist poetry movement still remains to be done. My goal for the readings I have conducted is that they contribute to this critical consciousness, in the conviction that increased critical understandings will not only insure that the history of the movement and the work of each of its poets holds a place within the American poetic consciousness but that they will also provide the energy that only principled criticism (and self-criticism) can inject into an ongoing movement that actively desires and imagines its own future. Each of the poets whose work I have explored has made a vital contribution to this movement and the present state of its self-understanding, and my hope is that these readings will aid in establishing the feminist critical atmosphere to historicize, analyze, and further energize the work of these and other poets and the movement as a whole.

Because of the deficit in feminist criticism of the feminist poetry movement, the critical model I have provided is in many ways simply groundwork, but I see important issues rising from this critical expedition and the resulting readings. First of all, especially after charting in some depth the scope of themes and formal strategies adopted by Grahn, Jordan, Anzaldúa, Klepfisz, Harjo, and Pratt, the idea of a women's tradition that does not rely on a single definition of "Woman" seems nothing short of indispensable. My consideration of these representative poets alone demonstrates the range of backgrounds and self-understandings that come into play in poetry that is always nevertheless united in the idea that women have some common areas to explore, some important and shared reasons for writing to, with, about, and even for each other as women. The central, necessary critical attitude requires reading for "Woman" with the understanding that "she" may or may not appear in expected ways. Critics and readers may expect feminist poets to adopt provisional definitions of gender in order to converse with each other about their common experiences of gender, but they must also realize that these poets will always write about their diverse individual experiences, whether they explicitly address issues of women's community or not. It is fundamental that we give unwavering attention to the ways that feminist poets both locate themselves subjectively in relation to their own histories and experiences as well as promote notions of and participate in women's (and other kinds of) community. In this process, we can chart both the more solitary, lyric-based practices of introspection and self-understanding as well as the performance-oriented and hybrid practices, like coalitional voice and the lyric-narrative, which root feminist poets in the integral interaction of writer, text, and reader/listener(s) and promote feminist identification and action.

This nexus of poetic possibilities is apparent in the readings I have undertaken here. The need to define a self and pursue survival has led Grahn to establish the centrality of personal memory and a commitment to fighting what seem like overwhelming odds against the oppressed; Jordan to list and assert her rights; Anzaldúa to double back within her experimental text in search of some sense of a core self; Harjo and Klepfisz to burrow deeply into their specific heritages in search of a self that can withstand devastating historical violence and celebrate cultural traditions; and Pratt to examine the fragments of her own personal history looking for some ongoing, surviving center (however fictive). At the same time, these poets constantly search for community for its potential to unify and empower individual women. Grahn celebrates feminist community through narrative, "commonality," and coalitional voice. Jordan and Pratt insist on telling their own stories only within larger narratives, narratives that relate the "hidden" histories of oppressed groups. Anzaldúa writes within and against fragments of historical texts, shaping her "mestiza" consciousness in relation to multiple historical forces. Klepfisz is only able to state some sense of self by working from deep within Jewish history and culture and the Yiddish language and rewriting them; her self is only evident through textual movement between past and present, between herself and her historical communities. And when Harjo combines lyric and narrative and turns to the prose poem, she situates her own struggle in more than one cultural world and alternately defines gender through each of them; she has to create her own distinct political vision, drawing on multiple cultural resources, in order to achieve some sense of synthesis of all the places from which she comes.

When each of these poets calls on a sense of an ongoing, surviving self—through the lyrical "I"—she understands the necessity of self-assertion to survival, and the necessity for some sense of subjectivity that withstands the storms of division and marginalization. However, as Pratt puts it, they constantly seek to move back and forth "between more than one self, more than one end to the story" (1990, 115), highlighting the ways that continual self- and communal-definition require writing and rewriting the story. This desire to explore incessantly the space between self and other, and to insist on celebrating difference, at once contains the feminist poetry movement and further destabilizes it. But this destabilization, in my reading, is a positive force, preventing stasis and exclusion, promoting continued exploration and redefinition. To put it another way, it simultaneously defines the movement and drives it forward.

This paradox proves to be perhaps the central identifying characteristic of feminist poets as a movement, for these very patterns of poetic exploration—which heavily emphasize difference—themselves mark these poets as a community. While the concept of "sisterhood" dominated in early analyses of feminist poetry, and implied the suspension (or the nonexistence) of difference, these poets welcome difference, within and between women, and indeed understand it in Lorde's sense, that is, as a "dynamic human force" that "enhances" subjectivity and the relations between individual selves. These poets, in contrast, see themselves as a community, but only because they are involved in the same set of activities: understanding the ways their gendered experience results from oppressive structures and practices that dominate political life; writing their lives fearlessly into poetry, always attentive to the flux of self-definition; and entering into community/coalition by conversing with each other in their poetry as well as in their prose and their activism.

This notion of community means that criticism of feminist poetry must rely on both a poetic and sociological/political understanding of what goes on within any given poem. The poem holds its own meanings but ultimately always also relates to the sense of community the women create textually and intertextually. As Muriel Rukeyser understood it, "the poem as object" must be usurped in favor of a notion of the poem as an exchange of energy that carries "the capacity to produce change in existing conditions" (1949, 185–86). The women's poetry movement thus becomes significant both as an aesthetic current within the larger stream of American literature and as a strategic social/political practice within the ongoing struggle of the larger women's movement in the American context. The idea of the women's poetry movement as a movement is and will remain relevant precisely because these women poets see themselves as important to some poetic and political work that relies on and yet surpasses their own individual poems.

This very attention to difference as constitutive of literary and/or political community indeed belongs to a vital trend in American poetry at the end of the twentieth century, and the feminist poetry movement may be said to have made a fundamental, if not the central, contribution to this evolution. Indeed, far from being truly revolutionary in any isolated sense, feminist poetry's very attention to the possibilities of a communal role for poetry that nevertheless celebrates and uses difference identifies this movement with the changes in American poetry overall—the "racing convergence of tributaries" whose "origins and nature . . . are not just personal but communal" (Rich 1993, 130, 175). And these readings of feminist poets, this critical study, highlight the relationship of the feminist poetry movement to this larger transformation of ideas about poetry and poetic practices in yet another very important way, for all of these feminist poets also relate to other poetry subcultures that locate themselves in opposition to the poetry establishment and understand the communal force of poetry central to their cultural work on identity and difference.

Of course, this happy recognition that feminist poets are at least a part of, if not on the cutting edge of, a shift in American attitudes toward poetry does not entirely negate the continued power of the historically empowered institutions of American poetry to interfere with the distribution and recognition of what is happening on what their arbiters understand as "the margins." Again, Rich's perceptions elucidate this state of affairs and point out how the neglect of women's poetry specifically extends even into counterestablishment circles. She recalls meeting in the late 1980s with a poet with whom she had participated in antiwar poetry readings during the Vietnam years; according to Rich, this poet wanted to know where she went after that burst of literary comraderie in the 1960s, saying, " '*You disappeared! You simply disappeared.*' " The irony of the word "disappeared" is not lost on this reader; however, the deeper irony lies in Rich's statement that the feminist poetry movement had actually made her "feel more apparent, more visible—to myself and to others—as a poet" (1993, 164–65). The task of maintaining an outer-directed oppositional stance toward the poetry establishment and its various enclaves remains important, but Rich's experience of a vital, inspiring literary movement among women, and the experience and work of the poets examined here, illustrates that the feminist poetry movement clearly has maintained its own terms of conversation and its own (however evolving) standards for poetic expression. The necessary impulse to pay attention to how the "center" of American poetry is defined by those with cultural and political power remains strong, but feminist poets in the years 1970–1990 certainly moved beyond any primary concern with simply finding a niche within a larger tradition bent on ignoring, or at least downplaying, their accomplishments.

The feminist poetry movement has not experienced, and shows no signs of approaching, a static state. In spite of a lack of critical attention from either establishment or feminist critics, the movement flourished greatly during the two decades after its inception, and continues to show signs of strength and promise and even the potential to influence the American poetry scene in a radical fashion. My hope is that the project I have conducted here will enhance this strength and assist in carrying out this promise. My hope is that it will work in both the outer-directed and inner-directed critique of the women's movement, carrying along its oppositional project of revising the American literary tradition and, most significantly, aiding feminist poets and their readers in understanding the forces at work in their own literary communities and thereby fostering the continued work of feminist poetry itself. Finally, in the spirit of energetic conversation that has characterized this movement from its inception, I extend this work as an invitation to other poets and critics to explore further the importance of feminist poetry to both women's and American literature.

Notes

Introduction

1. The Lamont Prize for Poetry is awarded annually by the Academy of American Poets for a second volume of poetry. The poet must by nominated by the publisher with whom the book is under contract.

2. I use the somewhat neutral term "establishment" to refer to the most centralized forces within contemporary American poetry as a culture industry. This consists of the "mainstream," established poets and critics who work in and through culturally sanctioned organizations like the American Academy of Poets and publications like the *American Poetry Review*. It is not surprising that feminist poets often have a much more pointed view of what they consider to be the hegemonic nature of this "establishment." A prime example is Joy Harjo's reference to the "poetry mafia" (1989, 8).

3. For instance, though Pratt gave the money she received from the Lamont Prize to several gay and lesbian activist organizations, she was very pleased with the idea of "all the little libraries, all over this country, that are going to order this book because it's on the list of award winners for next year" (Zipter 1990).

4. A partial listing includes Paula Gunn Allen, Alta, Gloria Anzaldúa, Lorna Dee Cervantes, Chrystos, Cheryl Clarke, Jan Clausen, Wanda Coleman, Judy Grahn, Susan Griffin, Joy Harjo, June Jordan, Irena Klepfisz, Audre Lorde, Janice Mirikitani, Pat Mora, Cherrie Moraga, Robin Morgan, Pat Parker, Marge Piercy, Margaret Randall, Adrienne Rich, Wendy Rose, Carol Lee Sanchez, Kitty Tsui, Nellie Wong, and Mitsuye Yamada.

5. Anzaldúa has published in, among others, *Conditions* and *Ikon*; Harjo has also published in *Conditions, Heresies,* and the *Woman Poet*; Jordan has frequently published in *Ms.* and for years has written a regular column, often about feminist issues, in the *Progressive*; Klepfisz has also published in *Sinister Wisdom* and *Womannews*; Pratt has published in *Bridges* and *Sinister Wisdom,* among others. Most of their volumes of poetry have been published by small "minority" presses, if not by feminist presses. The intertextuality of their works (quoting one another, speaking to one another) is notable, as I will demonstrate in chapter 1. These poets relate heavily to their marginalized racial/ethnic and/or

lesbian/bisexual communities, in which they address feminist issues regularly. Thus, for instance, Harjo has been published often in a wide range of Native American publications, while Jordan has appeared in African-American journals like *Callaloo*, Klepfisz in the Jewish journal *Tikkun*, and Pratt in *Gay Community News*.

Chapter 1. The Life of the Movement

1. Other anthologies published in 1973 or within the next two years include Barba and Chester 1973, Gill 1973, Goulianos 1974, Iverson and Ruby 1975, Kaplan 1975, Segnitz and Rainey 1973, and Stanford 1973.
2. These two lines also inspired the title of the anthology *The World Split Open: Four Generations of Women Poets in England and America, 1552–1970* (Bernikow 1974).
3. Silliman discusses the fate of those who are institutionally "disappeared" from "the public discourse and consciousness of poetry" (1990, 149).
4. Brooke Adams (1980) maintains that three phases of distribution provided this network with its readership base: 1967–70, when feminists found out about feminist publications primarily at local meetings; 1970–72, when women's centers replaced the local group meeting; and post-1972, when the feminist bookstore became the primary source of information. My own research suggests that these phases were not so neatly distinct and that the press itself became a self-perpetuating network through its own substantial advertising in virtually all its publications, including books.
5. Rich has always published with W. W. Norton. *Diving in the Wreck* was significant because it marked her coming out as a lesbian feminist.
6. The *Second Wave*, based in Boston, illustrates well; see Wright 1972 and Williams 1971. See also *Awake and Move* 1, no. 3 (June 1971), which urges feminists not to compare their oppression to that of blacks; and a special issue of *It Ain't Me Babe* on racism in the women's movement (1, no. 7 [1970]). Many of these newspapers also include stories about and notices of movement activities with women in prison.
7. The editorial statements in the editions of *Conditions* published in the 1980s chronicle just one publishing collective's fight for survival as public funds dried up or were withdrawn.
8. Hannah More's assessment is representative; she wrote of women that the "lofty epic, the pointed satire, and the more daring and successful flights of the tragic muse, seem reserved for the bold adventurers of the other sex" (1855). If women wrote poetry at all, it had to be in what were then considered the less important forms, like the lyric. I am grateful to Carole Myers for our ongoing discussions about the

changing attitudes toward women writers in eighteenth- to twentieth-century England and America.

9. See announcements of poetry readings in *Majority Report* 2:3 (July 1972): 9; *off our backs* 1:5 (December 1975): 16; *Feminist Communications* 3:1 (September 1976); and *Feminary* 5:23 (November 23, 1974): 5.

10. See, for example, notices for the "Southeastern Women's Festival" (held near Nashville), *Feminary* 6:14 (August 6, 1975); "A Women's Outdoor Cultural Festival" (Chapel Hill, North Carolina), *Feminary* 6:11 (May 25, 1975), 2; and "The First Women's Multi-Media Festival" (Los Angeles), *Everywoman* 2:16 (November 12, 1971), 14. Judy Grahn and Pat Parker recorded their immensely popular Olivia Records release *Where Would I Be Without You?* at the latter.

11. Brodine's language is very reminiscent of Paulo Friere's when he describes the way revolutionary social action emerges in the dialectic in which action produces reflection, which produces more action (or "praxis," as he terms it); see Friere 1974. This connection illustrates the links between radical feminism in the United States and other liberation movements, especially in Latin America, where Friere's philosophy has deeply informed especially Marxist/Christian-influenced fronts like the Sandinistas in Nicaragua. Not coincidentally, feminist poets were very interested in the Nicaraguan revolution; Adrienne Rich, Jan Clausen, June Jordan, Joy Harjo, and Susan Sherman (among others) visited Nicaragua during the 1980s.

Chapter 2. Judy Grahn's Poetics of Commonality

1. I will refer to Grahn's collected works (1978) rather than to the now out-of-print original publication of each series of poems under examination here. These include *Edward the Dyke and Other Poems,* with drawings by Wendy Cadden, Brenda Crider, and Gail Hodgins (San Francisco: Women's Press Collective, 1971); *The Common Woman,* with drawings by Wendy Cadden (Oakland, California: Women's Press Collective, 1973); *A Woman Is Talking to Death,* with drawings by Karen Sjholm (Oakland, California: Women's Press Collective, 1974); and *She Who: A Graphic Book of Poems with Fifty-four Images of Women,* with drawings by Wendy Cadden and Karen Sjholm (Oakland, California: Diana Press, 1977).

2. Flyer insert, *Mother Lode,* no. 4 (Spring 1972).

3. In *The Highest Apple* (1985), Grahn defines the tradition she discusses as "Lesbian" rather than as feminist, and her use of the term "Lesbian" is both specific and general. That is, she interprets all of the nine poets she discusses (including Emily Dickinson) as specifically lesbian because they loved/love women erotically, but she grounds her critical perspective in a definition offered by Mary J. Carruthers (1983). Ac-

cording to Carruthers, "These four poets have voices that are bold, even arrogant, in their common, urgent desire to seize the language and forge with it an instrument for articulating women. Not all women writing today write this kind of poetry, not all poets who are Lesbians are Lesbian poets, nor all Lesbian poets always lesbian" (293). Quoted in Grahn 1985, xix. While Grahn goes on to ground her observations in a reading of Sappho and to call for an examination of openly lesbian writing, she also makes many more general statements about the writings of woman-identified, or (in my term) feminist, writers.

4. In light of her stance of the early 1970s, the fact that Grahn published *The Work of a Common Woman* with a progressive but not exclusively women-run press (the Crossing Press) has been overlooked. In more recent years, she has also published extensively with Beacon Press. Grahn and Arnold's "separatist" goals were tactical, specific to a crucial period of strategizing for a strong feminist cultural and political base in the early days of the women's liberation movement. As Grahn says in *The Highest Apple* (1985), the writer needs a "strong home-base" from which "she can approach the world at large as somebody in particular" (58).

5. In Brady and McDaniel 1980, Irena Klepfisz (herself a veteran of women's publishing) asserts that "women's studies departments generally don't emphasize feminist presses . . . The focus is primarily on material that is coming out of the commercial presses." Brady responds: "I think that many women teaching in women's studies programs are not educated about the necessities and hardships of the feminist presses" (79).

6. All of the first editions of the works Grahn eventually collected in *The Work of a Common Woman* were accompanied by striking pen and ink drawings, many of them by Wendy Cadden, Grahn's coworker in the San Francisco women's movement. These visual images further root the *Common Woman* poems in physical experience by adding a distinct facial expression to each woman and add depth to the poems. The pictures nevertheless stand on their own and are not merely incidental or ornamental to the poems. They emphasize Grahn's commitment to art that reached women on many levels and in multiple ways; as her poems were designed to be read either silently or publicly, so were her poems not the only expression in any of these three books. Rather, they stand beside other expressions that also invite response from readers/viewers. Nevertheless, because they do not contribute to the performance aspects of "The Common Woman," and the visual arts fall outside the scope of the project, I will not discuss them further here.

7. Grahn later used "Crow Dikes" to accompany Ereshkigal, the owner of a lesbian bar and "queen" of the lesbian underground culture in *The Queen of Swords* (1987). Grahn notes that crows "often accompany the goddess of death in mythology, and represent the world of spirits from the land of the dead" (169n).

8. Grahn experiments with "feminine" rhyme, an Old English term for words that are, as Grahn puts it, "two-syllable, unimportant, used only for humor, not worth listing" (1978, 76). This is an instance in this plainsong, and the second plainsong is the poet's substantive attempt to revise this notion/practice as a positive and playful one for feminist poetry.

Chapter 3. Feminist and Black Arts Strategies in the Poetry of June Jordan

1. Jordan was a contributing editor for *Chrysalis* when Lorde was the journal's editor. Their poetics differ greatly, and comparing the two also highlights Jordan's emphasis on class as an underexplored fact of oppression. Of Lorde's assertion that "poetry is not a luxury" (which became something of a maxim in the women's movement in the late 1970s), Jordan once said, "I'm not sure that I know what Audre is saying. Certainly she's speaking as a poet. I know that most women are not poets . . . For many people, and for many women, especially Black women, in this country, poetry is a luxury" (1981b, 90). Lorde's essay "Poetry Is Not a Luxury" was originally published in *Chrysalis*, and later appeared in *Sister Outsider* (1984).
2. In his study of the development of the "jazz aesthetic" in the poetry of Amiri Baraka, William J. Harris notes that Baraka uses the insistent, even wild, rhythms of jazz "to move the reader/auditor, to make him/her want to dance." *The Poetry and Poetics of Amiri Baraka: The Jazz Aesthetic* (Columbia: University of Missouri Press, 1985), 106.
3. Moynihan's report was released in 1965. For Jordan's prose response to the vein of rhetoric used in this report, see the essay "Don't You Talk About My Momma!" (1993). Jordan says the effect of Moynihan's vocabulary is the idea that the African-American family is itself to blame for its problems because it fails "to resemble the patriarchal setup of White America" (67).
4. Jordan recalled that, when she showed this poem to a friend, he suggested that she remove her mother since all the other violators were male. She refused (1981b, 91). Elsewhere she has said that her point was the violation of self-determination, no matter by whom, which perhaps indicates why the poem made feminists uneasy (Deveaux 1981, 138).

Chapter 4. Survival as Form in the Work of Gloria Anzaldúa and Irena Klepfisz

1. Anzaldúa and Klepfisz worked together as contributing editors for the lesbian feminist journal *Sinister Wisdom*, 1984–1987. They have stated each other's importance to their work and provide another example of

the importance of intertextuality among feminist poets. See Klepfisz 1990b, xi; 1990a, 171. See also Anzaldúa's poem for "Irenita" Klepfisz, "Poets have strange eating habits" (1987, 140–42).

2. I am relying on Bruce-Novoa's definition of these terms here: bilingualism means that poems are in one language or the other, while interlingualism refers to sections in which two languages are mixed. According to Bruce-Novoa, " 'Bilingualism' implies moving from one language code to another; 'interlingualism' implies the constant tension of the two at once" (1985, 226).

3. See Maria Damon (1993), who develops a definition of nostalgia as "a proactive creation of collective experience" rather than a "foggy mystique" attached to historical artifacts, which helps in the denial of contemporary reality, and in which alienation is a necessary element (113).

4. Damon explores the various definitions of the avant-garde—as formal tradition, historical moment, and "series of names"—and arrives at a use of the term to connote a wide spectrum of activity of "(op)position one can occupy at any time and whose contours are contextually determined" (1993, ix–x).

5. Anzaldúa has elsewhere commented extensively on the shamanic use of metaphor as a kind of healing device. See "Metaphors in the Tradition of the Shaman" (1990b, 99).

6. Anzaldúa understands that the question is not just one of different languages but of the correct version of any given language. See June Jordan's "Nobody Mean More to Me than You And the Future Life of Willie Jordan" (1986, 123–40).

7. Leonard Diepeveen (1993) coins the term for Modernist poems in which the poet suspends her/his own voice with "exact borrowings from another text" (vii). Diepeveen maintains that quotations "simultaneously affirm, antagonize, and feed off of their sources" (17).

8. The two volumes, now out of print, are *Periods of Stress* (New York: Out & Out Books, 1975) and *Keeper of Accounts* (Watertown, Mass.: Persephone Press, 1982). These were later published together as *Different Enclosures* (London: Onlywomen Press, 1985), which also included the fictional diary, "The Journal of Rachel Robotnik." Both volumes were gathered again, together with a collection of eight new poems titled after the collection itself, as *A Few Words in the Mother Tongue* (1990).

9. Klepfisz says that she had begun to grow concerned about the increasing commercialism surrounding Holocaust material when she was writing her own early poetry about the Holocaust (1990a, 168).

Chapter 5. History, Myth, and Empowerment in Joy Harjo's Poetry

1. I will use the term "Native American" to refer to the diverse indigenous tribal cultures of North America, as well as to call upon the con-

sciousness, however variously defined, developed across tribal lines particularly by Indian writers and activists. Many of these writers and activists use the terms "Indian," "Native American," and "Native" interchangeably; for the most part I follow their lead, although "Native American" is the term I use most often.

Though she is of mixed Indian and non-Indian ancestry, Harjo is a member of the Creek Nation, based in Oklahoma. Harjo herself calls upon specifically Creek history and myth but also relies on broader Native American concepts she has received from and helped shape with other Native American writers.

In her comments on "giving back" racism, Harjo says she tells young Indians "the next time they are in a restaurant, or in a store, and they are treated as a lesser people, they must turn it back in their mind—just give it back. I don't mean act racist, but in their mind say: 'This is your weakness, this is not mine'" (1994, 50).

2. Paula Gunn Allen's comments on the relative unimportance of memory and tradition among feminists are also instructive: "Rejection of tradition constitutes one of the major features of American life, an attitude that reaches far back into American colonial history and that now is validated by virtually every cultural institution in the country. Feminist practice, at least in the cultural artifacts the community values most, follows this cultural trend as well" (1986, 210).

3. See also the comments of the Hopi feminist poet Wendy Rose (1990, 127). She shares Harjo's view that little crossover exists between Native and feminist political philosophies.

4. The problem of language is illustrated in that younger generations of Native Americans often do not know any tribal language; Harjo is no exception (1987, 94). Rather, for these younger generations, tribal languages have been entirely supplanted so that English becomes their "native" tongue. Younger poets, then, do not rely on tribal linguistic structures but on ceremonial and story forms and content, especially natural imagery that has importance to the life of the tribe traditionally. Audre Lorde provides a corollary among African-Americans; she stated that she used the rhythms but not the actual words of African languages (1981, 11).

5. Harjo writes: "I love language, sound, how emotions, images, dreams are formed in air and on the page. When I was a little kid in Oklahoma I would get up before everyone else and go outside to a place of dark rich earth next to the foundation of the house. I would dig piles of earth with a stick, smell it, form it. It had sound. Maybe that's when I first learned to write poetry" (1981, 8). While Harjo's understanding of the force of nature in poetry is primarily informed by Native American metaphysics, it resembles Romantic ideas of poetry expressed by nineteenth-century figures like Emerson, who understood nature to be finding expression in his linguistic utterings. As James McCorkle puts it, Emerson placed himself "in the universe" and listened for " 'the

spirit of the thing' to give it back in the form of language." McCorkle also identifies one of the leaders of the feminist poetry movement, Adrienne Rich, in this tradition (1990, 20).

6. Among the more well known of the poets in this group are Luci Tapa-honso, Linda Hogan, Louise Erdrich, and Wendy Rose. For a sense of the breadth of form and theme in contemporary Native American women writers, see Green and Allen. Green 1984 is one of the first and most complete anthologies of contemporary Indian women writers, and Allen 1989 continues this work.

7. The Lorde quote is from her essay "The Transformation of Silence into Language and Action" (1984, 41). Harjo goes on to say that she has felt silenced within the women's movement: "Maybe it comes from being a mixed-blood in this world. I mean, I feel connected to others, but many women's groups have a majority of white women and I honestly can feel uncomfortable, or even voiceless sometimes. I've lived in and out of both worlds for a long time and have learned how to speak—those groups just affect others that way—with a voicelessness" (1990b, 61).

8. Jaimes 1992 is a provoking introduction to the way the professional-ization of history and its reliance on theories of "manifest destiny" and "progress" aided American officials who wished to write the history of treatment of Native Americans to the benefit of the goals of the U.S. government.

9. These poems are from *The Last Song* (1975) and *What Moon Drove Me to This?* (1978), both of which are now out of print. Selections of poems from these volumes appear in Green 1984, 127–45.

10. Harjo has indicated that she considers herself a transmitter of experiences that "take shape in (the) subconscious," so that finally "the sheer weight of memory coupled with imagery constructs poems" (1989, 10). Thus she sees herself at once as the cultural bearer of experience and vision as well as the artist who shapes their expression.

11. Harjo has spoken of the "warrior spirit" in ordinary people like Jacqueline Peters or Anna Mae Pictou Aquash: "I believe those so-called 'womanly' traits are traits of the warrior. Vulnerability is one, you know . . . I've known some of the greatest warriors in my life. They've stood up in the face of danger and in the face of hopelessness. They've been brave—not in the national headlines, but they've been true to themselves, and who they are, and to their families. Their act of bravery could have been to feed their children, to more than survive" (1989, 11).

Chapter 6. Motherhood, Eroticism, and Community in the Poetry of Minnie Bruce Pratt

1. See the editorial statement in *Feminary* 10:2 (1979): 2–3.

2. In her poststructuralist treatment of "lesbian : writing," Meese quotes

Nicole Brossard, who says, "A lesbian who does not reinvent the word is a lesbian in the process of disappearing" (1992, 4).

3. See also McMillen 1992. For a historical exploration of the deep connections between racism and sexism in the South, see Andolsen 1986.

4. "Mother-woman" is Kate Chopin's term for those nineteenth-century southern women who understood submissive wife and motherhood as their highest duty (1984, 51).

References

Adams, Brooke. 1980. "The Chador of Women's Liberation: Cultural Feminism and the Movement Press." *Heresies* 3, no. 1:73.

Alarcon, Norma. 1990. "The Theoretical Subject of *This Bridge Called My Back* and Anglo-American Feminism." In *Making Face, Making Soul/Haciendo Caras: Creative and Critical Perspectives by Women of Color,* edited by Gloria Anzaldúa. San Francisco: Aunt Lute.

Allen, Paula Gunn. 1986. *The Sacred Hoop: Recovering the Feminine in American Indian Traditions.* Boston: Beacon Press.

———. 1989. *Spider Woman's Granddaughters.* Boston: Beacon Press.

Anaya, Rudolfo A., and Francisco A. Lomeli, eds. 1989. *Aztlán: Essays on the Chicano Homeland.* Albuquerque: University of New Mexico Press.

Andolsen, Barbara Hilkert. 1986. *"Daughters of Jefferson, Daughters of Bootblacks": Racism and American Feminism.* Macon, Ga.: Mercer University Press.

"Angry Arts For Life/Against the War." 1967. *Ikon,* July 4, 14–15.

Anzaldúa, Gloria. 1983. "Speaking in Tongues: A Letter to Third World Women Writers." In *This Bridge Called My Back: Writings by Radical Women of Color,* edited by Gloria Anzaldúa and Cherrie Moraga. New York: Kitchen Table/Women of Color Press.

———, 1987. *Borderlands/La Frontera: The New Mestiza.* San Francisco: Aunt Lute.

———, ed. 1990a. *Making Face, Making Soul/Haciendo Caras: Creative and Critical Perspectives by Women of Color.* San Francisco: Aunt Lute.

———. 1990b. "Metaphors in the Tradition of the Shaman." In *Conversant Essays,* edited by James McCorkle. Detroit: Wayne State University Press.

Anzaldúa, Gloria, and Cherrie Moraga, eds. 1983. *This Bridge Called My Back: Writings By Radical Women of Color.* New York: Kitchen Table/Women of Color Press.

Arnold, June. 1976. "Feminist Presses and Feminist Politics." *Quest* 3, no. 1 (Summer): 26.

Asante, Molefi Kete. 1990. *The Afrocentric Idea.* Philadelphia: Temple University Press.

Avi-ram, Amitai F. 1987. "The Politics of the Refrain in Judy Grahn's 'A Woman Is Talking to Death.'" *Women and Language* 10, no. 2:38–43.

Backus, Margot Gayle. 1993. "Judy Grahn and the Lesbian Invocational Elegy: Testimonial and Prophetic Responses to Social Death in 'A Woman Is Talking to Death.'" *Signs* 18, no. 4 (Summer): 815–37.

Bambara, Toni Cade, ed. 1970. *The Black Woman: An Anthology*. New York: New American Library.

Barba, Sharon, and Laura Chester, eds. 1973. *Rising Tides: Twentieth Century American Women Poets*. New York: Washington Square Press.

Bernikow, Louise. 1974. *The World Split Open: Four Centuries of Women Poets in England and America, 1552–1970*. New York: Random House.

Biggs, Mary. 1990. *Cannot Be Refused: The Writing and Publishing of Contemporary American Poetry*. New York: Greenwood Press.

The Black Maria Collective. 1983. "Black Maria: Our Herstory." *Black Maria* 4, no. 3:6–7.

Braderman, Joan, et al. 1977. "From the First-Issue Collective." *Heresies* 1, no. 1 (January): 2–3.

Brady, Maureen, and Judith McDaniel. 1980. "Spinster Ink: An Interview." (Interview with Irena Klepfisz.) *Sinister Wisdom* 13 (Spring): 77–80.

Brito, Silvester J. 1984. "Change in American Indian World Views Illustrated by Oral Narratives and Contemporary Poetry." *Explorations in Ethnic Studies* (July): 27–39.

Brodine, Karen. 1979. "Politics of Women Writing." *Second Wave: A Magazine of New Feminism* 5, no. 3:6–13.

Brooks, Gwendolyn. 1979. Interview with Juliette Bowles. In *In Memory and Spirit of Frances, Zora and Lorraine: Essays and Interviews on Black Women and Writing*, edited by Juliette Bowles. Washington, D.C.: Institute for the Arts and Humanities, Howard University.

Bruce-Novoa. 1985. *Chicano Poetry: A Response to Chaos*. Austin: University of Texas Press.

Bruchac, Joseph, ed. 1983. *Songs from This Earth on Turtle's Back*. Greenfield: New York: Greenfield Review Press.

Bulkin, Elly. 1978. "Review of She Who: A Graphic Book of Poems." *Conditions* 3, 111–16.

Bulkin, Elly, and Joan Larkin, eds. 1981. *Lesbian Poetry: An Anthology*. Watertown, Mass.: Persephone Press.

Bunch, Charlotte. 1977. "Feminist Publishing: An Antiquated Form?" *Heresies* 1, no. 3 (Fall): 24–25.

Carruthers, Mary J. 1983. "The ReVision of the Muse: Adrienne Rich, Audre Lorde, Judy Grahn and Olga Broumas." *Hudson Review* 36, no. 4 (Summer): 293–322.

Case, Sue-Ellen. 1988. "Judy Grahn's Gynopoetics: The Queen of Swords." *Studies in the Literary Imagination* 21, no. 2 (Fall): 47–67.

Chesman, Andrea, and Polly Joan. 1978. *Guide to Women's Publishing*. Paradise, Calif.: Dustbooks.

Chopin, Kate. 1984. *The Awakening*. New York: Viking Penguin.

Christian, Barbara. 1993. "Remembering Audre Lorde." *Women's Review of Books*, March, 5–6.

Clausen, Jan. 1976. "The Politics of Publishing and the Lesbian Community." *Sinister Wisdom* 1, no. 2 (Fall): 99.

————. 1989. *Books and Life*. Columbus: Ohio State University Press.

"Come to the Newly Organized Milwaukee Women's Poetry Co-operative." 1972. *Amazon* 1, no. 3 (July): 7.

Cone, James. 1972. *The Spirituals and the Blues: An Interpretation*. New York: Seabury Press.

Conte, Joseph M. 1991. *Unending Design: The Forms of Postmodern Poetry*. Ithaca, N.Y.: Cornell University Press.

Cook-Lynn, Elizabeth. 1987. "As a Dakotah Woman." (Interview by Joseph Bruchac.) In *Survival This Way*, edited by Joseph Bruchac. Tucson: Sun Tracks and University of Arizona Press.

Damon, Maria. 1993. *The Dark End of the Street: Margins in American Vanguard Poetry*. Minneapolis: University of Minnesota Press.

Daniels, Kate. 1991. "The Demise of the 'Delicate Prison': The Women's Movement in Twentieth-Century American Poetry." In *A Profile of Twentieth-Century American Poetry*, edited by Jack Myers and David Wojahn. Carbondale: Southern Illinois University Press.

————, ed. 1992. *Out of Silence*. Chicago: Triquarterly Books.

Davis, Angela. 1990. "Black Women and Music: A Historical Legacy of Struggle." In *Wild Women in the Whirlwind: Afra-American Culture and the Contemporary Literary Renaissance*, edited by Joanne M. Braxton and Andree Nicola McLaughlin. New Brunswick, New Jersey: Rutgers University Press.

DeShazer, Mary K. 1986. *Inspiring Women: Reimagining the Muse*. New York: Pergamon Press.

Deveaux, Alexis. 1981. "Creating Soul Food: June Jordan." *Essence* 11 (April): 135–40.

Diehl, Joanne Feit. 1990. *Women Poets and the American Sublime*. Bloomington and Indianapolis: Indiana University Press.

Diepeveen, Leonard. 1993. *Changing Voices: The Modern Quoting Poem*. Ann Arbor: University of Michigan Press.

Doty, Mark. 1991. "The 'Forbidden Planet' of Character: The Revolutions of the 1950s." In *A Profile of Twentieth-Century American Poetry*, edited by Jack Myers and David Wojahn. Carbondale: Southern Illinois University Press.

Echols, Alice. 1989. *Daring To Be Bad: Radical Feminism in America 1967–1975*. Minneapolis: University of Minnesota Press.

Eliot, T. S. 1965. "Tradition and the Individual Talent." In *Modern Poetics*, edited by James Scully. New York: McGraw Hill.

Erdrich, Louise. 1987. "Whatever Is Really Yours." (Interview with Joseph Bruchac.) In *Survival This Way*, edited by Joseph Bruchac. Tucson: Sun Tracks and University of Arizona Press.

Erickson, Peter. 1985. "June Jordan." In *Afro-American Writers After 1955*, edited by Thadious M. Davis and Trudier Harris. Detroit: Gale Research.

Erkkila, Betsy. 1992. *The Wicked Sisters: Women Poets, Literary History, and Discord*. New York: Oxford University Press.

Felski, Rita. 1989. *Beyond Feminist Aesthetics: Feminist Literature and Social Change*. London: Hutchinson Radius.

Fisher, Dexter. 1980. *The Third Woman: Minority Women Writers of the United States*. Boston: Houghton Mifflin.

———. 1985. "The Transformation of Tradition: A Study of Zitkala Sa and Mourning Dove, Two Transitional American Indian Writers." In *Critical Essays on Native American Literature*, edited by Andrew Wiget. Boston: G. K. Hall.

Fraser, Kathleen. 1977. "On Being a West Coast Woman Poet." *Women's Studies* 5:154–60.

Freedman, Diane P. 1992. *An Alchemy of Genres*. Charlottesville: University Press of Virginia.

Friere, Paulo. 1974. *The Pedagogy of the Oppressed*. New York: Seabury Press.

Gallagher, Tess. 1986. *A Concert of Tenses: Essays on Poetry*. Ann Arbor: University of Michigan Press.

Gill, Elaine, ed. 1973. *Mountain Moving Day: Poems by Women*. Trumansburg, N.Y.: Crossing Press.

giovanni, nikki. 1970. *The Women and the Men*. New York: William Morrow.

Grahn, Judy. 1972. *Edward the Dyke and Other Poems*. San Franscisco: Women's Press Collective.

———, 1978a. Introduction to *Movement in Black: The Collected Poetry of Pat Parker, 1961–1978*, by Pat Parker. Oakland, Calif.: Diana Press.

———. 1978b. *The Work of a Common Woman*. Freedom, Calif.: Crossing Press.

———. 1982. *The Queen of Wands*. Trumansburg, N.Y.: Crossing Press.

———. 1983. "From a Public Dialogue Between Grahn and John Felstiner, Professor of English, Stanford University, November 19, 1980." In *Women Writers of the West Coast: Speaking of Their Lives and Careers*, edited by Marilyn Yalom. Santa Barbara, Calif.: Capra.

———. 1985. *The Highest Apple*. San Francisco: Spinsters, Ink.

———. 1987. *The Queen of Swords*. Boston: Beacon Press.

———. 1989. *Really Reading Gertrude Stein: A Selected Anthology with Essays by Judy Grahn*. Freedom, Calif.: Crossing Press.

———. 1990. "Drawing in Nets." In *Conversant Essays*, edited by James McCorkle. Detroit: Wayne State University Press.

Green, Rayna. 1984. *That's What She Said*. Bloomington: Indiana University Press.

Griffin, Susan. 1982. *Made from This Earth: An Anthology of Writings*. New York: Harper and Row.

Halsey, Theresa, and Annette M. Jaimes. 1992. "American Indian Women: At the Center of Indigenous Resistance in North America." In *The State of Native America*, edited by M. Annette Jaimes. Boston: South End Press.

Harjo, Joy. 1975. *The Last Song*. Las Cruces, N.M.: Puerta del Sol.

———. 1978. *What Moon Drove Me to This?* Berkeley: Reed and Canvas.

———. 1981. "Bio-Poetics Sketch." *Greenfield Review* 9:8–9.

———. 1983. *She Had Some Horses*. New York: Thunder's Mouth Press.

———. 1984. "A Treatise on Loving Ourselves." *Sinister Wisdom* 24:158–62.

———. 1987. "The Story of All Our Survival." (Interview with Joseph Bruchac.) In *Survival This Way,* edited by Joseph Bruchac. Tucson: Sun Tracks and University of Arizona Press.

———. 1989. "A *MELUS* Interview." (Interview with Helen Jakoski.) *MELUS* 16 (Spring): 5–14.

———. 1990a. *In Mad Love and War*. Middletown, Conn.: Wesleyan University Press.

———. 1990b. Interview with Laura Coltelli. In *Winged Words: American Indian Writers Speak*. Lincoln: University of Nebraska Press.

———. 1993. Interview with Mickey Pearlman. In *Listen to Their Voices,* edited by Mickey Pearlman. New York: Norton.

———. 1994. Interview with Angels Carabi. *Belles Lettres* 9, no. 4 (Summer): 46–50.

Harris, William J. 1985. *The Poetry and Poetics of Amiri Baraka: The Jazz Aesthetic*. Columbia: University of Missouri Press.

H.D. 1925. *Collected Poems*. New York: Liveright.

Homans, Margaret. 1980. *Women Writers and Poetic Identity*. Princeton, N.J.: Princeton University Press.

hooks, bell. 1984. *From Margin to Center*. Boston: South End Press.

Howe, Florence, ed. 1993. *No More Masks: An Anthology of Twentieth-Century American Women Poets*. New York: HarperPerennial.

———. 1994. "The Poetry of Life." *Women's Review of Books* 12, no. 2 (November): 12.

Howe, Florence, and Ellen Bass, eds. 1973. *No More Masks: An Anthology of Poems by Women*. Garden City, N.Y.: Anchor.

Hutcheon, Linda. 1988. *A Poetics of Postmodernism*. New York: Routledge.

Ippolito, Donna. 1971. "Notes on a Writer's Workshop." *Black Maria* 1, no. 1:15.

Iverson, Lucille, and Kathryn Ruby. 1975. *We Become New: Poems by Contemporary American Women*. New York: Bantam.

Jaimes, M. Annette. 1992. "Sand Creek: The Morning After." In *The State of Native America,* edited by M. Annette Jaimes. Boston, Mass.: South End Press.

Jones, Kirkland. 1992. "Folk Idiom in the Literary Expression of Two African American Authors: Rita Dove and Yusef Komunyakaa." In *Language and Literature in the African American Imagination,* edited by Carol Aisha Blackshire-Belay. Westport, Conn.: Greenwood Press.

Jordan, June. 1969. *Who Look At Me?* New York: Crowell.

———. 1971. *Some Changes*. New York: E. P. Dutton.

———. 1974. *New Days: Poems of Exile and Return*. New York: Emerson Hall Publishers.

———. 1977. *Things That I Do in the Dark*. New York: Random.

———. 1980. *Passion*. Boston: Beacon Press.

———. 1981a. *Civil Wars*. Boston: Beacon Press.

———. 1981b. Interview with Karla Hammond. *Woman Poet* 90–94.

———. 1985. *Living Room*. New York: Thunder's Mouth Press.

———. 1986. *On Call: Political Essays*. Boston: Beacon Press.

———. 1989. *Naming Our Destiny: New and Selected Poems*. New York: Thunder's Mouth Press.

———. 1993. *Technical Difficulties*. New York: Norton.

Juhasz, Suzanne. 1976. *Naked and Fiery Forms*. New York: Octagon Books.

Kaplan, Cora, ed. 1975. *Salt and Bitter and Good: Three Centuries of English and American Women Poets*. Lawrence, Mass.: Two Continents Publishing Group/Paddington Press.

Kaye/Kantrowitz, Melanie and Irena Klepfisz, eds. 1989. *The Tribe of Dina: A Jewish Women's Anthology*. Boston: Beacon Press.

Klepfisz, Irena. 1975. *Periods of Stress*. New York: Out & Out Books.

———. 1979. "Criticism: Form and Function in Lesbian Literature." *Sinister Wisdom* 9 (Spring): 27–30.

———. 1982. *Keeper of Accounts*. Watertown, Mass.: Persephone Press.

———. 1985. *Different Enclosures*. London: Onlywomen Press.

———. 1990a. *Dreams of an Insomniac: Feminist Essays, Speeches and Diatribes*. Portland, Ore.: Eighth Mountain Press.

———. 1990b. *A Few Words in the Mother Tongue*. Portland, Ore.: Eighth Mountain Press.

Koolish, Lynda. 1987. "The Bones of This Body Say, Dance." In *A Gift of Tongues: Critical Challenges in Contemporary American Poetry,* edited by Marie Harris and Kathleen Aguero. Athens: University of Georgia Press.

———. 1981. *A Whole New Poetry Beginning Here: Contemporary American Women Poets*. 2 vols. Ann Arbor, Mich.: University Microfilms.

Le Tourneau, Gayle Dodson, and Annette Townley. 1974. "Transformations in the Politics of Aesthetics." *Second Wave: A Magazine of New Feminism* 3, no. 4:5–8.

Levertov, Denise. 1973. *The Poet in the World*. New York: New Directions.

Levi, Jan Heller, ed. 1994. *A Muriel Rukeyser Reader*. New York: Norton.

Lockett, Andrea. 1993. "Sister Difference: An Audre Lorde Memorial Conversation." (Interview with Barbara Smith.) *Belles Lettres* (Summer): 39–41.

Lorde, Audre. 1978. *The Black Unicorn*. New York: Norton.

———. 1981. Interview with Karla M. Hammond. *Denver Quarterly* 16 (Spring): 10–27.

———. 1982. *Chosen Poems*. New York: Norton.

———. 1984. *Sister Outsider: Essays and Speeches*. Freedom, Calif.: Crossing Press.

———. 1986. *Our Dead Behind Us*. New York: Norton.

Lowell, Amy. 1928. *Selected Poems*. Edited by John Livinston Lowes. Boston: Houghton Mifflin.

McCarriston, Linda. 1993. "Class Unconsciousness and an American Writer." *New England Review* 15, no. 2 (Spring): 65–75.

McCorkle, James. 1992. "Contemporary Poetics and History: Pinsky, Klepfisz, and Rothenberg." *Kenyon Review* 14 (Winter): 171–88.

———, ed. 1990. *Conversant Essays*. Detroit: Wayne State University Press.

McMillen, Sally G. 1992. *Southern Women: Black and White in the Old South*. Arlington Heights, Ill.: Harlan Davidson.

Marshall, Barbara. 1992. "Kitchen Table Talk: J. California Cooper's Use of Nommo—Female Bonding and Transcendence." In *Language and Literature in the African American Imagination,* edited by Carol Aisha Blackshire-Belay. Westport, Conn.: Greenwood Press.

Martin, Biddy, and Chandra Talpade Mohanty. 1986. "Feminist Politics: What's Home Got to Do with It?" In *Feminist Studies/Critical Studies,* edited by Teresa de Lauretis. Bloomington: Indiana University Press.

Martin, Joel. 1991. *Sacred Revolt: The Muskogees' Struggle for a New World*. Boston: Beacon Press.

Meese, Elizabeth. 1992. *Sem)erotics: Theorizing Lesbian: Writing*. New York: New York University Press.

"Memorial to Audre Lorde." 1993. *Ms.,* March/April, 58.

Michie, Helena. 1992. *Sororophobia: Differences Among Women in Literature and Culture*. New York: Oxford University Press.

Miles, Sara. 1981. "This Wheel's On Fire: The Poetry of June Jordan." *Woman Poet* 2:87–89.

Mora, Pat. 1993. *Nepantla: Essays from the Land in the Middle*. Albuquerque: University of New Mexico Press.

Montefiore, Jan. 1987–1988. " 'What Words Say': Three Women Poets Reading H.D." *Agenda* 25, nos. 3–4:172–90.

Montenegro, David. 1991. *Points of Departure: International Writers on Writing and Politics*. Ann Arbor: University of Michigan Press.

More, Hannah. 1855. *Works,* vol. 2. New York: Harper and Brothers.

Morgan, Robin. 1990. *Upstairs in the Garden: Poems Selected and New, 1968–1988*. New York: Norton.

Olsen, Tillie. 1983. *Silences*. New York: Dell.

Ostriker, Alicia. 1986. *Stealing the Language*. Boston: Beacon Press.

Parker, Pat. 1983. *Movement in Black: The Collected Poetry of Pat Parker, 1961–1978*. Trumansburg, N.Y.: Crossing Press.

Perkins, David. 1987. *A History of Modern Poetry*. Cambridge: Harvard University Press.

Piercy, Marge. 1982. *Circles on the Water*. New York: Knopf.

———, ed. 1987. *Early Ripening: American Women's Poetry Now*. New York: Pandora.

"Poetry Marathon." 1972. *Majority Report* 2, no. 3 (July): 9.

"Poetry Support Group." 1975. *Majority Report* 4, no. 21 (February): 10.

Pope, Deborah. 1984. *A Separate Vision: Isolation in Contemporary Women's Poetry*. Baton Rouge: Louisiana State University Press.

Pratt, Minnie Bruce. 1981. *The Sound of One Fork*. Durham, N.C.: Night Heron Press.

———. 1985. *We Say We Love Each Other*. San Francisco: Spinsters/Aunt Lute.

———. 1990. *Crime Against Nature*. Ithaca, N.Y.: Firebrand.

———. 1991. *Rebellion: Essays, 1980–1991*. Ithaca: Firebrand Books.

———. 1992. Interview with Elaine Auerbach. *Belles Lettres* 8, no. 1 (Fall): 32–36.

"Preamble to *Aphra*." 1969. *Aphra* 1, no. 1 (Fall): 3.

Randall, Margaret. 1990. "The Sixties/The Nineties: Looking Forward, Looking Back." *Ikon Second Series* 11:5–14.

Rexroth, Kenneth. 1971. *American Poetry in the Twentieth Century*. New York: Herder and Herder.

Rich, Adrienne. 1972. *Diving into the Wreck*. New York: Norton.

———. 1978. "Power and Danger: *The Work of a Common Woman* by Judy Grahn." Introduction to *The Work of a Common Woman*, by Judy Grahn. Freedom, Calif.: Crossing Press.

———. 1979. *On Lies, Secrets and Silence*. New York: Norton.

———. 1981. *A Wild Patience Has Taken Me This Far*. New York: Norton.

———. 1984. *The Fact of a Doorframe*. New York: Norton.

———. 1986. *Blood, Bread, and Poetry*. New York: Norton.

———. 1991. *Atlas of the Difficult World: Poems, 1988–1991*. New York: Norton.

———. 1993. *What Is Found There: Notebooks on Poetry and Politics*. New York: Norton.

Rose, Wendy. 1992. "The Great Pretenders: Further Reflections on White-shamanism." In *The State of Native America*, edited by M. Annette Jaimes. Boston, Mass.: South End Press.

———. 1990. Interview with William Balassi, John F. Crawford, and Annie O. Eysturoy. In *This Is About Vision: Interviews with Southwestern Writers*, edited by William Balassi, John F. Crawford, and Annie O. Eysturoy. Albuquerque: University of New Mexico Press.

Rukeyser, Muriel. 1949. *The Life of Poetry*. New York: A. A. Wyn.

———. 1978. *The Collected Poems*. New York: McGraw-Hill.

Sanchez, Rosaura. 1987. "Postmodernism and Chicano Literature." *Aztlan: A Journal of Chicano Studies* 18 (Fall): 1–13.

Sánchez, Sonia. 1970. *We a BadddDDD People*. Detroit: Broadside Press.

Segnitz, Barbara, and Carol Rainey, eds. 1973. *Psyche: The Feminine Poetic Consciousness*. New York: Dell.

Sexton, Anne. 1969. "Notes." *Aphra* (Fall): 5.

Sexton, Linda Gray, and Lois Ames, eds. 1991. *Anne Sexton: A Self-Portrait in Letters*. Boston: Houghton Mifflin.

Shaw, Robert B. 1973. *American Poetry Since 1960*. Cheshire, England: Carcanet Press.

Sherman, Susan. 1982–83. "Freeing the Balance: Activism and Art." *Ikon Second Series* 1 (Fall/Winter): 2–4.

Silko, Leslie Marmon. 1977. *Ceremony*. New York: Viking Press.

Silliman, Ron. 1990. "Canons and Institutions: New Hope for the Disappeared." In *The Politics of Poetic Form: Poetry and Public Policy,* edited by Charles Bernstein. New York: Roof.

Stanford, Ann, ed. 1973. *The Women Poets in English.* New York: McGraw-Hill.

Taylor, Verta, and Nancy Whittier. 1993. "The New Feminist Movement." In *Feminist Frontiers III,* edited by Laurel Richardson and Verta Taylor. New York: McGraw-Hill.

Trinh, T. Minh-ha. 1990a. "Interlocking Questions of Identity and Difference." In *Making Face, Making Soul/Haciendo Caras: Creative and Critical Perspectives by Women of Color,* edited by Gloria Anzaldúa. San Francisco: Aunt Lute.

————. 1990b. *Woman, Native, Other.* Bloomington: Indiana University Press.

Ullman, Leslie. 1991. "American Poetry in the 1960s." In *A Profile of Twentieth-Century American Poetry,* edited by Jack Myers and David Wojahn. Carbondale: Southern Illinois University Press.

Wakoski, Diane. 1980. *Toward a New Poetry.* Ann Arbor: University of Michigan Press.

Walker, Alice. 1983. *In Search of Our Mother's Gardens.* San Diego: Harcourt Brace.

Whitman, Walt. 1959. *Complete Poetry and Selected Prose.* Boston: Houghton Mifflin.

Williams, Maxine. 1971. "Women's Liberation and Nationalism." *Second Wave: A Magazine of New Feminism* 1, no. 1:18–20.

Wong, Nellie, 1979a. "Glows from the Dark of Monsters and Demons: Notes on Writing." In *Three Asian American Writers Speak Out on Feminism,* by Nellie Wong, Merle Woo, and Mitsuye Yamada. San Francisco: San Francisco Radical Women.

————. 1979b. "Toward the Rainbow" (poem). In *Three Asian American Writers Speak Out on Feminism,* by Nellie Wong, Merle Woo, and Mitsuye Yamada. San Francisco: San Francisco Radical Women.

Wong, Nellie, Merle Woo, and Mitsuye Yamada. 1979. *Three Asian American Writers Speak Out on Feminism.* San Francisco: San Francisco Radical Women.

Wright, Doris. 1972. "On Black Womanhood." *Second Wave: A Magazine of New Feminism* 2, no. 4:13–15.

Yamada, Mitsuye. 1987. "A *MELUS* Interview." (Interview with Helen Jakoski.) *MELUS* 15, no. 1 (Spring): 97–107.

————. 1979. "Invisibility Is an Unnatural Disaster: Reflections of an Asian American Woman." In *Three Asian American Writers Speak Out on Feminism,* by Nellie Wong, Merle Woo, and Mitsuye Yamada. San Francisco: San Francisco Radical Women.

Zipter, Yvonne. 1990. "Minnie Bruce Pratt Wins Lamont Prize." *Hot Wire,* January, 1.

Index